CEME[...]

Water poured from the skies in [...] le
blue Toyota Corolla in which the teenage couple was
parked. A rainy night in the Buhler Plains Cemetery only
added to the romance as they fumbled with each other's
clothing. The graveyard, with its tombstones made of
concrete covered in drooping daisies and tulips and
roses, was the perfect place for young love to blossom.

The young boy kissed the girl as he helped her peel
down her pants, first one leg, then the other. Hungry for
closer contact, he rid himself of his jeans and lay on top of
her in the backseat, loving the feel of her body so close to
him, uninhibited by clothing. So focused was he on the girl
that he did not hear the footsteps approaching through
the patter of rain and the passionate whirring in his brain.
When the door opened, he jumped up, startled.

He couldn't see the man, but the dome light outlined
the bush axe just before it bit into the boy's scalp, cutting
deeply. The girl screamed, putting up her arms to defend
herself, but not before the axe raked across her leg. The
axe kept coming as the young couple tried desperately to
avoid its jagged edge. They were unsuccessful, the axe
ravaging the boy's arms, his hands, as he tried to protect
the girl; the ferocious man wielding the weapon was
determined to hack them to bits.

BLOOD BATH

SUSAN D. MUSTAFA
and
TONY CLAYTON
with
SUE ISRAEL

PINNACLE BOOKS
Kensington Publishing Corp.
http://www.kensingtonbooks.com

Some names have been changed to protect the privacy of individuals connected to this story.

PINNACLE BOOKS are published by

Kensington Publishing Corp.
119 West 40th Street
New York, NY 10018

All Kensington Titles, Imprints, and Distributed Lines are available at special quantity discounts for bulk purchases for sales promotions, premiums, fund-raising, and educational or institutional use. Special book excerpts or customized printings can also be created to fit specific needs. For details, write or phone the office of the Kensington special sales manager: Kensington Publishing Corp., 119 West 40th Street, New York, NY 10018, attn: Special Sales Department, Phone: 1-800-221-2647.

Pinnacle and the P logo Reg. U.S. Pat. & TM Off.

ISBN-13: 978-0-7860-2133-8
ISBN-10: 0-7860-2133-0

First printing: August 2009

10 9 8 7 6 5 4 3 2

Printed in the United States of America

For the victims

Genesis

On November 5, 1968, deep in the heart of bayou country, a monster was born.

Connie Lynn Warner

In late summer 1992, Louisiana residents were busily preparing for Hurricane Andrew, which had come through Florida and into the Gulf of Mexico only a few days before. There's nothing that can raise tensions in the middle of a humid Louisiana summer faster than a strong, approaching hurricane, and residents of Baton Rouge and its suburbs hurried to stock up on last-minute supplies—water, gasoline, nonperishables, and plywood and tape to protect vulnerable windows. Andrew had carved a destructive path over the Bahamas and through the lower parts of Florida and was lurking in the Gulf, carefully choosing its next victims.

The townspeople in Zachary, a small town about fourteen miles northeast of Baton Rouge, were not as concerned as those who lived in lower-lying areas closer to the coastlines.

Connie Lynn Warner was a bit concerned, though not about the hurricane. She was worried about the black man she had seen peeping into the windows of her home in Oak Shadows subdivision. Connie had made a report to the police and had not seen the man since, but still, she worried.

Connie had moved to the subdivision only four years before, attracted to the pretty rows of starter homes, which lined the streets of the neighborhood—streets named Job and Saul and Eli, Leviticus and Numbers, their names taken from the Bible. Connie lived on Job Avenue, on the corner, in a pretty pale-brick home with a single carport and large yard. A privacy fence ran along the back edge of her property, separating her home from the backyards of those on the next street.

After many years of living with her parents, Jack and Betty Brooks, Connie was excited that she was finally making it on her own. She had divorced her husband when her daughter, Tracy, was only a baby. Zachary was the perfect place to raise the child around whom Connie had built her world.

In 1992, Zachary was much smaller than it is today, quiet and charming with old family homes situated on large properties in neighborhoods that lined country roads. There were not many commercial structures to be found beyond the town's small business sector. The Zachary Police Department (ZPD) sat amidst a few businesses on the main road in the center of town. As Baton Rouge experienced the exodus of many middle- to high-income families searching for better schools in which to educate their children, the town experienced a boom, and construction accelerated.

But in August of 1992, Zachary still retained its small-town appeal, complete with low crime rates and friendly neighbors who enjoyed easy accessibility to Baton Rouge when things became too monotonous.

Connie was unaware that the safe neighborhood filled with other single mothers and families just starting out had already become fodder for a man who lived just down Highway 964 in St. Francisville, a man who liked to watch light-skinned women with dark hair.

Oak Shadows subdivision runs alongside Azalea Rest Cemetery, whose majestic oaks proudly cast shadows over the edge of the subdivision when the sun is positioned in the west. With huge roots sprawling above ground, these expansive oaks also provide shade for those buried in rows beneath their branches. Flowers and toys surround graves whose markers denote time lines back through the 1800s.

While the dead peacefully rested, young mothers in Oak Shadows subdivision hurried about their lives in blissful ignorance of the danger that lurked in the shadows of the cemetery.

Connie couldn't have been happier when she bought her home. Finally she had a place where she and Tracy could build a life. That accomplishment had been difficult. She had gone into her marriage with high hopes, only to find herself alone with a child to raise. She had gotten a job with the Louisiana Department of Health and Hospitals as an accountant, but she was laid off shortly after she moved into Oak Shadows because she didn't have a college degree. Upset by this setback, Connie once again enlisted her parents' help, and they agreed to take care of her bills while she concentrated on earning her degree. In 1990, Connie graduated from Southeastern Louisiana University in Hammond, equipped with the diploma that would ensure her future. She soon found another job with the state, and she and Tracy at last had the financial security that Connie had worked so hard to achieve. Connie's worries were put to rest—until she saw the man peeping into her window.

Connie was not one to go out much, especially at night. Her poor vision did not allow many excursions after dark because it was too difficult for her to see clearly. She went to work and went home, unless Tracy had an activity she needed to attend. Connie always made time to go to Tracy's basketball and football games, proud that her daughter had been chosen for the cheerleading squad. But mostly her evenings consisted of cross-stitching and sewing and watching television.

Although very attractive, with her curly brown hair, pretty green eyes, which were partly hidden behind large hard-rimmed glasses, and her open, friendly smile, Connie preferred to stay home. She chose to devote her life to her seventeen-year-old daughter and was happy with her simple existence. She had worked hard in her forty-one years and was content with the peaceful life she had created.

A steamy night in August, one week before her forty-second birthday, would change all of that. Someone was watching, waiting for the right moment to strike. Police are not sure when Connie Warner's world was invaded by an unknown man bent on her destruction—if it was August 23 or 24. But they know that she was alone that weekend. Tracy had gone to stay with her boyfriend, Andre Burgas, although Connie thought her daughter was staying at a friend's while going through orientation at Louisiana State University (LSU). Connie knew the importance of a good education, and she was proud that Tracy would soon be attending the university.

Just five days before Connie disappeared, a husky black man who lived in St. Francisville, less than twenty miles up the road from Oak Shadows subdivision, lost his job with the Cecil Graves automobile dealership. Connie did not know this man, but he had worked in the construction industry in Zachary throughout the late 1980s and early 1990s. He knew the area well. He knew the subdivision. He was drawn to it through the beautiful young women who lived there.

He liked watching them.

And he was filled with an unending yearning to possess just one of them. The loss of his job only perpetuated the anger and rage he felt inside—the feelings of incompetence, of not being good enough. Though he tried, he could not keep a job or get the women he desired to take notice of him.

On that hot August weekend, the man's hunger took on its own life, stirring and whirling about inside him like the hurricane that lingered in the Gulf. So he drove to

Oak Shadows subdivision, determined to take possession of the slender woman upon whom he had spied.

Connie sat alone in the house on Job Avenue, cross-stitching what could possibly have been her vision of herself and Tracy—a Southern room with a lady and a young girl dressed in ruffled gowns with a window opened wide to a view of the world. The television provided a distraction from the needle that slowly wove in and out through the pattern. Perhaps it was a knock at the back door that prompted Connie to hook the needle in the pattern and lay it on the floor in front of her. Perhaps she opened the door to investigate a noise, nervous about the Peeping Tom. There were no signs of forced entry, but telltale clues within the house would later provide a picture of what happened next.

It was about nine o'clock on the evening of August 24 when Tracy returned home. She noticed immediately that her mother was not there, but the teenager was not too concerned because the television was on. She thought that perhaps Connie had gone to visit a neighbor and would be home shortly.

By 10:30 P.M., when Connie still had not come home, Tracy became worried and called her grandparents, but she could not reach them. She had noticed that things in the home were out of place. Tracy ran to several of her neighbors' houses and asked if they had seen her mother. They had not.

By 11:30 P.M., she finally got in touch with her grandparents. Jack Brooks rushed right over. Tracy showed him the washer and dryer, which appeared to have been pushed back, and pointed out spots of blood on the utility room floor. On the carport, Jack noticed three buttons that looked as if they had been ripped from a shirt. He looked in Connie's 1989 Chevy Cavalier and saw vomit on the backseat. Very worried, Jack called the police.

Officer D.L. Courtney was the first to arrive. He questioned Jack and Tracy, and then began to inspect the home. Sergeant Bruce Chaisson arrived next.

"Connie would not just go off at night without letting Tracy know where she was," Jack assured Chaisson. "She wouldn't do that."

The hood of the car told the officer that this was not just a case of a woman going out for the evening. There was brown hair stuck to the hood, where marks indicated that someone had lain across it. There was vomit on the right corner. The side of the car was dusty, but outlines in the dust indicated that someone had slid across the car from the passenger's door to the driver's door. Chaisson found vomit in the backseat, as well as part of a belt buckle. He also saw the three lavender buttons.

"Those belong to a striped blouse my mom always wears," Tracy said. "And this door—it's always locked. My mom never leaves a door unlocked, even when she's here."

Chaisson examined the carport door and found no signs of forced entry. Opening it, he went into the utility room, where he noticed three blood spatters on the floor between the door and the washing machine. The washer was out of place, as if someone might have grabbed hold of it to keep from being pulled out of the house. Another piece of broken belt was found on the dryer.

Connie's bedroom revealed more clues. The mattress of the bed had been pushed against the nightstand; the bottom drawer, where Connie always kept a can of Mace, was partially opened. The top sheet, which Connie always tucked in, was tangled in the middle of the bed, indicating that some sort of a struggle had occurred there. Connie's glasses were lying on the floor. Detectives later found a small bloodstain on the carpet beside the bed. A pair of pink pants and white panties bearing bloodstains were also entered into evidence.

Chaisson was convinced that Connie was missing and possibly harmed. He and other officers secured the crime scene. Tracy and her grandparents waited anxiously for Connie to come home, staring at the phone hoping for a call, pacing back and forth, asking everyone who knew Connie if they had seen her. But Connie never came home.

The vomit on the front of the car and in the backseat verified that Connie had been alive when she was taken. The buttons ripped from her shirt found lying on the ground indicated that she had put up a fight. Connie did not go with her attacker quietly—yet no one in the small neighborhood heard her cries. Her keys would never be found. A witness would later tell police that he had seen a man carrying a bundle walking toward Connie's car that night, but the man had then placed the bundle into another vehicle parked behind hers—a red Buick.

Jack, Betty, and Tracy would never know exactly how it had happened, but they would eventually know who had done it—although the man who had so cruelly destroyed their lives would never be officially linked to Connie's murder. Any clues that might have surfaced with the discovery of Connie's body would be washed away by a hurricane.

Andrew roared through Baton Rouge on August 26, although its strength was diminished by its journey from the coast to Louisiana's capital city. By the time Baton Rougeans were huddled in their homes, taking cover from the storm, Andrew's winds were only seventy miles per hour, not enough to do serious damage to homes and residents. The storm moved on to the north, leaving behind some downed trees and homes without electricity for several days. But this hurricane would have a major impact on the investigation of a murder that happened only miles from Baton Rouge. Connie Warner's body, exposed during the storm, would rapidly decompose, and clues to her attacker would disappear with Andrew. Meanwhile, Connie's parents and daughter would spend endless nights waiting for news that she had been found, hopefully alive.

For nine days, they waited.

On September 2, a truck driver discovered Connie's corpse on Sorrel Street, near downtown Baton Rouge. Her badly decomposed body, found by the Capitol Lake, close to the state capitol building, did not offer much in the way of evidence for police. They could only determine that she had died from a skull fracture, apparently from a beating of some kind. There was no other evidence, no fingerprints or tracks in the grass, no DNA. Nothing. Andrew had washed away any clues that could have led police to the killer.

After Connie's death, Tracy moved in with her grandparents once more and tried to go on with her life. It was difficult because there were no answers, no reasons why, no arrests. Connie was simply gone, and so was her killer. It would be eleven years before her family would get some inkling as to who had committed this despicable act. Eleven years of wondering.

But someone did know, and after he had dumped Connie's body by the lake, he felt the satisfaction that comes with power, the power to hold a human life in his hands, the power to make another human being succumb to his whims. He had held the light-skinned woman, had felt her hair, had run his fingers along her cheekbones as she begged for mercy. He had made her his. His appetite had been appeased.

For a while.

It is possible that Connie Warner may not have been this man's first victim, although it is widely thought that she was. A young LSU student, Melissa Montz, had disappeared many years before, in 1985, as she was jogging along River Road in Baton Rouge. Her decomposed body had been discovered close to the LSU golf course by a golfer retrieving a ball. She had been strangled. And another woman, Joyce Taylor, had been murdered in her home in Baton Rouge, stabbed to death just three months before Connie's abduction. Joyce had been a physical education teacher at the man's high school.

Connie's death was a shock to the small community of Zachary, a warning of things to come. But residents in Zachary and Baton Rouge would not know for many years that they had a much larger problem. A problem bigger than just one murder.

If this man was indeed responsible for Melissa's and Joyce's deaths, then Connie's murder made three, and a serial killer had been born on that night in Oak Shadows subdivision. A killer who would hold a vast area of Louisiana in a grip of terror for many years to come. No one was safe.

But back then, ignorance was bliss.

The Cemetery

The young man crouched low beside his car, surrounded by the dead, hiding among them. He was usually
comfortable there, but not on this cool November night
in 1992. It had been only three months since he had left
the woman by the lake, but he hadn't forgotten the feel
of her—the taste of forbidden fruit. He had come back to
Zachary for more. Even though the cool night air blew
across the tombstones, he was sweating. He had ridden
the girl's bicycle hard to get back to his car. He heard the
footsteps getting closer, saw the glare of flashlights illu-
minating the graveyard. He had to make his escape.

He jumped into his red Buick Electra, revved the
engine, and sped out of the Azalea Rest Cemetery, heading down Highway 964. The police officers followed. The
man threw his blue jacket out the window as he drove,
determined to outrun the officers. They caught him at
Shellmire Lane.

"Turn around and put your hands up," an officer commanded. The man complied. They had him.

The house in Fennwood subdivision, just across the
highway from Oak Shadows, had looked like an easy
mark. The man had been watching it. The golf course located behind the affluent homes had made watching easy.
He had thought no one would be home, but the owner

had arrived unexpectedly. The husky black man had tried to be friendly.

"Hi," he'd told the frightened owner. "I'm looking for Monroe," he said before running out of the house and jumping on the bike. The owner called police, who arrived immediately and gave chase.

The man they arrested would make bail in two days and soon return to Buhler Plains Cemetery, located just behind Azalea Rest.

Water poured from the skies in steady streams over the blue Toyota Corolla in which the teenage couple was parked. They didn't care. April always brought rain to South Louisiana, and 1993 was proving to be no different. A rainy night in the Buhler Plains Cemetery only added to the romance as they fumbled with each other's clothing. The graveyard, with its tombstones made of concrete covered in drooping daisies and tulips and roses, was the perfect place for young love to blossom. They were determined to complete their union as the heat between them fogged the windows, and the rain pelted the top of their vehicle.

The young boy kissed the girl as he helped her peel down her pants, first one leg, then the other. Hungry for closer contact, he rid himself of his jeans and lay on top of her in the backseat, loving the feel of her body so close to him, uninhibited by clothing. So focused was he on the girl that he did not hear the footsteps approaching through the patter of rain and the passionate whirring in his brain. When the door opened, he jumped up, startled.

He couldn't see the man, but the dome light outlined the bush axe just before it bit into the boy's scalp, cutting deeply. The girl screamed, putting up her arms to defend herself, but not before the axe raked across her leg. The axe kept coming as the young couple tried desperately to avoid its jagged edge. They were unsuccessful, the axe ravaging the boy's arms, his hands, as he tried to protect the girl; the ferocious man wielding the weapon was determined to hack them to bits.

As suddenly as the attack had begun, it stopped. The man had spotted headlights coming his way. He grabbed the keys from the ignition and ran into the night, skirting in and out of the tombstones he knew so well, hidden by the darkness. The teenagers, in shock and afraid he would come back, locked the car doors.

Officer Troy Eubanks had passed by the cemetery only seconds before and noticed the light from the car shining in the darkness. He turned around to investigate, thinking that no one in his right mind would be in the cemetery on a night like this. Eubanks approached the car carefully and was startled when he shined his flashlight into the window and saw two half-dressed kids covered in blood. The girl started screaming, "It's him! It's him!" Eubanks understood her fear and turned the flashlight on himself so the hysterical girl could see his uniform. The girl cautiously unlocked the door.

Eubanks saw the severe laceration on the boy's head and called for paramedics. The teenagers were transported to separate hospitals, while police searched the cemetery, but they were unable to find any footprints or other clues of value because the rain had washed away any trace of the man with the axe. Only the backseat of the Corolla, covered in blood, gave witness to the fierceness and determination of the would-be butcher.

It would be six years before the girl would identify her attacker in a lineup. But it was too late by then. The statute of limitations for attempted murder was prescribing. The man she identified would be allowed to stay on the streets—free to roam about and kill at will. His name was Derrick Todd Lee. His family called him Todd.

Derrick Todd Lee

"Don't you move, Tarshia. You're gonna scare the birds."

Tarshia moved, wiggling about in the tree, the sound of her movements rustling through the leaves.

"Didn't I tell you not to move?" Todd warned, irritated with his little sister and wondering why he had brought her along. "Next time, I'm leaving you at home."

But he never did. Todd liked bringing Tarshia along when he went bird hunting. He brought her with him most everywhere, and Tarshia loved that her big brother with the big smile let her hang around. She liked him, even though they squabbled a bit. Her mother and stepfather would often laugh and say, "That Todd and Tarshia, they argue and fuss today, and then tonight they're back talking."

A year younger, Tarshia was smarter than Todd, catching up to him in the fourth grade when Todd was held back. He had always been a little slow in school, and Tarshia had fun teasing him that year. "Miss Hammond's gonna give you a paddlin' when you don't know how to spell your spelling words." Tarshia would laugh. She never misspelled her words. "Miss Hammond said I'm the smartest girl in the class. I got an award, and you're gonna get a paddlin'."

Though she teased him, she loved Todd—loved that he

took her horseback riding on the horse their stepfather had given him, loved that he let her hang around him, that he took her through trails in the woods around their home. Together, the two of them would gather old sheets to make tents in the yard. They liked to pretend they were camping out, and Tarshia would make sandwiches or pile leftovers onto plates to eat inside their tent. Tinita, their older sister, and Debra, their younger sister, would play with them sometimes, but Todd and Tarshia had a special bond. They shared the same father, although they didn't know him.

In 1968, Samuel Ruth and Florence Lee were living with Florence's mother in St. Francisville, Louisiana. They were only together for a couple of years and never married, but Florence gave birth to Derrick Todd Lee and Tarshia Lee during that time. Florence was only seventeen when Todd was born and didn't even bother to list Samuel as the father on his birth certificate. Samuel soon took off to reunite with his first wife, Rosetta Ruth, with whom he had fathered five children.

It would be many years before Todd and Tarshia saw their father again, but perhaps that was for the best. Samuel Ruth had problems—severe mental problems. Samuel would go on to father three more children, one with his first wife and two with his second. It would be the testimony of his second wife that would result in his arrest for attempted manslaughter in 1991. Todd and Tarshia were lucky. They had Coleman Barrow.

Florence's luck with men changed when she met Coleman, and when the couple wed, Coleman became a father to her children—a real father. He worked long hours driving a cement truck to provide for the family. He spent what time he could with the children, teaching them right from wrong, playing with them. He and Florence raised them in the church, taught them about God, about sin. Theirs was a normal family life set amidst a backdrop of beauty.

They made their home on the outskirts of St. Francisville in the little settlement of Independence in a small grouping of houses and mobile homes off Blackmore Road, known to the locals as Lee's Quarters. They lived in a nice brick home in an alcove filled with trailers that housed many extended family members. Aunts, uncles, and cousins lived next door and across the street and down the block. Kenny Ray Lee, a cousin whom everyone called Ray, lived just across Highway 61, and he and Todd would often play together, basketball and baseball and sometimes whaling away on drums. Todd played the snare. Together, the two boys marched in the band at school, and on weekends they fished at the sandy-bottomed Thompson Creek, which ran just behind Todd's house. And though the red clay beneath the sand often muddied the water in the summertime, turning it to hues of rust, the boys would gather their fishing poles and sit on the banks of the creek waiting for hungry fish to nibble on their lines.

Ray was a year older than Todd, and was about ten when he first heard the rumors. Todd was peeping into the windows of homes in the area, looking at girls, at his cousins in a way that nine-year-old boys shouldn't be looking. Todd liked to watch girls just as he liked to watch birds. "Shhh, Tarshia, don't you move." Todd never moved when he was watching. He knew how to be very still, even at nine.

Growing up in St. Francisville should have been magical for the young boy, but the area was steeped in old Southern traditions with reminders of the past whispering through the breezes that blew through oak alleys and rolling hills. Although many envision all of Louisiana as flat, swampy land, St. Francisville begins the foothills to the Appalachian Mountains. Numerous antebellum homes dot the landscape, beautiful plantations such as Hemingbough and Greenwood. It is rumored that Todd's ancestors worked as slaves on Greenwood Plantation, which later came to be owned by Connie Warner's sister.

The Myrtles is another relic of the past along Highway 61. This plantation is reputed to be one of the most haunted houses in America—its reputation due in part to the numerous murders that have taken place there. Nestled among the others is Butler Greenwood Plantation, whose current owner was married to a former warden of the Louisiana State Penitentiary at Angola, a warden who tried to kill her.

Many secrets lie hidden throughout the small town that has never experienced the commercialization that other cities do. There are gas stations and fast-food restaurants and salons, like other towns, but old architectural structures stand alongside red-cobblestone sidewalks in the downtown area, and history can still be felt in the lines of the homes whose wide porches invite neighbors over to drink iced lemonade during humid Louisiana afternoons. Life is just a little slower here. Everyone knows everyone and their business. But the lines between the races—black and white—are ever present, and the plantations serve as a constant reminder. There is separation here between the wealthier white landowners and the blacks who live together in clusters and boast a larger population than whites.

Because their heritage is felt so strongly in this town, black boys are taught at an early age to stay away from the white women. They are the "forbidden fruit and will do nothing but get you in trouble." Even lighter-skinned blacks, the Creoles, are not to be messed with. Children are taught to stick with their own kind, in both white and black households. West Feliciana High School still hosts separate black and white proms, almost fifty years after desegregation. But though the township clings to such outdated modes of thought, St. Francisville is a wonderful place to live, and the locals are rather snobbish about the piece of paradise they call home.

Locals aren't the only ones enamored of its beauty. Every year, St. Francisville attracts thousands from around the country who are drawn to this charming reminder of the past, regardless of the fact that this particular part of the South prospered on the backs of so many who were enslaved to bring wealth to plantation owners. Even John James Audubon took up residence in St. Francisville for many years because the vast bird population provided so many opportunities for him to capture nature at its finest in his paintings.

Todd liked to explore the wonderful setting into which he was born. The children in Lee's Quarters were not allowed to play inside during the day, so they all spent a lot of time in the outdoors. Todd spent many hours at his cousin's house watching Ray's family work in the garden. He looked up to Ray's father, Robert, who was Florence's brother, and to his maternal grandfather. He also respected Coleman, happy that he had a father in his life who paid attention to him, who had given him a train for Christmas when he was a small boy. He liked to watch it go round and round the track. Everyone knew, however, that Todd was just a little slow.

In school, Todd was placed in special education classes, his inability to learn as fast as the other children evident early on. But in the 1970s, many black children were labeled slow learners and placed in special classes. Todd's IQ was tested regularly, sometimes slipping below seventy, the standard measure of retardation, but mostly staying above—between seventy-five and ninety-one throughout his school years. And in physical education classes, he did well, always dressing out and participating. If he got into the occasional scuffle with other kids, he just walked away and quit playing. Ray can remember several instances where Todd could have gotten into a fight, but didn't. "He only fought when someone got in his face," Ray recalls. "But mostly he walked away."

Todd's second cousin Betty had a different perspective.

"I done seen that boy's temper all through growin' up.
That boy had him a temper."

Todd was arrested for the first time three days after his
thirteenth birthday for burglarizing the Sweet Shop on
Highway 935, just off Blackmore Road. He pled guilty to
simple burglary, was placed on probation, and was ordered to make restitution. His violent temper went on
record when he was sixteen. He was arrested by the St.
Francisville Police Department (SFPD) and charged with
attempted second-degree murder after a fight with another teenager, Roy Raiford. Todd had tried to cut him
with a knife. There would be no disposition in that case.

When he was seventeen, Todd's propensity for peeping
into the homes of others finally got him into trouble. In
February of 1986, Alfred Lee, along with Florence, went to
the West Feliciana Parish Sheriff's Office (WFPSO) to
report that Todd had been peeping into the windows of
Alfred's house. "He's also been peeping into my sister An-
gelina's house," Alfred told police. "He starts looking in my
window around eight o'clock at night. This has been going
on for about two weeks, and I'm sick and tired of it."

Although he experienced these arrests as a teenager,
Todd was never required to spend any time in a juvenile detention facility.

Todd met Jacqueline "Jackie" Denise Sims, his future
wife, when she was thirteen. She had moved to St. Francisville from California to live with her father, Henry Sims,
after her mother, Doris, had passed away. Jackie was six
months younger than Todd. She liked the boy with the big
smile, and the two soon became friends. Todd was nice to
her. He didn't hang around girls much, not the ones at
school, preferring to play with his female cousins at home.
He didn't hang out with the other boys either. He had
enough friends within his family to keep him occupied,
and they accepted him, understood him. He didn't have
to worry about what they thought. But Jackie was different.
She liked him. She was quiet and smart. He didn't have to

try hard to impress her, but he liked to impress others. Later on in life, he would spend a lot of time bragging about the women he'd had, the women who wanted him.

Todd dropped out of school in the eleventh grade, and in 1987, he began his love affair with the town of Zachary. He went to work for Kellogg Brown & Root Construction (KBR) as a pipe fitter helper in the small town and would become very familiar with the area. He would work for the company until the middle of 1988.

Jackie and Todd dated throughout high school and married in 1988, soon after she graduated. Their wedding was a big affair, with the whole family present. Liz Lee, the owner of Liz's Lounge, drove the happy couple away from the wedding in her fancy blue-and-white Cadillac. Nine months later, they had a child, Derrick Todd Lee Jr., and Todd was faced with the responsibility of supporting a family. But by September of 1988, Todd would again find himself in trouble and would plead guilty to the unauthorized entry of an inhabited dwelling.

Doris Lee was born in November of 1992, just a few months after the deaths of Joyce Taylor in Baton Rouge and Connie Warner in Zachary. The family was complete, a boy and a girl, and Jackie tried to keep everyone happy.

Todd worked hard, sometimes driving cement trucks, sometimes pipe fitting. He took his children to parks and to the zoo in Baton Rouge, and if he didn't come home occasionally, well, he was a man, and was entitled to do what he wanted.

He liked to hang out in the local bars, drinking Bud Light and bragging about his girlfriends. He and Ray would go to Cat's and Price's Bar in St. Francisville or to Bailey's Lounge and Liz's Lounge, located not far off the road that leads to Angola. Jackie made life easy for Todd. She didn't complain too much and soon adjusted to his roaming. The marriage had deteriorated somewhat after the birth of their first child. Although they had intercourse on occasion, there was not much intimacy or real communication in the marriage. Jackie had heard rumors about other women, but she preferred to ignore them. Eventually, "I just quit caring and went on with my life," she would later admit.

Todd had always been fascinated by women, but he didn't care about the ones who came on to him in the bars. They were too easy. He wanted the other ones—the ones with the pretty dark hair and fair skin. The ones who were smart, with the high cheekbones. The ones he considered to be high society. The forbidden ones. Those were the ones he watched.

And Jackie, tucked away at home to care for the children, was oblivious.

Randi Mebruer

The three-year-old little boy wandered around the yard aimlessly, hoping that his friend next door would come out to play. He was hungry, but he couldn't find his mommy. They had watched movies together before he fell asleep the previous night, but when he awoke, she wasn't there. He had looked on her bed, but no mommy—just a lot of sticky red stuff. He had searched in the bathroom and kitchen and living room. She wasn't there, so he went outside.

"Mom, Michael's outside. Can he come over and play?" Cathy Morris looked at her young son and replied, "Make sure it's okay with his mom." Cathy waited a few minutes, then went outside to make sure that the boy's mother, Randi Mebruer, had said it was okay.

"Did you tell your mother where you are?" she asked Michael.

"Mommy's lost. I can't find her," the little boy cried.

"It's okay, honey. I'll find her for you," Cathy said, knowing that Randi would be home. She would never leave Michael alone.

Cathy reached for Michael's hand and walked across the yard to the house next door. The kitchen door was open, so she went inside with the little boy. Cathy saw the blood on the floor, but she thought Randi must have cut herself.

"Randi? Randi, where are you?" she yelled. There was no answer. Cathy moved into the living room and noticed more blood on the floor. She began to worry. "Randi?" she called. Hoping that Randi was in the shower, Cathy hurried to the bedroom, where she saw even more blood on the bed. She scooped Michael into her arms and ran to get her husband, Robert.

"Robert, there's blood all over Randi's house, and I can't find her," Cathy frantically told her husband. Together, they went back to the house. Robert knew immediately that something was terribly wrong and called the police.

The pretty pale-brick home was located on Saul Avenue, the main road into Oak Shadows subdivision. Randi lived there alone with her son, having divorced his father, Michael Sr., two years earlier. Hers was the fourth house from the end. The houses across the street separated Saul from Job Avenue, where Connie Warner had been abducted six years before. But Randi had always felt safe there, surrounded as she was by the neighbors with whom she had made friends.

Randi was a friendly girl. At twenty-eight, she had a good life. She worked at Synergy Home Health Care in Baton Rouge, a job that made Randi feel good about herself. She liked helping others, but she also liked to have fun. Her arrangement with her ex-husband to have joint custody of little Michael worked out perfectly. Michael got to spend time with both of his parents, and during the time that he was with his father, Randi could go out with her friends in Baton Rouge.

She was a pretty girl, petite and slender, with brown hair and big brown eyes. She liked to work out with ankle weights and barbells and did so on a regular basis. She had no trouble attracting men and enjoyed their attention. She had received roses from an admirer just a week before. Randi had several boyfriends, but one in particular was on her mind this week in the middle of April 1998, the one who had given her flowers. She had met him at Ricky B's Lounge on South Sherwood Forest Boulevard in Baton Rouge on April 10. They made a date for the following night.

Brian Duby arrived at Randi's house that Saturday evening right on time. He took her to Mike Anderson's Seafood restaurant, where they dined on the succulent seafood for which Louisiana is famous. Randi and Brian talked throughout dinner, getting to know each other, before they went to Glen's Bombay Club, where they drank and danced for a while.

Their next stop was Affects lounge. By the time they left the club, around 1:00 A.M., both were feeling the effects of the alcohol and the beginnings of romance. Brian drove Randi home, and the two spent the next few hours making love. Brian promised he would call, and he did the very next day. And the next. He wanted to see her again, but he was scheduled to go to Fort Dodge, Iowa, for a construction job. He told Randi he would be back on April 20 and promised to see her then.

Randi was excited about Brian and looked forward to his return. But sometimes she missed her ex-husband. She had told him that, just a few weeks before when he came over to visit with their son. They had shared a tender moment, one of many they had shared throughout the years. Though they were divorced, they got along well, and Randi was happy that Michael spent so much time with their little boy, even though he lived in Mississippi. Michael was scheduled to pick up his son on April 19.

April 18 started out like any other Saturday. Randi got up, fixed her son breakfast, then set about catching up on housework. Saturdays were the only day she really had time to clean. She began by taking the burners off the stove to scrub underneath, then headed into her bedroom to tackle a pile of clothes that needed attention. A little after noon, she left to run errands, renting some videos for later on, and returning home in time to make Michael his supper. She talked to his father for a while on the phone, double-checking to make sure that he would be there on Sunday.

Randi spent the evening watching Disney movies with little Michael. As the final credits rolled, Randi smiled as she looked at him sleeping. She picked up her young son and carried him to bed, carefully tucking the covers around him.

"Good night, Michael. I love you," she might have whispered as she kissed him. Had she known that would be their last kiss, their last "I love you," she might have sat beside his bed just a little longer, holding close this little boy she loved so much. But she couldn't know, so she returned to the living room to check her Lotto ticket. The local news program broadcast the results at nine fifty-nine each night. Disgusted that she hadn't won, again, Randi crumpled up the ticket and pitched it onto the coffee table. Her luck was about to go from bad to worse. Someone had been watching her. Another man who thought she was pretty.

Todd was not in a good mood. He had been laid off from Ascension Ready Mix just two days before, and Consandra Green, his girlfriend, had been giving him problems. They were always arguing, but this night was worse than usual. They had spent the afternoon barbecuing with friends and then headed off to Bailey's. Then it was on to Liz's Lounge, just up the street. Liz Lee had been a teacher at West Feliciana High when Todd had been a student there and had been friends with Jackie's father, but she was not related to Todd's family. Archer Lee, Liz's son, was a detective with the city police and had been keeping his eye on Todd throughout the years. Todd liked Liz, even though she was a feisty old lady who didn't like any kind of trouble in her bar.

And Todd was trouble, but the girls who admired the way he always dressed so sharply liked his kind of trouble. So did Consandra, but not on this night. She was sick of watching Todd flirt with other women and told him so. Upset and tired, Consandra left the bar about 10:30 P.M. and went home. Todd drove to another favorite hangout, the Hideaway Lounge in Alsen, a small settlement just north of Baton Rouge. He sat at the bar and drank, his anger and frustration building. He thought about the girl he had been watching. The one in Oak Shadows. Todd downed his beer, picked up his money from the bar, and headed for the door.

As he drove north on Highway 964, he thought about the pretty lady with the little boy. He smiled as his mind worked over the details—how she would look, how she would feel. He wondered if she would fight. The excitement made him accelerate. Already he could feel the wildness stirring within as he thought about how he would kill her. He parked his truck in a familiar spot, the Outskirts Lounge at the corners of Highways 964 and 64 in Zachary. Todd took off on foot, his heart pumping as he made his way stealthily through the shadows.

Randi prepared for bed. She might have thought about Brian and how nice he had been. It was only two more days before he would be back in town, and she couldn't wait to see him. Her friends said she was excited about him. Michael had assured her that he would be there to pick up the baby. She closed her eyes and fell asleep.

Did she next hear a knock at the door? Had she left it unlocked? Was she in bed when Todd, dressed in his red shirt, black jeans, and snakeskin boots, entered her home? No one would ever know, but no signs of forced entry would be evident.

It is not known how Randi Mebruer was killed as her body has never been found. What police discovered when they arrived was blood. Lots of it. The headboard of the bed was covered in red, as if Randi's head had been smashed against it. Her contact lenses lay in a puddle on the floor; smudges of blood surrounded the light switch. The living-room floor revealed a scarlet trail, smeared, as if she had been dragged across it. Still more blood was found on the floor of the kitchen, pieces of Randi's hair mangled in the gore.

As Todd pulled the helpless woman from the house, her blood spilled again onto the carport near a trash can liner, an object that would hold the clue that would solve her murder five years later. Semen, carelessly ejaculated onto the liner, would eventually be linked to the DNA of a serial killer.

Randi simply vanished. Her car, which she usually parked in the center of the driveway, was out of place, parked to the left. Her keys and the five-pound barbells she worked out with, like Randi, would never be found.

Todd disposed of Randi's body as easily as he had killed her, with no thought that she was human, a real person with hopes and dreams and love in her heart. To him, she was nothing. He had accomplished what he had set out to do. He had possessed another white woman. He had watched the blood run from her body. He had felt the release spill from his. He was once again free of the terrible hunger. Todd drove straight to Consandra's, ready to make up. He hated it when she was mad at him.

Little Michael slept peacefully through the night.

Michael Sr. would soon find himself a suspect in the murder of his ex-wife. He arrived in Zachary the next day to pick up his son, only to discover that Randi was missing, the condition of her home suggesting that she had been harmed.

"She would not leave Michael alone," he told police. "She's a good mother. I talked to her just last night, around seven. She was telling me about a new guy she was seeing. Everything seemed fine."

"Do you know this guy's name?" Detective Louis Banks asked him.

"No, but maybe her friend Tammy would. She works with Randi."

Michael would be called back to Zachary for questioning again and again. Police would learn that he'd had surgery on his foot just days before Randi's disappearance and was still in some pain. Michael assured them that he and Randi got along fine, neglecting to mention until the middle of May that he and Randi had still been intimate on occasion, and had made love about a week and a half before she was taken. Police asked him about fights they'd had in the past, but Michael insisted that aside from the occasional spat, they were friends. Michael seemed to be honest and sincere, but police would gain more insight into him through his other former wife, who stated that their marriage had been fraught with arguing and violence.

Samantha Mebruer told police that she and a friend had followed Michael one day, and when he spotted her, Michael had jumped out of his car and said, "I've been in the marines and could kill y'all, bury y'all, and nobody would find y'all."

Samantha said that Michael had a drinking problem and had been in Parkland Hospital for seventy-two hours one time to combat his alcoholism. The Zachary police gave Michael a second look, talking to his coworkers and his girlfriend, Holly. She alibied him for the night in question. Still, they kept Michael under their radar for

years. Although they had no evidence, the police were
suspicious of him.

Michael took his son back to Centerville, Mississippi,
to raise him alone, wondering if Randi would ever come
back. From the condition of her home, he didn't think
so. He tried to explain to Michael Jr. why his mommy
had disappeared.

There was one detective with the Zachary Police Department who knew why Randi had vanished. He knew
who had done it, knew that she was dead. He felt it in his
gut. And he would spend years trying to prove it. His
dogged pursuit of his suspect would eventually get him
removed from the case. And it was not Michael Mebruer
he was after.

David McDavid

It was a cold night in February 1997, a little after nine o'clock, and Sergeant Roderick Ennis was patrolling Oak Shadows subdivision with his headlights turned off. There had been numerous calls to the Zachary police station about a prowler. Ennis noticed a man wearing a blue warm-up jacket with the hood pulled over his head walking by the corner of Job and Eli. The man looked back as Ennis got closer, and Ennis knew immediately that he did not belong in the neighborhood. Ennis knew because he lived there. He pulled over.

"What are you doing?" he asked the man.

"My truck broke down, and I'm goin' to my girlfriend's to use the phone," Todd responded.

"What's her name?"

"I dunno."

"Where does she live?"

Todd again answered, "I dunno."

Ennis asked Todd for picture identification. He said it was in his broken vehicle. He was fidgeting now.

As Todd tried to put his hand in his pocket, Ennis noticed a sheath for a knife on the man's right side. Ennis patted him down. The sheath was empty, but he found a folded knife in the front pocket of Todd's starched blue jeans. He found brown work gloves in his back pocket, but no wallet or keys. He asked for Todd's name, then ran a check on him. It came back with no warrants. Ennis brought Todd back to his truck, which was parked beside the cemetery, and again asked for identification. Todd reached into his brown Chevrolet truck for his driver's license and gave it to Ennis. Satisfied, Ennis let him go. Todd started the truck right up and drove away. He would not be arrested on this night. Ennis had no cause, although he was very suspicious.

David McDavid, a detective with the ZPD whom everyone called Mac, was on call the night of July 31, 1997. When his phone rang, he was summoned to Oak Shadows subdivision in reference to a black male Peeping Tom. He was asked to assist uniform patrol. Mac jumped into his truck, already suspecting who the culprit was he would be looking for. He had chased Todd before. He had chased him for years. He already suspected him of Connie Warner's murder and of the brutal hacking of the kids in the cemetery. Mac had been in uniform back then, but Todd had a history of peeping into windows in the area. Mac had no doubt that Todd was his man, but he couldn't prove it. As he hurried to join the chase, he worried. He knew that the women in that neighborhood weren't safe. This time it was a house on Numbers Avenue, right behind the house where Connie had lived.

As Mac was riding through the area, another call came in from Willow Creek Apartments, also referred to as Divorce Row, about a half mile farther up the road. A black male was standing in a kiddy pool looking into the window of an apartment. By the time Mac got there, the man was gone. Mac continued to ride down Highway 964 and turned in to Fennwood subdivision, just across the highway from Oak Shadows. On the main road, he spotted Todd running across the street. He shined his light on him, but Todd kept running. He was headed for the

Junction Lounge. Mac followed and saw Todd's truck in the parking lot. He ran the plates, just to be sure.

Todd took off toward the woods. Mac called for tracking K-9s and put an officer with night vision in the cemetery. The officer spotted Todd tiptoeing in between trees and graves, looking this way and that, trying to see if the officers were nearby. Todd ran toward the highway, then squatted, looking up and down the road. Another officer approaching from the north saw Todd running toward him. Todd didn't see the officer until it was too late.

Todd, who said that his truck had broken down and he was looking for a phone, was apprehended. He was wet and covered in mud. He was brought to the station and booked on six counts of criminal trespassing, two counts of being a Peeping Tom, and resisting an officer. His boot print matched perfectly to the ones set in mud outside the window into which he had been peeping. As usual, Todd was dressed to the nines. And as usual, he would be bailed out quickly.

Mac took Todd's offenses personally. He had grown up just three houses down from Betty Brooks and had been friends with Connie Warner's daughter, Tracy. No one wanted to find Connie's murderer more than Mac, who had joined the police department as a reserve in 1984. He had spent many years as a reserve before joining the force full-time and finally being promoted to detective in 1997.

Mac was a friendly man with a good sense of humor. He was handsome, with graying brown hair and a salt-and-pepper mustache, which gave him a distinguished air. He was muscular and trim, with a ready smile that immediately put frightened victims at ease. Criminals, though, were not at ease around Mac as he had a steely side that let them know that he meant business. The law was not meant to be broken, and Mac had little tolerance for repeat offenders.

He had even less tolerance for Todd. He knew that Todd had been peeping in the area earlier that year.

Todd pled guilty on January 14, 1998, to two counts of being a Peeping Tom for the July incident. He was placed on supervised probation for one year. Probation was not enough to keep him away from Oak Shadows, and on April 18, Todd returned to Saul Avenue to the home of a mother and her young son.

Mac knew immediately. "I knew that he was involved in Randi's murder, in Connie's murder, in the incident in the cemetery. Wholeheartedly I knew." And on April 20, Mac, along with Officer Kling and Detective Banks, headed to Highway 61 to a house in Starhill, near St. Francisville, to question Todd. They conducted a cursory search of his home, with Todd's consent.

Todd was advised of his rights and informed that the officers were investigating anyone who had been arrested before in that area. Todd told them that he had been at Bailey's with Consandra, then had gone to the Highland Bar and on to the Junior Food Mart. "Then we went back to Highland, but we got in a fight. Consandra went home, and so did I. I stayed there for about a half hour; then I went to Hideaway Lounge in Alsen."

"I know what you're doing," Mac told Todd as he headed into his bedroom. "I know what you're doing, and I'm going to get you."

Todd shadowed Mac as he peered into the closet. Todd's side was very neat, shirts and jeans starched and pressed, in contrast to Jackie's disheveled side. "He was on top of me when I looked at his clothes. So much so that the hairs on the back of my neck stood up," Mac said. "Then he asked us to leave."

Mac would interview Consandra the next day, an interview that would convince him even further that Todd was responsible for what had happened to Randi. Todd's path would have placed him on Highway 964 at the entrance to Oak Shadows subdivision at the established time of

Randi's abduction—between 10:30 P.M. and 2:30 A.M.
A neighbor would come forward to say that she had heard
a loud noise, which sounded like a muzzled shotgun blast,
around midnight.

The owner of the Outskirts Lounge, close to Oak
Shadows, would tell officers that the guy who had been
arrested for peeping in the area had been parking his
two-toned brown or champagne truck in the bar's lot
and had taken off on foot several times over the last
three weeks. On another occasion, he had seen the
truck parked at the Daiquiri Depot across the street and
had watched the driver get out of it at about 9:00 P.M.
The truck was still there at 1:00 A.M. when the owner
left. That was on a Wednesday. He saw it again on a
Thursday when he left the club about 3:00 A.M. He remembered the truck from when Todd was arrested the
year before.

It would be years later that a confidential source would
come forward to say that Todd had come to his home
about midnight just a night or so after Randi's disappearance. Todd asked him to take a ride with him to his
house, and the confidential source agreed. The source
got into Todd's pickup and watched as Todd opened the
console and placed a long-barrel revolver inside. They
drove to Starhill and stayed at Todd's house for only a few
minutes before driving back to the source's home.

On the way, Todd informed the source that the
Zachary Police Department was harassing him over a
missing woman. Police had not informed Todd that
anyone was missing. It was the next day as the confidential source was watching TV that he saw the first reports
about Randi's abduction. It was the woman Todd had
told him about the night before.

* * *

Mac, along with Sergeant Ray Day, who had been one of the first officers at the scene to investigate Randi's disappearance, would spend many years trying to get enough evidence to arrest Todd. In 1999, they would enlist the help of the Louisiana Attorney General's Office (AG's office), which would work with the Zachary police to solve the cold cases that had occurred at Oak Shadows. As the years passed, these two men would become more and more frustrated with the knowledge that a murderer was free in their midst, and they could do nothing about it. They knew him—what he had done, what he was capable of doing, and where he lived. But they could do nothing. There was not enough evidence to stand up in court. At least that's what they thought.

But locked away in an evidence locker in the ZPD station was a trash-can liner containing the DNA of the killer. It had not been tested, though, and that simple mistake, among others, would cost many women their lives.

Still, the two men, each in his own way, would keep Todd in their sights.

Mac, because of his single-minded determination that Todd had killed Connie and Randi, would be taken off the case for a year. Other officers in charge felt that the culprits were ex-husbands or boyfriends. Mac would again become involved with the cases in 2002 when he was promoted to lieutenant. But in 2001, Mac would become convinced that the man he had chased for years had set his sights on Baton Rouge. He knew from the start the name of the South Louisiana Serial Killer. It was Derrick Todd Lee.

But no one would listen.

Derrick Todd Lee—The 1990s

"I got to do the right thing, Tarshia. I got to," Todd said.

"You're giving the baby your name?" Tarshia couldn't believe it.

"It's the right thing to do. I gotta do right by my kid," Todd replied.

Consandra was pregnant, and everyone in the Lee family already knew. Todd had made no secret of the fact that he had a steady girlfriend. He'd been staying at the apartment they shared in Jackson, Louisiana, just down Highway 10, two or three nights each week. Now she was pregnant, and he was determined to give the baby his name.

The two had met at the Highland Bar in March of 1997 and had hit it off. Todd soon began spending more and more time with Consandra, and although Jackie knew, she didn't care. She enjoyed the peace and quiet when Todd was away. Although he could be very charming at times, even chasing her around the house to get a hug now and again, the marriage had become quite stormy.

There had been the incident in February of 1990 when Todd had twisted her arm and thrown her out of the house. She had filed a restraining order against him then. In May, he had gotten into a fight with her dad, Henry, and had been arrested for disturbing the peace.

Jackie forgave him for those incidents and took him back. In November of 1992, Jackie filed an absent parent form against Todd, stating that he had walked out on her and the children, and in early 1993, she requested action against him for criminal neglect of family. Todd came home. The couple would get along for a few months, but in June of 1993, Jackie complained to the St. Francisville police that Todd was beating and choking her. In February of 1997, Jackie would make a complaint that Todd was fighting with her because she had been talking on the telephone. She called police again in December of 1998, claiming that Todd had hit her.

The early 1990s were not good years for Todd's biological father either. Samuel Ruth had been hospitalized many times during his life for mental disorders. He had been diagnosed with manic-depressive disorder and was considered psychotic. He liked to preach the Bible to anyone who would listen, and, like Todd, he drove a truck for a living. He had a history of violence toward the women in his life. By 1991, he was divorced from Rose Marie Williams, who claimed that he had physically abused her. Police in Gretna, Louisiana, a suburb of New Orleans, arrested Ruth by the end of that year for attempting to murder Rose. He had grabbed his gun, pointed it at her, and pulled the trigger repeatedly. Luckily for Rose, the gun did not fire.

Samuel's mental problems surfaced while he was being held over for trial. Guards at the prison where he was housed reported that he refused to wear clothes and could often be spotted naked in his cell, washing his face in the toilet. Samuel was ruled incompetent to stand trial. For the most part, he was incoherent. He was committed to a mental institution until he was able to stand trial. In 1997, Samuel would be moved to a long-term facility where he would spend another five years before a judge deemed him competent. He would eventually

plead guilty to attempted manslaughter and be released
in a plea bargain. During the course of his care, Samuel
reported to his doctor that his family had a history of
mental illness. But though Todd, his biological son,
would occasionally fight with those he loved, no one suspected that it was anything more than that.

Todd's temper would definitely improve in 1996 when
Jackie's father died in an explosion at the Amoco plant,
where he worked. Jackie received about a quarter of a mil-
lion dollars in a settlement. Todd was in heaven. Overnight
he could dress the way he wanted, buy the cars and trucks
he wanted, spend money in bars, attract women. And he
did. Suddenly all the girls in his local hangouts wanted to
talk to him. He dressed sharply in expensive shirts, de-
signer jeans, and snakeskin boots. His neck was adorned
with gold chains. Todd enjoyed the attention and knew
how to sweet-talk the girls. They were attracted to his good
looks and his money, although he never spent a lot on
them. He was known, though, to occasionally buy the bar
a round. He liked the image that having money created for
him. But even the money didn't stop the secret life he led.

Although Todd was constantly in trouble with police,
his mother and sisters did not usually see the darker side
he kept hidden from them. They knew he had been a
Peeping Tom, but they thought he had grown out of
that. They knew he had a temper, but he'd always had
that. In 1990, Todd and Florence had gotten into an argument over money that Todd said Florence owed him.
The dispute had led to the police being called.

And on another occasion, Tarshia filed a complaint
that Todd had tried to break into her home. When
Tarshia refused to let him in, Todd had taken the glass
out of the front door, put his hand inside, and unlocked
the door. When Florence got home, she berated Todd
for coming into the house without permission. Todd

started threatening Tarshia, telling her, "You keep it up, and you're gonna get an ass whipping like nobody ever had. You got that?" But even though they fought occasionally, Todd loved his family and bought Florence a brand-new van with the money Jackie had received.

Jackie was quiet and preferred to stay home with the children, while Todd enjoyed being out and carousing. She minded her own business and kept to herself, ignoring the rumors she heard. She and Todd had finally bought a home with the settlement money, and she was comfortable there. It was a nice brick, three-bedroom house with a large yard, almost an acre, on Highway 61 in an area south of town known as Starhill. The house, located next to the home of Todd's uncle Robert, would become a permanent stain on the landscape, a reminder to anyone traveling toward St. Francisville of the evil that had grown up in the town.

Jackie had never really been happy with Todd, but she was very loyal to him, and she loved him in her way. He was the father of her children. But he had been in and out of trouble since they had wed, and she preferred a more peaceful life. Todd had been arrested in Zachary, in St. Francisville, and in Lake Charles, where they had lived for a while. He had been in and out of prison. She didn't understand why he did the things he did.

In July of 1993, Todd was convicted of simple burglary and was sentenced to four years of hard labor. He was remanded to the custody of East Baton Rouge Parish, where he spent the next two years within its prison system. He signed up for parole in July of 1995 and moved to Lake Charles, where he would be arrested two months later on Peeping Tom charges. Todd was sentenced to 120 days, but the sentence was suspended and he received two years of unsupervised probation.

Todd was arrested again three weeks later when he decided to take a ride with his cousin Robert Lee Welcome and their friend Sean Simpson. The young men were going to the store to get cigarettes when Todd spotted some Salvation Army bins and decided to avail himself of some of the contents, including five bundles of clothing and a gray suitcase. Unfortunately for Todd, local police were patrolling the area and watched the men empty the bins. As Todd and his cohorts left, the police gave chase and captured them as they turned into a private driveway on the corner of Third Avenue and Sixth Avenue. The burglary and theft charges would be reduced to misdemeanors.

Todd would soon return to St. Francisville, where he would enjoy the luxuries his wife's money afforded. One of those luxuries was Consandra. But Todd and Consandra's relationship was even stormier than his marriage. Where he had fought with Jackie at home in private, he and Consandra aired their differences in the many bars in which they partied. Todd had what many men fantasize about—a wife at home and a girlfriend he could stay with whenever he wanted. Both of these women, who had become used to his comings and goings at all hours, would never suspect what he was really doing when they found themselves alone. Todd convinced both women that the police were out to get him; so each time he was arrested was simply another example that the police had a vendetta against him.

But then Consandra got pregnant with Dedrick Lee, the illegitimate son Todd had insisted must have his name because he liked to do the right thing. The tension began to build. With Dedrick's birth in July of 1999, Todd now had the responsibility of two families—two women nagging at him, three children to feed. And the money that he had enjoyed was gone—spent on clothes, gold chains, and the numerous vehicles he went through. But Todd had already found someone new on whom to focus his attention: Collette Walker.

Collette Walker

Downtown St. Francisville is picturesque, a step back in time to the Old South. St. Ferdinand Street leads the way past the West Feliciana Historical Society, housed in a Greek Revival structure built in 1896, to the Grace Episcopal Church, constructed in 1827 and surrounded by a lacy wrought-iron fence that allows visitors a glimpse of the beautiful church on the hill. Grandmother's Buttons, which specializes in making jewelry from beautiful antique buttons, makes its home in the old bank building, which was built in 1905, and is just around the corner from the Georgian Revival courthouse, built the same year. In the midst of this historical ambiance, the more modern St. Francisville Square Apartments provide lodging for those who want to enjoy the beautiful tree-shrouded area. With its redbrick townhouses trimmed in white and single-storied duplexes, this apartment complex affords its residents serenity under a blanket of oaks. A brick apron at both entrances welcomes residents home.

And until June 21, 1999, thirty-six-year-old Collette Walker had enjoyed living there. But on that day, she had an unexpected encounter in the parking lot close to her front door as she was leaving for the local Cracker Barrel convenience store. The man was so quiet that she was startled by his approach. He was black, well-dressed, and good-looking.

"Do you live in that apartment?" Todd asked, pointing in the direction of her home.

"What?" This man made Collette nervous. He had come from the parking lot and had walked up so quietly.

"Was that your boyfriend that just left?" the man continued. The girl with the flawlessly fair complexion was pretty, and Todd had been watching.

"Where are you going? You wanna go for a ride across the river to get a beer?"

"I'm not going anywhere but to the store and back," Collette responded, amazed that the black man was trying to pick her up in the parking lot.

"Will you go out with me Sunday night?" Todd pressed on.

"No. I'm not going anywhere this weekend." Hoping that the man would leave her alone, Collette began walking to her car.

"Can you gimme a ride to my car? I was visiting a friend and need a ride over there," Todd said, pointing toward the post office. Collette told him no and left. She was nervous about the encounter, so she took her time at the Cracker Barrel, chatting for a while with some police officers who were there. Hoping that the man would be gone, she returned home.

As she unlocked her door, Todd walked up from around the corner of the building. He asked her again for a ride. Collette said no. "You'll make me walk?" Todd asked. Collette closed the door.

Two days later, Collette was entering her apartment, when Todd appeared suddenly and followed her inside. He asked for a glass of water or a beer. Nervous and not quite knowing what to do, Collette got him water. Todd sat down on the couch as if he had every right to be there.

"Do you date black guys?" he asked.

Collette didn't want to offend him, so she told him that another black guy had asked her out once, but she had told him that they could only be friends because she didn't date black men.

"I bet a lot of black guys ask you out. I bet they like the way you look. I been wantin' to ask you for a while. That's why I been comin' in the store the last two months."

Collette worked at Feliciana Seafood and suddenly realized where she had seen him before.

"I think we should go out of town, but we gotta make sure no one knows 'cause I like to keep my business to myself," Todd told her. "What would your family think if you dated a black man?"

"They'd probably disown me," Collette responded, wondering how she was going to get rid of him.

"That's what the last white woman I dated said. She'd pick me up, and we'd spend the weekend at her apartment. No one ever knew," Todd bragged. "I know that white women fantasize about being with black guys, and I'm telling ya, if you was with me, no one else would matter no more. You would want just me."

Collette couldn't believe that this man was sitting on her couch, telling her these things. She watched in disbelief as he turned off the lamp. She turned it back on.

"Look, if you need money or help in any way, I take good care of my white women 'cause they know how to take care of their men. Black women don't treat their men right. They just want 'em to pay the bills. Come on," Todd pled. "Go out of town with me tonight."

"No," Collette said.

"Why not?"

"You might be one of those crazy people who would kill me and throw me on the side of the road."

Todd laughed. "If that's how I am, I could rape you right now, and no one would know, because I'm in your apartment."

Todd turned the lamp off again. Collette turned it back on. "You really have to go," she told him, more uncomfortable than ever.

"Give me a ride."

"No."

Todd wrote his phone number on a piece of paper and handed it to Collette. "Call me Todd, and don't tell anyone I was here. I really don't like people knowin' my business." He asked for a hug. When Collette didn't respond, he reached over to hug her, then left the apartment. Worried about the man who had been in her apartment and wanting to get out of there, Collette took a ride to the store.

The next night, he was back. It was late, around 11:30 P.M., and Collette's daughter wanted to get her fingernail polish from the car. Collette was standing at the door to keep an eye on her, when she got a funny feeling. She looked around but didn't see anyone. As her daughter came back, Collette saw Todd move away from a nearby tree.

"Is that your daughter? She looks just like you," Todd said. "I was looking for Apartment 13C."

Collette became very uncomfortable because she knew that he had been hiding behind that tree. He wasn't looking for an apartment. He was watching her home. The other times he had been there, she had thought that he was just walking through the complex. This time, she knew better. Collette got her daughter inside and hurriedly closed and locked the door.

A few days later, Collette ran into her neighbor Diane, who asked her about the black guy who had been hanging around. Diane said that the man had told her that he and Collette were dating, that he was waiting for her. Todd had asked Diane if she would talk to Collette about him, and then tried to follow Diane into her apartment.

She immediately told him to leave. Diane said she was worried because she had seen the man trying to look through a window into Collette's apartment. Collette called the police.

Assistant Chief of Police Archer Lee responded to the call. He had seen Todd hanging out in Liz's Lounge in the past, and he knew that Todd was being looked at for the Randi Mebruer murder. The St. Francisville police had received numerous Peeping Tom calls through the years, but Collette was the first time they had a solid lead. Todd's shoe print, which they collected from outside the window, was enough.

In a small town, news always travels fast, and Archer Lee was well aware of Todd's history—the fights with Jackie, the incidents in Zachary. He was glad to be able to pick him up finally.

"Todd never knew how I knew what was happening, that Collette had talked to me," Archer explained.

"How you know I was there?" Todd asked during the interrogation.

"I saw you over there," Archer responded. Todd just assumed that he had been videotaped, but when the case for stalking went to trial and Todd listened to Collette and Archer testify, he immediately began talking with his lawyer. Todd changed his plea to guilty in exchange for a plea bargain.

In December of 1999, Todd was sentenced to six months in West Feliciana Parish Prison, but that sentence was suspended. He was placed on supervised probation for two years. Collette was very upset by the plea bargain, and the fact that Todd would not spend any time in prison. But she needn't have worried, because by February of 2000, Todd's probation would be revoked and his sentence made executory. Todd was about to become violent again—this time with Consandra.

* * *

Archer Lee got the call, but it came from his mother, not the police station. Liz was working in her bar that February night. She had owned Liz's Lounge for almost fifty years. Liz treated her patrons with the same authority that she had exercised on the teenagers at West Feliciana High School, where she had taught for many years. Back then, she had been married to Archer's father, who was a farmer. Liz would teach during the day and work the bar at night. During the week, she always closed early. She lived next to the bar in a redbrick house that used to be the old schoolhouse for black children, long before desegregation. She had attended school there and had developed a fondness for the quaint building.

Liz's face was wise but unlined. With the gift of seemingly eternal youth, which many black women enjoy, Liz's beauty could not be erased by age. Neither could her memories. Liz could tell you what life was like when blacks in St. Francisville were treated with disdain by many of the whites. She remembered separate bathrooms and eating quarters. She remembered going to the Laundromat to wash clothes, only to be told she could not by a white woman who was already there.

"What are you doing?" the white woman asked as Liz began to load the washer.

"I'm washing my clothes," the young Liz told her.

"Not in there, you're not," the woman replied. "I just used that one, and I don't want no nigger to use it behind me."

Liz tried to ignore her and loaded the washer. The woman picked up a Coke bottle and hit Liz over the head with it. Liz hit her back. It wasn't long before police showed up at Liz's door and asked her to explain her actions. Liz stood her ground, telling the sheriff what had happened. "If you take me to jail, you'd better take her too." Rather than fight with Liz, the wise deputy let the matter drop. But such were the things that blacks in the area had to put up with.

Over the years, Liz watched the progress, the successful integration of blacks and whites, but in St. Francisville, that integration has been slower and more on a surface level for both blacks and whites. Growing up a generation later, Archer, too, felt the contempt that is barely veiled through smiling lips and shared public restrooms. He had always been fascinated with police work and began his career in corrections. In the late 1980s, he applied to the police department. Unfortunately, although he had been highly recommended, the police chief never called. "One of the lawyers that worked with the department told me that the chief had said, 'As long as I'm here, there will never be a black man on this force,'" Archer recalled. "Luckily, when Kenny Simmons took over as chief, he hired me a week later."

Archer sometimes hung out at his mom's bar, although he did not drink. He just liked to keep an eye on things. He would often see Todd cuddling up to Consandra, not caring who saw him. "He was so bold," Archer said. But on that night in February of 2000, Todd wasn't feeling especially loving and began beating Consandra in the parking lot just after she pulled in.

"I did not want to talk to him. I was trying to get out of my car, and he pushed me back in," Consandra stated to police. "I tried to get out again, and he pulled me out of the car by my hair. He started beating me in the face. He was sitting on top of me. I was begging him to stop hitting me, but he kept doing it. Someone pulled him off of me. As they were holding him, he started stomping me in the face with his cowboy boots. He got loose and started beating me in the face again. They pulled him off of me the second time."

Liz had seen Consandra run into the bar, her face bruised and bleeding. "We hid her behind the DJ booth on the stage," Liz recalled. "When Todd came in looking

for her, I called Archer. Todd even went into the ladies'
room, trying to find her."

When the police arrived, Todd, in an attempt to
escape, tried to run over an officer with his vehicle. He
was arrested for assault and battery, aggravated flight,
simple criminal damage to property, and attempted first-
degree murder of a police officer, a charge that would
later be dropped. Todd would spend the next year in
prison. For a while, women in the area were safe.

Collette would not forget this man who had stalked
her and, in just a few years, would make a call to a multiagency homicide task force that was investigating a serial
killer. She had watched the news programs about the
murders, and she had a feeling about who had done it.
In 2002, she would call a special hotline to report that
she knew who the killer was. She just knew it was the
same man who had stalked her. Again, no one would
listen.

Dannie Mixon

Dannie Mixon got the call shortly before seven in the evening.

A young woman had been raped and murdered on Greenwell Springs Road in Baton Rouge while her children played in another room. Her husband had come home from work to discover her mutilated body. Valerie Davis had been raped, strangled, and stabbed to death with a kitchen knife.

Dannie Mixon lived only a few miles from the victim's home. He jumped into his car, aware that he could get to the crime scene quickly. He had been working homicide for the East Baton Rouge Parish Sheriff's Office (EBRSO) for years, and as he always did before entering the scene of a murder, Dannie mentally prepared as he drove. No matter how many times he encountered the realities of what human beings could do to one another, he never got used to it. Each case affected him deeply, especially the senseless ones, the ones that involved women and children. But no matter how much he had prepared, Dannie was not expecting the brutality he was met with as he entered the house on Greenwell Springs Road, so close to his own home.

Valerie's body lay on the bedroom floor, surrounded by evidence of a bloody struggle. The wounds the knife had inflicted made an eerie pattern across her chest. Her husband had pulled the butcher knife from her left breast. A lamp cord was wrapped around her neck. One of her nipples had been bitten off. Dannie swallowed a lump in his throat.

It was getting late when Dannie and his partner, Bill Strickland, along with other sheriff's deputies, decided to call it a night. They had gathered all the clues they could, and the coroner's office had taken the woman's battered body away hours before. Disappointed that nothing solid had surfaced, Dannie turned to his partner. "Well, Strick, I'll meet you at ten in the morning, and we'll start going door-to-door."

The next day, they began knocking on doors in the quiet tree-lined subdivision, asking neighbors if they had seen anyone who looked suspicious hanging around the day before. No one recalled seeing anything unusual. After a few hours of getting nowhere, the detectives headed to Charlie's Barbecue to have lunch before resuming their canvass of the area. As they worked their way through tender barbecued ribs, a man approached them. "Are y'all working on that murder?"

"Yeah," Dannie replied. "You got something for us?"

"Well, yesterday I was in the Villa Oaks Grocery, and there was a crazy son of a bitch in there with headphones on. He had some crazy eyes. You might wanna ask someone there about him. He was telling Rita, the cashier, that he needed some medicine for a nervous condition. He looked like he was on drugs."

"Thanks, man," Dannie said as he turned to Strick. "Let's go talk to her."

The two men headed to the store and went directly to the office to inquire about the incident. Dannie turned toward the entrance while he waited for the manager and observed a man walking into the store. Dannie watched him for a moment, noticing his eyes—eyes that had the look of a crazed beast. The man saw Dannie looking at him and turned around to leave the store. The instincts that Dannie had relied on for decades— that feeling in his gut—took over.

"I knew it was him. There are millions of people in this country, and I knew it was him," Dannie recalled. "He walked out and started heading back toward the scene of the crime a few blocks away."

"Let's get him," Dannie told Strickland.

The two men followed their suspect, staying a short distance behind him. A few blocks later, they pulled alongside, and Dannie jumped out of the car, grabbing the man before he could run. Dannie shook him down, put him in the car, and then called the station to report that he was bringing in a suspect. "I had no probable cause to bring him in, nothing. I just felt it, knew it. It's like some kind of ESP."

Dannie spent six hours interrogating David Puryear. He prayed with him. He drank 7UP with him, ate cookies with him. He played the father-confessor role, and his suspect finally broke, admitting that he had killed the woman. David told Dannie that he had escaped from the Southeast Louisiana Mental Hospital in Mandeville, just days before, and that his brother-in-law had once lived in the same house occupied by the victim and her family on Greenwell Springs Road. He shared his sexual fantasies with Dannie while fondling himself, then explained what had happened.

"I saw her sunbathing in the yard, so I said, 'How are you? You're really looking good today.'"

"Fuck you," Valerie had responded, irritated with the man who had disturbed her.

"Fuck you," David said; then he grabbed her and dragged her into the house. A struggle ensued, and Valerie cut David on the knuckle of his hand with a piece of glass in a desperate attempt to save her life. "You're not gonna kill me," she bit out as she fought.

David went to the kitchen, looking for a weapon as

Valerie tried to escape. He came back with a butcher knife and stabbed her repeatedly in the chest before grabbing a lamp and yanking the electrical cord to use as his final weapon. He strangled the twenty-five-year-old mother of two babies before raping her.

"I wanted to kiss her on the mouth, but there was too much blood, so I kissed her on the cheek and left," David recounted nonchalantly.

By ten that night, police had matched the teeth prints on the victim's breast and the blood to Dannie's suspect. Case solved. In one day. "This was the most brutal murder I had ever seen," Dannie said, "until Derrick Todd Lee."

But this day in April of 1984 was not the first time Dannie had pulled a rabbit out of his hat by acting on his own particular brand of ESP.

Years before, Baton Rouge cocktail lounges were being plagued by a series of rapes at closing time. Two men had been entering local lounges carrying a sawed-off shotgun and a pistol and raping the patrons or the barmaids in front of those who had lingered for that one last drink. One would hold a gun to the head of the victim while the other committed the rape, then vice versa. They had already hit seven places, raped seven women, before one particular night in September when Dannie and his then partner, Dudley Williams, drove up on a stakeout at Sammy's Lounge on Florida Boulevard. About seven Baton Rouge city police units were parked in the lot, hoping to apprehend the rapists.

Dannie observed the stakeout for a moment, then looked across the street into the parking lot of the Happy Note Lounge. He was very familiar with the case, as it had received intense publicity. One of the victims had been the girlfriend of a local television station news anchor. As Dannie looked around, he noticed a vehicle parked in the lot across the street. He could barely make out that two men were slumped down in the car. He decided to check it out.

As he and Dudley approached the vehicle in their patrol car, Dannie got that feeling, the one he always got when he knew he was onto something. "Grab the shotgun, Dudley," he said.

Dannie ordered the men out of the car, noticing that they both wore topcoats, even though it was still September and not yet that chilly outside. He saw one of the men reach for a gun. "Dudley!" he yelled. Dudley cocked the shotgun while Dannie watched the driver of the vehicle assessing Dudley's massive frame. At six foot seven, Dudley was intimidating enough without a gun. The two men threw down their weapons. Dannie and Dudley had them. While Baton Rouge police officers watched from across the street, the two sheriff's detectives rolled right in and busted the rapists. Dannie's intuition had paid off then too.

Dannie was a flatfoot, a slow and methodical detective who had been in law enforcement for almost fifty years before he would encounter the most difficult case of his life—the hunt for a serial killer. When he was young, he had wanted to become a history professor and had earned his degree in history and government from LSU in 1960. But he had to work while in college, so he got a job as an intern, a clerk in the Bureau of Identification photo lab. Soon he found himself to be a fingerprint technician.

In those days, everything was done by hand. There were no computer databases to plug fingerprints into for identification. Dannie looked at thousands of fingerprints every day, matching point for point on left hands and right hands in order to find matches. It was in that lab that he learned to be methodical, to take his time and track down every clue. Those lessons would stay with him throughout his career.

After college, Dannie went straight to the sheriff's

office and worked in the juvenile division before rising to the rank of lieutenant. Then it was on to detective, a job he loved. Peter Falk as Columbo was his hero, and he fancied himself to be the kind of cop he watched on television every week, hard-nosed and smart, but with a heart. Dannie worked with the East Baton Rouge Parish Sheriff's Office for twelve years before moving to the Louisiana Attorney General's Office as an investigator for the next five years.

"That was a nightmare," Dannie said. "There were major public corruption cases going on, and I was gone from home all the time." After a reduction in force, Dannie returned to the sheriff's office, working homicides and general investigations for many years, helping crack several major cases, including the Ski Mask Rapist, John Simonis, who had terrified Baton Rouge by raping young girls in their homes.

Dannie spent the last years of his career as an investigator once again with the attorney general's office, and it was there that this seasoned detective was assigned the cold cases of Randi Mebruer and Connie Warner in Zachary. It was 1999, and when Dannie took that first trip to Oak Shadows subdivision, he had no idea that he was about to become entrenched in the biggest criminal case in Louisiana history.

Dannie's first step was to review the files from Connie and Randi's murders with David McDavid. Mac gave Dannie and his partner, Kurt Wagner, all the information he had on his suspects. There was no viable suspect in Connie's murder, but in Randi's, there were two—Michael Mebruer and a young black man who had been caught peeping into the homes of women in the neighborhood. Dannie immediately fixated on Michael Mebruer.

"I hated him, and I persecuted the son of a bitch," said Dannie, whose face turns red and tone becomes blustery at just the thought of the man. "He was the beneficiary on Randi's life insurance policy, and the Tuesday following her death, he was trying to cash it in. I knew that he had beaten his former wife, who he had three kids with. I knew that he was still sleeping with Randi and that they had talked for about forty-five minutes on the night she disappeared. I knew that he liked to prey on weak women. I spent months and months breaking down every telephone call he made. But the problem was, he had bunion surgery right before she died. We couldn't break his alibi. But for a long time, I thought he was capable of her murder, and I hated his guts."

Dannie knew that Mac had searched Todd's home right after Randi's murder, and while he focused much of his time on Michael, he also kept his sights on Todd. Mac was convinced that Todd was the killer, but Dannie kept plugging away on Michael, even asking for a sample of his DNA, a request that was refused. However, by March of 1999, the Zachary police had an opportunity to put Todd away for as many as five years. Had they been successful, the lives of many women and the heartache of a community may have been spared.

On March 29, Todd pawned a gun he had stolen while he was helping his cousin move. The .22-barrel rifle belonged to his cousin's boyfriend, who noticed it missing after Todd left the house and called the East Feliciana Parish sheriff to report the incident. The owner of E Z Pawn on Airline Highway in Baton Rouge called Dannie to report that he had a stolen gun in his possession. He said that it had been pawned by Derrick Todd Lee. Dannie went right over but soon learned that the pawnshop owner could not release it to the attorney general's office. It had to go to the city police or sheriff.

"Get with the Baton Rouge police and get that gun," Dannie told Mac. Two days later, Dannie saw the rifle standing upright in the corner of Mac's office. "Good job. At least we can get this son of a bitch off the streets," he'd told Mac.

"We decided to do a project exile and turn it over to the Feds," Dannie later recalled. He hadn't been so sure that Todd had committed the Zachary murders, but Dannie knew he was a Peeping Tom. Todd had an extensive record, and Dannie wanted him put away.

But that was not to happen. The gun simply disappeared. It had not been placed into evidence. "So when we were gonna bring it to the Feds, the gun was just gone. God strike me dead if I'm lying," Dannie said. "Mac screwed it up. The gun surfaced several months later. Mac finally found it one day, but it was too late. We were going after Derrick for felony possession, but the chain of evidence had been broken. It was useless. The Zachary Police Department tried to keep it quashed, but we could have had him. He would have been off the streets for years, not raping and murdering all those women."

Finally, in late 1999, after making no further progress toward solving the Warner and Mebruer murders, the Zachary police asked the FBI to do a behavioral profile on their killer. They thought the murders and the incident with the teenagers being hacked with a bush axe in the cemetery were connected. The FBI didn't agree. It was determined that there was no connection at all between Connie and Randi's deaths, nor were they connected to the cemetery. Even when the young female victim involved in the cemetery case identified Todd as her attacker in a lineup, nothing was done.

"The case was prescribing. The statute of limitations would have been up in a month, and the Zachary police chief, Drew Burke, discouraged detectives from going forward with the case," Dannie said.

Todd evaded arrest and would be allowed to wander about South Louisiana searching for pretty women. But with his later convictions for stalking Collette and beating

Consandra, Todd would spend the beginning of the new millennium where he belonged, in prison, and Louisiana women could rest peacefully at night for a while longer.

It would be two years before Dannie really began to piece together the fact that Todd was a serial killer, two years of chasing down lead after lead, two years of sifting through crime-scene evidence, two years of tracking Michael Mebruer's every move. It would be September of 2001 before he got an inkling that a serial killer was on the prowl, and that maybe the killer was the man he had been keeping an eye on. At that point, Dannie gave up on Michael Mebruer as his main suspect.

"I thought Mike Mebruer was a wimp. I called him a titty baby. I didn't think he had the mentality to be a serial killer," Dannie explained. "I became convinced that Derrick Todd Lee was the killer."

And so, in the years to follow, Dannie began to compile a timeline of Todd's life—a timeline that would one day be used to correlate Todd's prison history, vehicle ownership, and work record to a series of murders of bright and beautiful women, murders that were bringing a city to its knees.

Gina Wilson Green

Although Todd had been sentenced to four years' hard labor for the incident with Consandra, he was released through diminution of his sentence from Dixon Correctional Institute in January of 2001. West Feliciana sheriff's deputies would immediately pick him up on a court hold, and Todd would serve another month at the West Feliciana Parish Prison. On February 18, he would be released. Agent Lamar Goodfellow, Todd's probation officer, warned Todd that he could not go anywhere around St. Francisville Square Apartments. He was required to wear a monitoring device until June. But by April, Todd would violate curfew and would plead guilty to aggravated flight from an officer.

Goodfellow noted that Todd's attitude was poor, he and arranged for a meeting with his disgruntled charge in May. Todd had disconnected the monitor twice during his probation. On May 23, he was found guilty of violating his parole, but the parole board only reprimanded him. Todd owed three years on his original sentence, and although that sentence should have been enforced, the parole board gave him his freedom.

In August, an agent with the Bureau of Alcohol, Tobacco, and Firearms (ATF) called Goodfellow to inform him that they would be charging Todd with pawning the stolen gun from two years before. Goodfellow immediately notified Todd and set up a meeting with the ATF. Todd refused to talk without his lawyer and would never officially be charged with the crime.

Goodfellow got another call from the West Feliciana Parish Sheriff's Office on September 11, 2001. As the World Trade Center was being attacked by terrorists, and while a nation was mourning its dead, Todd was roaming around St. Francisville Square Apartments, looking for Collette. He had been warned not to go back there. Todd denied the accusations, stating that he had been nowhere near those apartments. His tension was building. Todd could not have Collette, so he headed to Baton Rouge, to Stanford Avenue.

Gina Wilson Green lived on Stanford Avenue in a pretty bungalow that had been built in the Craftsman Style of the 1940s. This street was a hubbub of activity, as it was only blocks from LSU. Traffic was usually unbearable, especially during the early mornings and late afternoons as students hurried to and from classes, but the pleasant beauty of the street, filled with early- to mid-twentieth-century Arts and Crafts charm, was much desired among locals. Many of the homes had been restored, and young families, single women, and students leased or bought the homes as soon as they were vacated. Luxurious old houses, resonating with the character of yesteryear, lined the LSU lakes closer to campus. Old Baton Rouge families and university faculty, who enjoyed watching students jogging, biking, and sunning by the lakes, occupied these homes. All were unaware that a predator was riding up and down Stanford Avenue searching for pretty, dark-haired girls. And Gina was prettier than most.

Originally from Natchez, Mississippi, Gina had moved to Baton Rouge after marrying her high-school sweetheart. She wanted to become a nurse, attracted to the idea of helping people, and began her career at Our Lady of the Lake Regional Medical Center. Soon becoming a nurse of infusion, Gina was now qualified to give patients medication to ease their pain and treat their illnesses. Gina knew all about pain. She had suffered a kidney disorder as a child that required numerous medical procedures. She was a teenager before her disorder was brought under control, and she wanted to help others the way the doctors and nurses had helped her throughout her childhood.

Gina also knew the pain of divorce. Her first marriage ended after ten years, and her second ended in 1999. At thirty-nine, she found herself alone and sometimes sad, but she worked hard not to dwell on her pain. She was still young and beautiful, with silky brown hair, a slender build, pronounced high cheekbones, and a stunning smile. Men were attracted to her sense of humor and upbeat attitude.

By September of 2001, Gina's life was in perfect order. She had a great job as the general manager of HCS Infusion Network, wonderful friends who loved her, and a charming bungalow in the heart of Baton Rouge. She had recovered from her divorce and was enjoying a life filled with possibilities. Gina had much to look forward to, but she had begun to worry lately. Nagged by the sneaking suspicion that someone was watching her, she told a friend how she felt just a month before.

On September 22, she told her mother. It would have been easy for someone to watch Gina. The side porch of her bungalow had been converted into a glassed-in sunroom. Anyone could hide behind the bushes or crepe myrtles in her yard and peer in at her as she sat with a cold drink and looked out over her yard. She had nothing concrete to report to her mother, just that she felt like she was being watched. It was just an uneasy niggling in the back of her mind, a sense of foreboding. And she was right.

Todd's problems were compounding, and when he couldn't handle the stress, he always went on the prowl.

It had been a long time since Randi Mebruer—almost three years—but he hadn't forgotten the feeling of power, the feeling of a white woman dying beneath him. He couldn't get near Collette, so he focused on Gina.

Although Gina was plagued by uneasiness on September 22, she dismissed her mood and went for a ride on her bike around the LSU lakes. When she got home, she felt better, invigorated by the exercise. Gina took a shower and called Amy Sanders, her sister.

"What are y'all doing?" Gina asked.

"Just hanging out," said Amy.

"Well, I'm coming over to play with Julia."

Gina loved Amy's two-year-old daughter and enjoyed spoiling the little girl. She jumped in her car without bothering to put on any makeup and headed to Amy's. The sisters spent the evening together. They went to dinner at On the Half Shell, a local restaurant specializing in delectable raw oysters. Gina gave Julia a bath soon after they returned home, tucked her in bed, and then she and Amy settled in with a movie. Amy walked Gina to her car at 11:30 P.M. and watched her drive away. It was the last time she would see her sister alive.

The alarm sounded on Stanford Avenue at 3:47 A.M. on September 23, startling Gina out of her sleep. Worried, she walked around the house, checking doors and windows, looking in closets and turning on lights. Nothing appeared out of the ordinary, and she reassured her security company that everything was all right. It was a false alarm. Still slightly worried, Gina tossed and turned for a while before falling asleep.

Cloaked in darkness, Todd watched from a distance, upset that the alarm had sounded in time to foil his plans. He stood very still, just as he had when he was young and quietly peeped into the windows of his cousins' homes as they undressed for bed. He would be patient.

* * *

Gregg LeBlanc was worried. It had been very busy that morning of September 24, and Gina hadn't shown up for work. She was Gregg's boss and friend. He knew that something must be wrong. Gina was very responsible and always called on the rare occasions that she had to miss work. He called her house repeatedly, leaving message after message. Gina didn't answer the phone. She didn't call back. As the morning wore on, Gregg became more nervous. He watched the clock as the minutes and hours ticked away, but each time he tried to leave to check on her, another patient needed him. It was after 12:30 P.M. when he finally got into his car and headed to Stanford Avenue.

Gina's BMW was parked under the carport in its usual spot. Gregg knocked on the door, calling out her name. He opened the mail slot. "Gina, Gina, are you in there?" He whistled for her, like he always did. He got no response. He tried the door. It was locked. Gregg walked down the concrete driveway that ran along the side of the house. He peered through the glass portion of the back door, yelling her name now and knocking hard. He could see through the house to the front door where Gina's keys hung in the door.

Still, no answer.

Gregg looked around for a spare key. Gina had told him once that she kept an extra one underneath a flowerpot, but he couldn't find it. He tried the door. It was unlocked.

He walked through the kitchen and into the living room. He called out Gina's name again, scared but hoping that she was in the shower, and just hadn't heard him. He moved into the small hallway that led to the bedrooms. He saw Gina lying in bed.

"Gina?" he said as he walked into her bedroom. That's when he saw it—Gina's right arm dangling down from the bed.

Being a registered nurse, Gregg immediately recognized the signs of death in Gina's arm and hand. They were too stiff. He backed out of the room, needing to get away from the sight of his friend lying there. He made it to the living room before he dialed 911 on his cell phone. Then, in a state of shock, he called the office.

"I've found Gina. She was at home. Oh, my God, she's dead!"

Detective John Colter took the call about a possible homicide. Uniformed police, an EMS vehicle, and the coroner's vehicle were there when he arrived. Coroner Louis Cataldie and his assistant, Don Moreau, escorted the detective to the master bedroom. Gina was still lying in her bed, covered up with a sheet. Colter immediately noticed the bruising and abrasions around her throat. He waited until crime-scene technicians finished processing the body, then began searching for clues.

A note from the victim's yardman requesting payment had been dropped through the mail slot in the foyer. Colter noticed black thong panties in front of the television in the living room. A pair of black panty hose was lying by one leg of the sofa, a black skirt by the other. A silver chain belt lay on the floor by Gina's skirt. Colter observed a beer in the kitchen sink.

In the hallway, he saw two hoop earrings and a bracelet on the floor, along with a shoe and a clump of pretty brown hair. As he looked into the master bedroom, Colter saw a black bra and a blue nightshirt on the floor by the bed. Along the wall, he saw a blue bath towel folded on the floor. As the scene was processed, a blue striped shirt would be found on a chair next to the kitchen table. It had what looked like blood around the collar and down the front. The handset to Gina's cordless phone would be found underneath a night table by her bed. Her cell phone and identification cards were missing.

It is not difficult to imagine what happened to Gina. Her clothes told the story. Gina had dropped her nightshirt on the floor by her bed as she pulled on a cute blue shirt and black skirt on Sunday morning. Perhaps she heard a knock on the door. The back door was unlocked, and there were no signs of forced entry. The back door led into her kitchen, which is where her shirt was found. The kitchen led into the living room of the rectangle-shaped house. Her skirt, panty hose, and panties were ripped from her there. Gina, with her fragile build, had not stood a chance against the two-hundred-pound Todd.

Her earrings and bracelets came off in the hallway as Gina fought, while this man who had watched her for a month, who had intruded into her world, callously raped her before he wrapped his big hands around her neck and squeezed her life's breath from her body. A feces smear on the carpet marked the spot of her death. Todd then picked her up and laid her gently upon the bed, this beautiful woman who had become his. He covered her nakedness with the sheet before he left through the back door. Sated.

The autopsy report would reveal that Gina had indeed been raped, both vaginally and anally, before being manually strangled. No semen would be found in her body.

Baton Rouge Police immediately began trying to track Gina's cell phone. Colter contacted Cingular Wireless with subpoenas to obtain Gina's cell phone records. It was discovered that the phone was still on and being used. Colter asked Cingular employees to help him find it. On September 27, William Reed, the regional director for Gulf States Security Asset Protection, set about tracking the phone.

A signal from Gina's phone hit a tower close to the Mississippi River Bridge that day. That particular tower's range included an area from north of the bridge to the east, almost to Plank and Chippewa Streets. Reed drove to the area and called the field engineer in Metairie, Louisiana, who had reported the original signal. When Reed got to a location where he had the same signal as Gina's phone, he used a tracking process called Trigger Fish to lead him to the phone. The program led him to Choctaw Street, part of the warehouse district in Baton Rouge.

Reed followed the signals until he found himself behind what was once the Ready Portion Meat Company. He looked around for a few minutes until he spotted a credit card—the name on it was Gina Wilson Green. Reed called the police. After searching the area, police discovered not only Gina's cell phone, but her checkbook, other credit cards, identification papers, and a towel from her home. Todd had tossed his trophies just blocks from where Connie Warner's body had been found nine years earlier.

Zachary police officer David McDavid would soon get his first hint that the man he had been trying to tie to Connie and Randi's deaths had found more fertile ground. But it would not be until July of the next year that residents in Baton Rouge would learn that a serial killer was roaming in their midst. Baton Rouge women would soon understand the meaning of fear.

The residents of Stanford Avenue were already concerned. And they had good reason to be. Gina was not the first woman who lived on Stanford Avenue to have been murdered. Four years earlier, Eugenie Boisfontaine had been abducted while walking around the LSU lakes. Her body would not be found for three months. Eugenie had lived just a few houses from Gina.

Just two days after Gina's murder, Jackie filed another domestic violence complaint against Todd. He would spend the month of October in the West Feliciana prison. Lamar Goodfellow would request that Todd be held for parole violation. Todd was brought before the parole board on the "flight from an officer" charge in the middle of October. Again, he would only be reprimanded. Again, he would be set free to stalk the women of Baton Rouge and the surrounding areas. Eventually he would make his way back to Stanford Avenue.

But in late September of 2001, as the cooler air began replacing the unrelenting humidity, no one thought about serial killers. Unbeknownst to anyone, Baton Rouge had not one, not two, but three serial killers raping and killing women during the 1990s and the early years of the new millennium. The year 2002 would force enlightenment. It would begin with the death of Geralyn Barr DeSoto.

Geralyn Barr DeSoto

The young girl leaned over her journal, pen moving slowly as she poured her broken heart onto the pages. She tried to fight back the tears, but the pain pushed them from her eyes, smearing the ink as she wrote. Although she had many people in her life who loved her, she felt so alone.

Geralyn Barr DeSoto was not alone. She had her mother and father, Melanie and John Barr, with whom she was very close. She had her sisters, Brandi and Heather. She had her aunt Belinda, who was her confidante. She had Jonathan Soileau and Robbie Simon, friends with whom she worked at the Accounts Services Department at Louisiana State University. And she had her husband, Darren, the cause of her feelings of alienation and aloneness.

Unknown to Geralyn, she also had someone else in her life, someone who passed by her home on Louisiana Highway 1 every afternoon as he left the Dow Chemical Company plant, someone who watched her, someone who plotted while waiting for the perfect moment to attack. Geralyn was definitely not alone, but she felt like she was.

Darren, whom she had married while attending LSU, had not turned out to be the man of her dreams. She loved him, and she tried hard to make the marriage work, but Darren had a volatile nature. She was accustomed to love and support from those in her life, not the cursing and shouting and shoving that became her existence soon after the marriage began. Geralyn was young, only twenty-one, with her dream of being accepted into LSU's Physical Therapy School close to a reality. School was her escape, her time away from the sadness that enveloped her home.

Home was where she felt so alone. When she was with Darren. When she wanted a hug, but she received a tirade instead. Accusations. Demands. Questions. Even sex was not what it had once been, not as romantic, not as loving.

Jonathan and Robbie had become tired of listening to her complaints. "If you are not going to do anything about it, then we don't want to hear it anymore," they had told her after she related a story from the previous evening about being stabbed in the leg with a fork. They were concerned for her and felt that she should leave the marriage, but that was not an option for Geralyn. She had made a commitment, and she loved Darren. Leaving would be the equivalent of failure, and Geralyn did not like to fail.

The pen moved faster now as she painted a portrait of each day of her life. She wrote how endless those days seemed, how each was just a mirror of the one that had come before. It was the same story that has been repeated by victims of domestic violence across the world: He yells; he curses; he gets violent. He cries, says he sorry, and then speaks of love. Her pen described her feelings of being overwhelmed, frustrated, sad, scared—the secret thoughts she couldn't share with anyone. She wondered if she deserved this life, if she had done something wrong. She prayed for someone to rescue her. She longed for someone to hold her close and tell her everything would be all right. She wanted to go back home, to be with her mom and dad, where she felt loved. She bowed her head over the pages of the notebook and cried harder.

* * *

Darren loved Geralyn, loved her dark brown hair and her pretty eyes, loved that she was smart. But he didn't like being married—the nagging, the long talks that Geralyn had with him, the jealousy that consumed him. He didn't like her to have friends. He wanted her to himself, at home, where she belonged, cooking and cleaning and attending to his needs.

"Don't ever get married," he told young David Bradford, the boy who lived next door, and whom Geralyn sometimes tutored.

Darren worked long hours at XRI Testing at the Kaiser Aluminum & Chemical Corporation in Gramercy, about a forty-five minute drive from the trailer park where the couple lived. He left home about six o'clock each morning and didn't return until very late some nights. He liked for his dinner to be ready when he got home, and he liked to talk to Geralyn throughout the day on the Nextel radio phones he had bought for Christmas. He liked for her to go to bed at the same time he did each night. Darren always wanted to know where Geralyn was and when she would be home. But Darren could not know that there would be a day when she would not answer that phone, a day when he would walk into his home and find the body of his young wife lying in a pool of blood on the floor of their bedroom. Darren did not know that he would soon find himself the prime suspect in the vicious murder of the woman he felt he could not live without.

January 14, 2002, was a pretty day in South Louisiana, cold and sunny. The early-morning dew shimmered on the spent sugarcane fields on either side of Highway 1 as Geralyn made her way from the small town of Addis to LSU, eager to pay her tuition for the additional classes that would pave the way for her entry into graduate school. She could see the state capitol building in the distance as she crossed the bridge over the Intracoastal Canal and then the mighty Mississippi River. Geralyn called Jonathan and asked him to have lunch with her.

"I'm trying to save money, so I was going to bring my lunch today," Jonathan said. "I'll just see you when you get here."

Geralyn had a job interview scheduled for that afternoon and was in a happy mood as she pulled into the LSU Hart Parking Lot on Infirmary Road. Jonathan arrived at the same time, and the two began walking through the Enchanted Forest near the Greek Theatre, an area on campus where beautiful old oak trees line walkways and students sit on benches, talking, playing guitars, or studying for upcoming tests. They arrived at Thomas Boyd Hall, and while Geralyn paid her fees, Jonathan went upstairs to the Accounts Services Department, where they worked.

Exuberant about her job interview, Geralyn wanted to spend a moment with Jonathan, so she went upstairs and asked him to go to the third-floor breezeway to chat while she smoked a cigarette. They made harmless jokes about the little ladies who worked in their office and discussed her interview. Jonathan said good-bye and went back to work. Geralyn went home to get dressed.

Geralyn spoke with Darren on the phone early that morning to tell him about her interview. When he called later, about 10:30 A.M., she told him that she would start getting ready soon for her two o'clock appointment. She had bought a new outfit for interviews soon after she'd graduated in December. This would be her first time to wear it. Geralyn sounded happy about the prospect of getting the job.

On her way home from her visit with Jonathan, Geralyn stopped at the Iberville Bank, just a few blocks from the trailer park. When she got home, she ignored the messy rooms, although the thought flitted through her mind that Darren would be upset when he came home.

Instead, she e-mailed Dr. Eve Tyler at LSU, who had been advising her about how to get into graduate school. Dr. Tyler received the e-mail at 11:41 A.M.

I just wanted to thank you and the faculty for allowing me to attend summer classes, Geralyn wrote. *Becoming an OT is a desire like no other for me and I intend on doing everything I can to achieve that goal and dream in my life. Thank you for having faith in me and in my efforts to becoming an occupational therapist.*

Feeling hopeless, she picked up her notebook and began writing. She was barely hanging on. Again, her pen expressed her anguish. She begged for comfort, for someone to hold her close. She wanted her mom and dad to save her, but they couldn't know that she needed rescuing. She hadn't told them. The words she wrote—a premonition. She knew, somehow, that she would not be okay.

It was 11:50 A.M. when Geralyn heard a knock at her door. She logged off the Internet and moved to answer it. No voice cautioned her against answering. There were no raised hairs on the back of her neck. Nothing. Geralyn opened the door.

Todd passed the trailer park every day on his way to and from work. Situated off the service road that parallels Highway 1, the park was one of several dotting the roadway. Thirty-two trailers lined up like dominoes in a row through the park. Geralyn's was located on lot number nine, twenty-three trailers from the road traveled each day by a hunter searching for prey. There was nothing to attract Todd to the trailer park—no sign to beckon customers, no office to welcome visitors—but it is easy to imagine that Todd could have spotted the pretty, young Geralyn leaving the park in her shiny black Mustang.

Perhaps he followed her to the video store, where she liked to rent movies, to the corner convenience store, where she stopped to buy cigarettes, to LSU. He had spotted her, that is for certain, and he liked what he saw.

Todd had been laid off from his job at Dow Chemical on January 11 and was issued his final payroll check on January 14, the day that Geralyn was busy preparing for her interview. That morning, he sat under an oak tree outside of the plant gate and waited for his check to be brought to him. He contemplated the young girl he had been watching. It had been almost four months since the body of Gina Wilson Green had been found.

Much had happened to Todd during that time— Jackie had reported him to the police again. He had spent October in jail. Lamar Goodfellow had been on his back. He had been brought up before the parole board several times, but he had not been reincarcerated. Todd was grateful for that. Long nights in prison meant he could not ride around looking at pretty white girls, as he liked to do. And now Dow had laid him off. He had no money, and the kids needed to eat.

The stress was building.

Just one week before his probation ended, Todd drove away from Dow in Iberville Parish and into West Baton Rouge Parish, riding along the rail line filled with tank cars meant for the plant. A highway sign welcomed him to Addis. Remnants of the recently harvested sugarcane crop stretched for miles in the fields to his left. As he drove along, he passed through the red light at the intersection of Highway 990, by a hardware store, and by Dickie's Sportsman's Center on his way to the pale blue-trimmed trailer sitting on lot number nine.

Darren had not talked to Geralyn since the morning call. He assumed that she was still at the interview. It wasn't until about 4:00 P.M. when his coworker Clarence Knight said, "Hey, man. Are you and your old lady on the outs?" that Darren realized he hadn't heard from Geralyn.

"Why do you ask that?" Darren said.

"Because you haven't been on the phone with her all day," Clarence responded.

Darren replied that Geralyn was at an interview, but he thought she should be calling soon. Geralyn didn't call, and Darren began to worry. He called her Nextel phone, but no answer. He sent an alert on the phone, which would have beeped, letting Geralyn know to call him. She didn't call. He called their home phone. No answer. He called again and again. By the time he left work, between 6:15 and 6:30 P.M., Darren had become very worried. He stopped at a store to call again. Nothing. He sped home as fast as he could.

Pen in hand, Geralyn stared at the empty page, trying hard to be grateful for the life she had been given. Her father had told her that life was a gift from God to be cherished. But sometimes, she felt like she wasn't living. She was merely breathing. That breath was the only thing that made her feel alive.

The attractive black man at the door appeared to be harmless, so harmless that Geralyn handed him her cordless phone and waited while he placed a call to the Exxon plant, where he had previously worked. He smiled—a friendly smile that warmed his brown eyes. He did not have the eyes of a killer, and Geralyn was unsuspecting until the moment he rushed in and hit her in the face with the phone so hard that he fractured her skull, causing damage to her brain tissue. Those eyes, warm just seconds before, filled with rage as Geralyn backed away in terror through the hallway to the bedroom where she knew Darren's shotgun was kept.

She thought the gun was loaded.

It wasn't.

Todd stalked her down the hallway, his strength over-powering her as they struggled for the gun. Scrape marks from the barrel etched into the ceiling as Todd wrestled it from her. He threw the gun on the bed. Geralyn tried to get away while fighting desperately with the frenzied man. An avenue of escape, the back door, was only a few feet away.

Todd pulled the Old Timer Schrade knife from its brown leather sheath, the same knife he had sharpened to a razor's edge in front of his son Derrick Jr. many times. He stabbed Geralyn twice in the back as she tried to escape, then in the side, then in her left breast. Seven times he stabbed her while she fiercely fought for her life.

Todd was ready to go for the kill.

He raked the knife across her throat ferociously, slashing through skin and tissue and muscle, through the jugular vein, through the thorax. Terrified, Geralyn grabbed her throat in an effort to stem the blood, in an effort to breathe as she fell to the floor, dying.

With his brown leather Wolverine boots recording his footprints in blood, Todd viciously stomped his prey before he exited the home. Geralyn had opened her door that morning to find death waiting on the other side.

Darren knew something was wrong. Geralyn's car was not parked in the right place. She usually parked to the side of the driveway so that he could pull in beside her. Her car was parked in the middle. Geralyn would never park there, when she knew he would be coming home from work. He hurried toward the trailer, noting that the door was ajar about an inch. He walked through the living room toward the hallway, shutting off the constantly beeping phone as he moved carefully through the room, fearing what he might find. Then he saw her, lying on the floor in the doorway of the bedroom. He ran toward her, only seeing the blood around her head, the blood running in rivulets down the walls. His first thought was that she had committed suicide. The shotgun on the bed registered slowly, and he moved away from her to check the gun for shell casings. There were none.

He screamed and punched a hole in the wall. He didn't know what to do. He leaned down over his wife and raised her shirt, looking for a gunshot wound. Her body was cold, stiff. He saw two wounds on her back that did not come from a gun. He picked up her head. That's when he saw it. Her neck was open, slashed from ear to ear.

"Oh no!" he shouted so loudly that neighbor Stephen Bradford heard it from inside his trailer next door. Darren tried to find the phone to call 911, but he couldn't find it. He ran to Stephen's trailer and told him to place the call, then went back to the dreadful scene that would follow him forever. Stephen came in and found Darren leaning over Geralyn's body, his shoulders shaking violently but no tears wetting his cheeks. Geralyn's nightmare had ended. Darren's had just begun.

In the months before she died, Geralyn's pen began depicting thoughts about death. Tired and defeated, she felt that she could die. But that didn't seem to be a good solution either. She wrote that dying would only leave her alone again, still missing her family.

Darren DeSoto

It was overkill. Detective Freddy Christopher knew that immediately upon seeing Geralyn's body lying on the floor. His trained eye followed the trail of blood up the wall, where it ran in rivulets and into the bathroom, where spatters filled the sink and walls. He saw that a hole had been punched in the wall of the hallway. It was definitely overkill, and that kind of rage and passion usually indicated that the victim was very familiar with the attacker. Christopher closed off the crime scene until it could be processed, then went outside to talk to Darren.

He asked Darren to go to the Law Enforcement Center to answer questions. Darren allowed himself to be taken away. He was in shock, not quite knowing how to act. At times, his shoulders shook, but no tears came. At other times, he talked calmly with detectives. When Christopher interviewed him, Darren's shirt was still covered with blood.

"How did you get all of that blood on you?" Christopher asked.

"When I saw Geralyn on the floor, I lifted her upper body up from the floor. I had to see what was wrong."

"Why is your hand bruised?"

"I got angry when I saw her like that. I punched the wall," Darren explained.

Christopher asked Darren his whereabouts earlier that day, and Darren explained that he had been at work. "How long does it take to get there?"

"About an hour."

Christopher continued asking him questions, then called Darren's parents to ask them to bring him a change of clothes. Darren's bloodied clothing needed to be bagged as evidence. He was asked to come back the next day for further questioning. The questions were just beginning, and Darren's life was about to be turned inside out. He was the main suspect and, for most of the investigation, would be the only suspect. The West Baton Rouge Parish Sheriff's homicide department intended to be very thorough.

And they were, following lead after lead, interviewing every friend of Geralyn's they could find, interviewing Darren's neighbors and coworkers. Their investigation would convince them that Darren DeSoto was violent and abusive toward his wife. Geralyn's own words would come back to haunt Darren when police discovered a journal she had written in the week of January 26 of the previous year.

A vivid description of abuse emerged. She wrote how tired she was of the pain and the anger. She unknowingly described for police the hateful curses she endured. Her words demonstrated what it was like to live in a house where two enemies lived, a house where love had turned to anger, fear, dislike. She gave them her husband's motive to kill her.

Major Donald Horner would interview Darren the day after Geralyn's murder. Horner was an older detective with many years of experience in interrogating suspects. He used all of his tricks on Darren. Horner calmly sat back in his chair while Darren nervously fidgeted in a chair against the wall. Horner moved items back and forth on his desk, tapping them at times, as he slowly asked Darren about where he was the day before. The veteran detective moved in closer to talk about the marriage. He had already heard statements from witnesses about domestic violence. He touched Darren's leg, the contact making Darren more nervous. Horner touched him again, resting his hand close to Darren's knee. For hours, Horner questioned him, intimidating him by his very nearness.

"I've been married a long time, and with any marriage, there are problems. I know my wife has made me very angry at times. That's normal in a marriage," Horner shared, hoping to earn Darren's trust but never letting him get too comfortable.

Repeatedly Darren said, "I didn't kill her. I loved her."

Horner pushed on, but Darren would not break, insisting throughout that he had not done this horrible deed. Darren began to realize that the police really thought he had killed Geralyn, and that knowledge increased his discomfort. Finally his cell phone rang. He told his mother on the other end, "They think I did this. I think I need a lawyer." The interview was over.

Geralyn's friends provided clues for police.

Her maid of honor, Claire, told police that she and Geralyn had hung out together since grammar school. "Two weeks before the wedding, Geralyn showed me where Darren had physically abused her. A maid of honor is supposed to approve of the wedding. I didn't approve of this one," she said.

After the wedding, Claire noticed bruises on Geralyn from time to time. They saw each other on LSU's campus occasionally, but Claire began avoiding Geralyn two months before she died. "We always ended up talking about her marital problems, and it was very depressing for me. I offered to come get her one time after Darren had hurt her, but she was too afraid to leave and she was afraid that something would happen to me." Upon hearing of Geralyn's death, Claire just knew that Darren was responsible.

Another childhood friend, Amber, had introduced Geralyn to Darren. "Geralyn came over to my mom's house about a week after the wedding. She had a black eye," Amber told police. Again, in March of 2000, Geralyn visited Amber and showed her a large bruise on her chest, where Darren had hit her. Geralyn always called when Darren was at work and would tell Amber about the times he stayed out all night. Amber worried about her friend.

Jonathan Soileau told police about the time that Geralyn had showed him where Darren had stabbed her in the leg with a fork. Robbie Simon shared how Geralyn had left Darren after a particularly bitter fight the year before and had stayed with her for a short while.

Even Darren's friend and coworker Clarence, who would help to alibi him, knew that Darren got physically violent with his wife. "He told me once that he had hit his wife, but I let him know that I thought it was disgusting that he would hit a girl, so he never talked about it with me again," Clarence told officers.

The alibi that Clarence and other employees at the inspection company provided could not be broken. Darren had arrived late that morning, and Clarence had driven his truck to the gate to let Darren in, as he had been having trouble with his access card. Darren had left for lunch at 11:32 A.M., gone to the Sonic Drive-In, and returned at 11:54 A.M. He clocked out at 6:14 P.M. It would have been impossible for him to have made the forty-five-minute drive home, and then to have driven another forty-five minutes back without anyone noticing he was missing. He was in constant contact with his coworkers throughout the day. But still, police were suspicious, and Darren remained the prime suspect for the vicious slaying of his wife.

Darren was cooperative with police throughout the investigation. He described how serious Geralyn was about her schooling, how she liked to go to the mall, how they made weekend trips to see their families. "We had what I considered to be a close relationship. Geralyn was very open to talking about everything going on. I, on the other hand, tend to keep things more to myself," Darren explained, painting a pretty picture of the marriage for police. But they knew better.

Geralyn had detailed nights filled with screaming, being shoved against walls, objects being hurled at her. In her frustration, she wrote about how she had tried to make things better, how she had tried to talk to Darren, but he didn't want to hear what she had to say. She tried to use reason, to build a family, but he simply closed that door and walked away.

By May, four months after Geralyn died, Darren was becoming tired of the endless digging into his life, his past, his bank dealings, and his credit card purchases. He was tired of the questions, of having to deal with the endless pursuit by police. He just wanted to know who had killed Geralyn. He wanted his life back. He didn't want to deal with the suspicious looks from friends and coworkers. On May 4, Darren decided to get away for a while, so he joined some friends in a poker run on the Tchefuncte River in Madisonville, Louisiana. It was there that he ran into an FBI agent who knew his friends. He asked the agent if he could help with finding Geralyn's murderer.

"I'm just not happy with the way the sheriff's department in West Baton Rouge Parish and the state police are handling the investigation," Darren told the agent. "They think it's me, but I'm innocent."

Agent Stephen Slote informed Darren that he should take a polygraph test. "I've taken two," Darren said. "I did okay on the first one, except when they asked me if I had any knowledge of who killed Geralyn. The second time, I failed the whole test." Darren told the agent how Geralyn had died, that her throat had been cut from ear to ear, that she had been stabbed, that he had held her in his arms. "I'm the number one suspect, but I was at work all day. I shouldn't have even been a suspect at all."

On May 20, the West Baton Rouge Parish Sheriff's Office (WBRSO) received a letter from the FBI detailing the conversation. Darren wasn't helping himself.

Although he remained the prime suspect, by July, events occurring in Baton Rouge encouraged detectives—who had been working overtime for months to gather enough evidence to arrest Darren—to consider that someone else may have been responsible. Detectives in West Baton Rouge Parish began comparing notes of their murder with the murders happening across the river.

Women in Baton Rouge were being killed in their homes, horribly stabbed to death, raped, abducted. A decomposing body had been found along River Road, close to LSU; a woman from Baton Rouge had been found dead by Whiskey Bay, along the route of Interstate 10 from Baton Rouge to Lafayette; closer to Lafayette, a woman had narrowly escaped death after being raped, brutally beaten, and strangled.

Todd was decompensating, his vicious acts coming closer and closer together—sometimes just days apart—

in what would become known as the summer of terror.
Southeast Louisiana women were about to have their
freedom taken away. They would sleep with their doors
locked. They would arm themselves. They would take
self-defense classes. They would stay indoors at night and
become watchful of strangers. But they could not be protected, not by the police, not by their husbands. Todd
was watching, always waiting for the perfect opportunity.
His sadistic acts would unravel a police department and
tear a city apart at the seams.

Darren just wished that Geralyn were still alive, that he
could hold her, maybe tell her he was sorry. But it was
too late.

*Geralyn had spent a long time feeling like she was wandering
around in the dark. She knew that there was no magic switch that
could turn the light of their love back on. She wrote that she had
been alone in the darkness for so long that it seemed impossible to
fix their relationship. She finally gave up. The fight had left her
bruised and battered with scars she felt would never heal. In her
journal, she forgave Darren but stressed that she could never forget
those nights when fear and anger had turned her world upside
down. She longed to remember the good times, the love she once felt.
Loneliness had made her forget the innocent girl she once was. She
knew then that she would never have the life she wanted.*

It would be more than two years before Geralyn's
murder would be connected by DNA to the South Louisiana Serial Killer. Although Todd had taken her life, Geralyn had taken a piece of him as well. The evidence that
would give her husband, who had caused her so much
pain, his life back was waiting to be discovered underneath
her fingernails.

Christine Moore

By the middle of May 2002, Todd had once again lost his job. He had been laid off from his employment at Harmony Corporation, a division of Turner Industries. He had worked at Formosa Plastics, whose plant was one of many that lined the Mississippi River in and around Baton Rouge. As that spring rolled toward summer, Geralyn and Gina's deaths had become just another murder statistic. No one thought about them, except for their friends and families and the detectives working the cases. And no one thought they were related.

But Todd remembered. He liked to remember, to go over the details in his mind as he drove down Nicholson to the various short-lived jobs he held. He had not been satisfied with Geralyn. She had fought too much, and he had not been able to relieve himself with her battered body. Since her death, he had been busy, working at Exxon, JE Merit, and then Harmony Corporation, and occasionally losing his money at Casino Rouge.

Nicholson Drive parallels River Road, which winds along the Mississippi River. Sometimes Todd would take River Road instead of Nicholson because he liked the sight of pretty joggers running along the grassy levees, which protected the area from flooding. River Road reminded him of St. Francisville in the tranquility it offered travelers. Scenes of sugarcane fields, cows munching on clover in large pastures, Farr Park Horse Activity Center, and, farther down, the picturesque little Ebenezer Baptist Church accompanied Todd as he drove. He had been wondering what he was going to do. He and Jackie were heading straight for bankruptcy, and he had lost his job. He was broke, with nothing to do with his days except drive around looking for a girl to help relieve that feeling that was building inside him. Todd was about to go on a rampage. He needed to vent his frustration.

Christine Moore also loved the beauty of River Road. She loved to jog along the top of the levee to keep in shape and run off the stress of finals. She was working on her graduate degree in business at LSU, and by May 23, she had just finished another semester. While some students had to worry about getting good grades, Christine didn't. She was very smart. Originally from New Orleans, she had come to Baton Rouge to earn the second degree that would ensure her future.

Her father, Tony Moore, had found it difficult allowing her to move to Baton Rouge, even though LSU was only a little over an hour from home. But he was so proud of her—proud of her intelligence, proud of her ambition, proud of her beauty. And she was very beautiful. With big brown doe eyes, sweetly curved lips, cheekbones sculpted high, and creamy chocolate skin, Christine attracted much attention from the opposite sex.

Tony worked hard for the Sewerage and Water Board of New Orleans (SWBNO), but had worked even harder to raise his children in a loving environment. His was a close-knit family. All of his children had attended good colleges and had grown into good people. Christine was his baby, and although she was only twenty-three, she had already mapped out the road to her future. Sometimes when Tony got lonely for her, he would stand in front of the large framed photograph of Christine in her cap and gown, look at her, and smile. Tony Moore was a very proud father.

Christine loved her father too. She wanted him to be proud. She knew how hard he had worked to enable his children to have a good education, and she appreciated the things he had done for her. She was happy when she got her grades that May, happy that she had done so well. She was glad to have another semester behind her, although she loved attending school. She was a member of Delta Sigma Theta and had made lots of friends at the university. Christine felt she was a lucky girl.

As she jogged along the river, Christine often thought about how fortunate she was to have a family who loved her so much. She liked to dream about her future, what she would do with her master's degree when she finished school. She wanted to accomplish big things. She wanted to marry a man like her father.

Christine would usually park her car at Farr Park Horse Activity Center, which wasn't far from LSU—just south of Brightside Lane. Sometimes she walked around the park, enjoying the serenity offered by the trees and listening to cows lowing in the distance. Other times, she would lace her tennis shoes tightly, stretch for a moment, and then take off. She loved to feel the breeze coming off the river, stinging her face as she ran.

On May 23, that's what Christine was doing—enjoying the freedom from classes and jogging down River Road. She would never be seen alive again. On May 25, Christine's car would be found at the park just as she had left it.

Tony and the rest of Christine's family would be devastated as they waited and worried about what had happened to her. They knew she would not simply take off with someone. They questioned her friends, anyone they could think of who might know something, but they learned nothing. The police had no answers for them. They would wait twenty-four days to hear some news, and with each passing day that Christine didn't call, their hopes dwindled.

Christine's disappearance would only cause a slight stir in the press—a headline or two about a missing black LSU student. Eight days later, a gruesome murder would occur that would give the media much bigger fish to fry. Christine's disappearance would be lost in the frenzy— yesterday's news—until June 16, when churchgoers on River Road would make a startling discovery.

Ebenezer Baptist Church bears no resemblance to the larger, more cosmopolitan churches that compete for worshipers in Baton Rouge. Located in East Baton Rouge Parish, close to the Iberville Parish line, the small wood-frame church, its front porch decorated with a white picket fence, stands as a quaint beacon—a reminder to those who follow the winding path of the mighty Mississippi that God can always be found, even on lonely rural roads in the backwoods of Louisiana. A large pond behind the church affords members a peaceful setting for picnics and Sunday dinners on the ground while they visit and catch up on each other's lives. A wooded area offers an abundance of shade for these visits. On June 16, those woods would divulge a terrible secret.

Deacons of the church would sometimes gather in a small clearing on the side of the church to talk after services were concluded. They often gazed into the woods, their eyes following the small ravine that snaked its way toward Bayou Manchac. Occasionally they would pick up the discarded wine bottles and other refuse that had been left by stragglers who stopped for a rest on hot summer nights before continuing their journeys.

For the past couple of weeks, they had noticed dogs chewing on what appeared to be some bones in the ravine. The deacons naturally assumed they were from a deer or other large animal that roamed the woods.

But on this day, as they chatted with each other and watched the dogs, they became concerned about the bones and called the police. Tony Moore was about to get the answer he had dreaded. He was about to find out what had happened to his daughter, but that was the only answer Tony would ever get.

The Forensic Anthropology and Computer Enhancement Services (FACES) Laboratory at LSU would assist in the identification of Christine's remains. Forensic anthropologist Mary Manhein, also known as "the Bone Lady," determined the cause of death to be a skull fracture, possibly caused by blunt-force trauma. Christine's skeletonized remains would offer no clues as to who had left her there. The dogs had scavenged her body, and decomposition was complete by the time she was discovered.

The next day, a young woman named Rachel would call the Louisiana state police to tell them about a good-looking black man who had knocked on her door around midmorning. The man told Rachel that he was looking for John Smith, then forced his way into the house. Rachel threatened to call the police, and finally the man left. He drove off in a burgundy pickup truck. Todd was already looking for another victim.

Christine's murder would once again become swallowed up in the events of the following months. As rumors of a serial killer targeting students at LSU spread around the city, Tony Moore begged police to do everything they could to find his baby's killer. He became more and more frustrated as months passed by, and the focus of investigations turned to the white women who were being killed. Carrying the framed photograph of his beautiful Christine in her cap and gown, Tony walked into a television station in New Orleans. "Please help me," he said, tears clouding his eyes as he asked for the media's assistance. But there could be no help for Tony. The answers he sought would never be found.

Christine Moore would never be positively linked to the South Louisiana Serial Killer. But as that hot and horrible summer wore on, police became convinced that her death should indeed be included on an ever-growing list.

Charlotte Murray Pace

She fought so hard—punching and kicking and scratching—harder than she had ever had to fight before. She fought for her life, for her mother, for her dreams. Even as her blood ran from her wounds, she fought, exhausted and crying, but never pleading. The flathead screwdriver kept coming at her, again and again, but she could no longer feel the pain. She could feel death swirling, reaching out for her. She could feel the man over her, pounding into her, frenzied by the blood. He was a big man. Black. One moment of darkness in a life filled with light and vision. Even after Charlotte Murray Pace was gone, the screwdriver kept coming. Death was not enough to still the frenzy.

The little ballerina posed in her pink tutu with her hands on her hips. A big pink bow perched above the brown hair that swung as she danced. When the music began, she spun around, her toes pointed to the stage, her arms in an arch above her head. She danced too fast, faster than the others, exuberance causing her to spin and jump a step ahead of the other children. She finished first, her pink bow now hanging over one eye, hands on her hips proudly. Ann and Casey Pace, her parents, smiled. They knew it was not the most graceful performance, but their precocious daughter had done it again. She had finished first.

Murray liked to finish first. Throughout school, she excelled in academics, in athletics, in personal relationships. She was a people person, friendly and fun and into fashion. Murray knew how to dress and enjoyed making over her friends and her older sister, Sam. Her parents encouraged her. Casey, an attorney for the Mississippi Legislature, believed in setting high goals and instilled that belief in his children. Murray learned her lessons well, determined to make her parents proud. And she did. Casey was in awe of this adventurous, ambitious child. She was fun; she laughed constantly; she brightened his life.

But Murray was also stubborn and would argue with her parents to get her way, especially with Ann, who was charged with keeping her daughter's feet on the ground. Murray's teenage years were sprinkled with the normal spats between a mother, who tries to keep a child in check, and a young girl, who is ready to boldly face the world, unaware of its dangers, innocent of its hurts. But Ann, too, was in awe of this child of hers.

Already finished with her course work and with enough accumulated credits, Murray skipped her senior year of high school, ready and eager to begin her college experience. She moved away from her parents, who agreed that she was mature enough to head off alone, and she went to Jackson, Mississippi, to spend her undergraduate years at Millsaps College. After completing her bachelor's degree, Murray moved to Baton Rouge to work on her master's degree at LSU.

The transition was difficult for Murray. She realized that her childhood was slipping away, her memories only rivers flowing behind her. It had happened so quickly. She no longer lived in the comfort of her home. Her mother no longer slept in the next room. Murray was now surrounded by strangers' faces and an unfamiliar world. She wondered who would listen to her—her complaints, her worries, her dreams. Though often overwhelmed, she understood that now her life was in her hands, that she possessed the power to make her dreams come true, to make her parents proud.

Unexpectedly, she received a letter from her mother. Distracted by the matters weighing on her mind, she placed the letter in a folder. A few days later, she remembered it was there. She wasn't prepared for the emotions she felt as she read her mother's words. Tears ran down her face, leaving smudges of makeup on her cheeks.

Murray liked that Stanford Avenue was so close to LSU. She didn't want to move into the crowded apartment complexes that surrounded the university, preferring instead to live amongst the modest houses with pretty yards that lined the street. She wasn't aware that Eugenie Boisfontaine had lived just a few houses down from the house she chose, that Eugenie had been murdered in 1997, her body left to rot beside Alligator Bayou Bar in Bayou Manchac. She didn't know that her home would be watched, her comings and goings monitored. She didn't know that she wasn't safe. Rebekah Yeager, the pretty blond college student who became Murray's roommate and friend, didn't know either. But the September murder of Gina Wilson Green, who lived just three houses from them, gave the girls their first clue.

Stanford Avenue is not a likely place for a serial killer to choose as a hunting ground. But Stanford Avenue, like Oak Shadows subdivision in Zachary, held something that drew Todd—beautiful single women, women who would never give him a second glance, women he had to have. It made him feel good—powerful—to watch them, because he knew he held their lives in his hands. It was his secret thrill. To watch them without their knowing. To learn their daily routines. To plan how he would take them, hurt them. He liked to feel as though he knew them before he struck. It enhanced the fantasy, prolonged the ecstasy.

And Murray had just the look he liked—the shiny brown hair, the fair skin, the wide, friendly smile, and those beautiful cheekbones, which accented her loveliness. Todd decided to bide his time. It was easy. He had noticed her while watching Gina. He would save her for later.

The days leading up to May 31, 2002, were busy days for Murray. She was graduating on May 24, the youngest student ever to earn a master's degree in business administration from LSU. Again, she had finished first, and it was time to celebrate. The night before her graduation, she met her parents for dinner, excited that it was almost over, that she had been offered a great job in Atlanta. She had decided to stay in Baton Rouge for the summer instead of moving back home, as Ann and Casey would have liked for her to do. She didn't want to have to move to Mississippi and then on to Atlanta so soon afterward. Instead, she opted to move with Rebekah into a new town house on Sharlo Avenue, not too far from her home on Stanford Avenue. The pretty town house was just a short distance from the reminder of Gina Wilson Green, whose unsolved murder had become a distant memory, but sometimes it pricked at Murray's subconscious when she drove by Gina's house in her shiny black BMW.

Soon after the graduation ceremony, Murray and Rebekah went shopping, then began to pack their things into boxes, preparing to move. Murray noticed that her pocketbook was missing, but she wasn't overly concerned. She had too much to do. She was hosting a keg party for her friends, and then she and Rebekah had to spend the rest of the weekend moving their belongings. The girls couldn't wait to get into their new home, and they had big plans for the summer. Murray had worked so hard, and now it was time to celebrate before she buckled down in her new career. She would be a success. She just knew it. She already was. What she couldn't know was that the man was back, watching her as she loaded boxes, following her to her new home.

Through her tears, Murray smiled as she read the words her mother had written. Her heart warmed; she held the letter close. Sunshine, her mother had written. Music and stories. She loved Murray more than all of those things. Her mother had said she was able and beautiful, that she sparkled. Murray's eyes sparkled with love and tears as she put the letter in a special place. She wanted to read it over and over.

The morning of May 31 was sunny and hot, about 85 degrees, and Murray was in a good mood when she left home about nine to go to work in LSU's Center for Engineering and Business Administration (CEBA) Building. She and Rebekah were settling into their new place and had gotten almost everything unpacked. She liked that the town house had so much room, two bedrooms downstairs and one upstairs, which they were using as a guest room. She liked the privacy as her bedroom was on the opposite end of the house from Rebekah's.

When Rebekah called her at work about 10:30 A.M., Murray told her that she would be going home about noon. They had plans to go to their ex-roommate Grace's wedding, which was scheduled for the next day in Alexandria. Rebekah was to be a bridesmaid, and she was planning to leave later that night. It was 11:40 A.M. when Murray left work, heading to Benny's Car Wash to hose down her car. She liked to keep it clean, proud that at twenty-two she owned a BMW. It was 12:24 P.M. when she left the car wash.

Earlier that morning, Murray's neighbor Chris Ville-marette was leaving for work about the same time as Murray. As he was leaving, he observed a man walking on the street. Chris noticed that the man wasn't very tall, about five feet eight, and had nappy hair and a mustache. He wasn't sure if the man was Hispanic or some other ethnicity, but he noticed that he was wearing a green shirt and Dickies pants. He thought the man seemed out of place, mostly because he appeared to be dirty. Chris noticed that he kept looking back at Murray's house. He thought it was strange, but he would forget about it until he came home later that day and saw the crime tape around her home, the police scurrying about collecting evidence. He struggled to remember every detail as they carried what remained of the beautiful, young Murray from the town house. Other neighbors would also come forward to report a thin black man hanging around that morning. Still, others would mention seeing a white man.

Murray arrived home sometime shortly after 12:30 P.M., fixed herself a sandwich, and grabbed a bottle of Diet Dr Pepper. She sat on her couch to eat and had gotten most of the way through her sandwich when she heard a knock at the door. It is possible that the smiling black man who stood there asked to use her phone. He had done that before with Geralyn DeSoto. The phone from Murray's residence would never be found. Murray had no reason to fear the man as he appeared friendly, and although she could see the bulging muscles of his arms, he looked harmless. His friendly brown eyes smiled at her as she opened the door wider.

What ensued was perhaps the fight of Todd's life. He could not have expected this pretty young girl to fight so hard, to be so determined to live. He could not have known how she had fought hard all of her life to achieve her dreams. She was not going to let this man take those dreams away from her. But Todd was even more determined, and with each moment of resistance, his fury grew. Murray's blood would tell the tale as the fight progressed through room after room of her new town house.

Todd had hit Geralyn DeSoto in the head with her phone as he entered her home. Blood spatters on the cradle of the phone in Murray's home indicated that had possibly happened again. Or perhaps the enraged beast immediately began stabbing her, not with the knife he had used on other victims, but with a flathead screwdriver, a standard tool that would not ordinarily be considered a weapon.

In one instant, that screwdriver became the sole focus of Murray's existence. She had to stop it from coming at her. She had to stop it from gouging holes in her, from hurting her. So she fought. With every bit of her strength, she fought.

As the fight led from the living room to the hallway, Murray's blood began running freely down the walls, soaking into the carpet, and still she fought.

Into the bedroom—Rebekah's. Kicking and screaming. But the screwdriver kept coming. Into her eyes, her chest, her arms, as she tried to defend herself. Into her back as she tried to run.

Eighty-three times the screwdriver met its mark, taking another piece of her with each entry and exit.

Murray read the letter again and wondered how she could have ever fought with her mother. She knew that Ann had given her so much, yet Murray had said hateful things to her at times. She reflected on the bond between them, the love that could never be severed. At that moment, she felt at one with Ann, realizing that her mother had created the person she was today. She thought about her mother's gentle hands and her patience, how she had given Murray power and courage and made her a better person, how she had taught her life's valuable lessons. The words she had spoken in anger came back to haunt her, but her mother's letter made her realize that even the harshest words could not break the loving bonds that held them together.

I have to tell her. I have to tell her how I feel about her. I have to admit I was wrong. I want her to know how much I love her, even though I'm sure she already knows. I have to live up to her expectations. I want to be the beautiful girl she sees in me. I want to sparkle and shine for her. I have to do this alone, without her, so that she will be proud of me. God, please help me become the person my mother envisions I will be, Murray thought.

Murray fell to the floor of Rebekah's room, helpless to defend herself any longer, and the last vestiges of life began slipping away.

The beast who had watched her for almost a year, who had followed her to her new home, climbed on top of her to glory in his triumph. She was now his, this lovely young girl who so loved life. And he pounded into her, frenzied by the bruising, by the blood that had now ceased to flow, by the lovely neck now gaping open.

Still, he stabbed, the screwdriver relentless in its fury, until he felt the release. Evidence of his conquest, he spilled onto Murray's left buttock. The beast in him silenced, but only for a while.

Todd left Murray's home just as he had entered it. Unseen.

Rebekah got home at 2:00 P.M., coming in through the back door and calling Murray's name. She knew something was wrong before she got to her room. Murray's car was there, but she didn't answer. Rebekah saw blood everywhere. She felt the fear rise up in her just before she saw Murray on the floor of her bedroom, almost completely naked.

Rebekah screamed and jumped back before she ran out of the room, desperate to find the phone so she could call 911. Unable to find it, Rebekah ran to her car and with trembling fingers dialed the numbers on her cell phone. The operator told her to go back inside to see if Murray was still alive, to try to revive her. As Rebekah knelt in a pool of blood to help her friend, she saw the gaping hole in Murray's throat. She had to get out of that house.

She was waiting outside, the shock of what she had witnessed setting in, the image of her friend lying on her bedroom floor permanently imprinting itself in her mind, when she frantically motioned the police into the driveway. Rebekah would later move away from Baton Rouge, unable to deal with the horror that lived there.

By 2:11 P.M., uniformed officers and homicide detectives from the Baton Rouge Police Department (BRPD) had been summoned to the scene. Officers Earnest, Karras, Damon, and Busbin were the first to arrive. Rebekah identified her friend's body, although she was barely able to speak. The officers had a difficult time understanding her. They followed the blood through the living room, into the hallway, and into Rebekah's bedroom, careful not to disturb the scene. Even the more seasoned officers were shaken by what they saw when they entered that room. After they established that Murray was dead, they retreated to wait for the crime-scene technicians. Bright yellow crime-scene tape fluttered in the breeze as the officers secured the house.

Homicide detectives Johnson, Norwood, Vavasseur, and Green arrived next, then crime-scene technicians Julia Naylor and Adam Bechel and coroner Louis Cataldie. As the technicians worked, the detectives canvassed the area, interviewing neighbors, hoping that someone had seen or heard something. No one had heard anything, although several neighbors did tell the detectives about the man they had seen hanging around earlier that morning.

When Naylor and Bechel finished processing the scene, the detectives entered. In the living room, they noticed a blue plate with a partly eaten sandwich sitting on the arm of the blue sofa. They observed blood on the base that would have held the VTech phone. There was blood smeared on the living-room wall near the hallway. Blood ran down the wall of the hall about two feet up from the floor, then puddled into the carpet. The bedroom door was covered in red. Then they saw Murray.

She was lying between the bed and the dresser, legs spread, her shirt pulled up over her breasts. The shirt was saturated. Her face was bruised, mostly around her eyes, and torn down the left side. Two holes were observed in her throat, one very large in size. Multiple stab wounds were obvious on her breasts and stomach. Her hands bore witness to her struggle. The detectives would also find wounds on her back, holes driven into the shirt she had worn. The walls of the room were covered in blood, so much that Rebekah would later testify that it was "in places you couldn't imagine how it got there."

On the bed, they found her pants, gray, and bearing the Banana Republic logo, turned inside out amidst still more blood. Police found the bottom of a blender under the dresser close to Murray's hand, and scattered throughout the room were pieces of a broken iron. They discovered the top of the blender in a green container along the wall and the bottom of the iron, smeared with blood, beside it. The cord and the top of the iron would never be found. Nor would Murray's phone, her keys, or her purse. What police did find was the print of a Rawlings Zipstar tennis shoe, the kind that could be bought at Wal-Mart, size ten and a half.

It was 7:46 P.M., seven hours after Murray had made her sandwich, before her body was wrapped in the white homicide sheet, then placed into a body bag.

Though gone, Murray would always be surrounded with love. In the letter, Ann had wished she could blow hugs and kisses through time to keep her precious daughter warm when the nights seemed endless and the sun did not shine. She believed that was possible because Murray would live forever in her heart. She expressed her appreciation for the joy and wonder Murray had brought into her life. She could not know Murray would soon be gone or that her words would touch her child so deeply in the days before her death.

With Murray's passing, an insidious darkness crept into the city.

Eugenie Boisfontaine

Gina Wilson Green and Charlotte Murray Pace were not the first women who lived on Stanford Avenue to be killed, and by the time Todd went on his rampage in the early years of the new millennium, the other woman had been long forgotten. But in 1997, on a hot day in the middle of June, Eugenie Boisfontaine was reported missing. She lived just a few houses down from Gina in a garage apartment set back from the main house. At thirty-four, Eugenie (an old European name pronounced U-jha-nay) had been married and divorced and had moved to Baton Rouge a year earlier to be near some old friends.

A pretty woman, Eugenie's naturally dark hair had been streaked with blond highlights to complement her caramel-colored skin. Her thick eyebrows shadowed deep brown eyes, and her slightly crooked smile hinted at shyness. She was a slender woman who liked to take long walks around the LSU lakes, sometimes just enjoying watching students, sometimes trying to make friends with those who walked along the paths. Occasionally Eugenie could be spotted carrying a bottle of wine and two wineglasses. Perhaps she hoped that she would meet a new friend, one who would want to sit with her by the lake and while away sunny afternoons amidst the peaceful setting. And although Eugenie liked the finer things in life, she was often seen wandering around the lakes in a long dress and an old coat.

Until June 13.

What happened to Eugenie is still a mystery. Police do not know if she was taken from her home or if she was grabbed as she walked along the lake. Her sister, Susan Edwards, says it would have been very odd for Eugenie to open her door to a stranger. She led a quiet life and kept to herself, except for those times when she was lonely, when she walked the LSU lakes.

And it was at those lakes that clues would be found, clues that led police to suspect foul play. On June 14, a jogger found Eugenie's credit cards aligned in a circle on a path that followed the circumference of the lake. The jogger, a visiting professor, turned the cards over to security personnel, who then brought them to Eugenie's house and left them in a basket by her front door. When her family didn't hear from her, when she didn't answer their calls, they came to Baton Rouge to check on her and found the basket. They reported her disappearance to police and then hired their own investigator, who later found Eugenie's keys near the lake. But the credit cards and the keys were the only clues to be found. There were no signs of forced entry into her home, and her car was parked in its usual spot in the driveway.

That humid, sunny day in June was the last time anyone had any contact with Eugenie, and it would be several months before anyone had any idea what had happened to the quiet, young woman, whose apartment had yielded a reservation for a much-awaited trip to Europe. Eugenie was about to spread her wings, to explore the world on the day that her life was abruptly taken from her. And her family, her mother and father, her sister, Susan, and her brother, Kurt, waited and worried, praying that she would be found alive and unharmed. But as the days and weeks and months passed with no word of her, they found their hope dwindling. And then all hope was lost.

"It was on a Wednesday when the police called," Susan recalled. "They said they had found Eugenie, that they had matched her dental records to a woman they had found."

August 7 was a typical, sweltering summer day, almost two months since Eugenie's credit cards had been found. A woman who took in stray dogs, and walked them along an alley that ran beside the Alligator Bayou Bar on Bayou Manchac, made a gruesome discovery. Lying in the tall reeds that lined the bayou next to the bar was a woman's decomposed body, mostly hidden under a tire that had been purposely placed to conceal her. Iberville Parish sheriff's deputies sent the woman's remains to the FACES Laboratory at LSU for identification. Mary Manhein identified her from dental records.

Eugenie was dead. She had been lying in that water for months as the Alligator Bayou Bar's customers went in and out grabbing a few quick drinks after a long work-day or partying into the wee hours, unaware that just outside the bar a lonely woman lay decomposing in the water, just waiting for someone to find her, to give her family some answers. But like Christine Moore's family, Eugenie's loved ones have never received any answers. Her death haunts them to this day.

"It was really awful," Susan said. "I begged police to do something about DNA, to stake off the area, anything. I thought they might be able to find who did this by the DNA that was found. Joe Freeman, the coroner in Iberville Parish, told me they didn't have the money for DNA test-ing, that they didn't even have the money to buy body bags. Joe Freeman was a nightmare. He was so rude, and nothing was ever done."

Eugenie's case went into the numerous files police were accumulating of unsolved cases of missing and murdered women in the Baton Rouge area.

It would be many years before the DNA found on the shredded black panties that were wrapped around Eugenie's left leg would be tested, sent by the Iberville Parish Sheriff's Office (IPSO) to the Louisiana State Police Crime Lab. But according to Dannie Mixon, who at that time was working with the attorney general's office, those panties were then lost for several more years. "The state police tried to say that Joe Freeman lost them, but they were found by a police officer, Chris Romero, in a refrigerator in the police crime lab a few years later," Dannie recalled.

By July 2002, five years had gone by. The Baton Rouge Police Department suddenly found itself with two new murders on its hands—murders that were linked not only by DNA, but by the location where the victims had lived. Police recalled another victim who had lived on the same street. It was Eugenie's address that prompted police to pull out her file, wipe the dust off, and take another look. However, with the information at hand, the only link seemed to be the street where the victims lived and the fact that they were raped, although in Eugenie's case, her body was too decomposed to tell. Her shredded panties, though, gave that indication to police. Nothing else matched.

Gina had been strangled. Murray had been viciously stabbed. Eugenie had died from a skull fracture, from a beating of some kind. Gina and Murray had been left in their homes. Eugenie's body had been placed in Bayou Manchac, some fifteen miles south of Baton Rouge. But as new victims were linked to a serial killer preying on South Louisiana women and Todd's modus operandi expanded, many began to believe that Eugenie should be included on the list.

Todd was working in the vicinity of where Eugenie's body was found in the days prior to her disappearance. As a driver for Louisiana Ready Mix, Todd delivered cement over a large geographic area around Baton Rouge. Several times in the weeks before Eugenie's murder, Todd picked up deliveries of cement on Highway 30 in the towns of Prairieville and Gonzales in Ascension Parish. Highway 30 crosses Bayou Manchac. Eugenie was found on the east side of the Mississippi River, near Prairieville. Todd was known to enjoy hanging out at bars after work, so it is not inconceivable that he would have made his way to the Alligator Bayou Bar while working in the area. On June 12, Todd picked up a delivery in Prairieville from a company called Lonestar, but he did not show up for work on June 13, the day Eugenie disappeared.

After Todd's capture, several men who had been building a fence near Eugenie's residence in the week she disappeared reported seeing a man who looked like the man they had seen in news reports prowling around in her backyard when they returned from lunch.

But all of this was only circumstantial. All real evidence had disappeared into a muddy bayou, except for the DNA scientists had recovered from those shredded black panties. In late 2005, ReliaGene Technologies, Inc., released its preliminary findings after its analysis of the evidence. The DNA on the panties did not match Derrick Todd Lee's.

Dannie Mixon was still not convinced. "The MO is too similar to the others. And the close proximity of her house to Gina and Murray's is too coincidental. Mark my words. Derrick Todd Lee killed Eugenie."

But that's little consolation for Eugenie's family. "My mom can't even talk about it anymore. She can't deal with it," Susan explained. "It's just been so difficult. We'll probably never know where or why it happened."

And so many years later, as the Boisfontaine family still went through the motions of everyday life while dealing with their grief, Todd began traveling new territory, over the swamps that led away from Baton Rouge toward Lafayette.

Diane Alexander

Just a few miles to the east of Lafayette is a city seemingly suspended in time. Its inhabitants are mostly Cajuns or transplants who fell in love with the quaint city streets and small-town atmosphere. Or maybe even just the food, as Breaux Bridge is *la capitale Mondiale de l'ecrevisse,* or the "crawfish capital of the world." Known for its simmering crawfish pies, étouffées, and bisques, the city grew up around a small bridge built by Firmin Breaux in 1799.

Breaux was a landowner who wanted his family and friends to be able to visit each other without having to swim across Bayou Teche, so he gathered wooden boards and rope and built a bridge by tying the rope to pilings and oak trees at either end. Forever after, when weary travelers would ask directions of the townspeople, invariably the focal point would be Breaux's Bridge. And thus the town got its name.

Breaux Bridge is a peaceful place, an attractive alternative to its much larger and busier neighbor, mostly because of the serenity that lasts throughout the year, except in the spring when hungry visitors come from around the world to experience the annual crawfish festival. With a lower crime rate than most Louisiana cities, Breaux Bridge provides a safe haven and slower pace for the families who thrive within its boundaries.

Safe, that is, until it became the hunting ground for a predator searching for new game. Just over a month after Derrick Todd Lee savagely murdered Charlotte Murray Pace, a young woman named Dora saw a good-looking black man in a burgundy pickup truck in the parking lot of the local Wal-Mart. She glanced at him briefly before she drove to the nearby Taco Bell, where she saw him again. As she walked across the parking lot, the man approached her, extending his hand in a friendly manner.

"Hi, my name is Anthony. You're not from around here, are you?" he said.

Anthony grabbed Dora's arm and pulled her toward him. Before she escaped, Dora noticed that the light-skinned black man attempting to abduct her was masturbating with his free hand. Anthony bore an uncanny resemblance to Derrick Todd Lee. So soon after the death of Murray, Todd was still hungry and had come to Breaux Bridge, as many did this time of year, to feed.

But one woman in this town that winds quietly along the bayou would later prove to be the undoing of a serial killer. Todd was about to make his first serious mistake—a witness, a victim, who lived to tell the tale.

Diane Alexander softly hummed along with the gospel music playing on her radio as she prepared lunch for her teenaged son, Herman. She had gotten up early as usual and left about seven-thirty that hot summer morning of July 9. Instead of going to her job at St. Agnes Hospital, Diane headed out to run errands, glad that she was working a different shift than usual. Normally, she worked mornings, but this day she didn't have to be there until almost three. Herman had still been sleeping when she left, although he was supposed to leave for school at 8:00 A.M.

Diane went first to Sam's Wholesale Club in Lafayette, but the store wasn't open and she had to wait in the parking lot for a while. Next it was on to Wal-Mart to pick up some supplies for the house, then back to Breaux Bridge—to Hebert's Grocery, to the post office, to the Canal Gas Station. As she headed back down Highway 31, she remembered that she needed to go to the bank, so she passed Jeffrey Broussard Road, where the mobile home she had lived in for twelve years was located, and went to run her final errand. It was almost 11:30 before she saw the familiar Dead End sign close to her driveway. Diane climbed the steps to the porch and went inside. She set her purse on the counter and took off her wedding ring, careful as always to keep from getting it dirty while she was cooking. After going to Herman's bedroom to set up the ironing board, where she would smooth the creases from her uniform, Diane began making lunch, pleased that she had managed to get her errands done in time. Herman would be arriving home from the University of Louisiana at Lafayette while his lunch was still warm.

Her husband, Oliver, a delivery driver for Bayou Land Seafood, had left the day before to make a run. She didn't expect him home until later that evening after her shift had begun. She was in a good mood this steamy July morning, happy that she had been able to change her routine. She wasn't thinking about Murray Pace. She didn't know about Anthony or Dora or what had happened at the Wal-Mart close to her home just six days before. She was thinking about Herman and lunch. She was humming along with her music, praising God in her simple way as she went about her day. But then she heard a knock at the door.

The man seemed lost. Clad in blue-jeaned shorts and a white shirt, he stood on the lower portion of the porch. He was clean-shaven and neat, a light-skinned black man. Diane did not feel threatened.

"Hi, my name is Anthony. I'm supposed to be doing construction work for the Montgomerys," the man said. "Do you or your husband know them?"

Diane informed him that she didn't, so he asked if he could borrow a phone and a phone book to look up their address. Still, Diane was not frightened. She brought her cordless phone and a phone book to the man and closed and locked the door. Returning to the stove, Diane felt there was nothing out of the ordinary about the man who stood on her porch. She waited a few minutes and opened the door again.

Todd flipped through the phone book, his heart pounding as adrenaline coursed through his system. She was like the others. Diane was black, but she had the same high cheekbones, the average build, the dark hair. She was a nurse, judging by the uniform she wore when she left for work each day. He had been watching her. He had thought about what he would say, how he would get her to talk to him. He knew that even though he was husky, his eyes that smiled and his friendliness would not frighten her, at least not until his demeanor changed, at least not until he wanted her to be afraid. That was what fed him, what made him alive—the fear.

And the blood.

The death.

He watched the doorknob turn, then opened the storm door to hand Diane the phone. It was time.

Gospel music could be heard from the open doorway. "I sing with a gospel choir," Todd said to Diane, asking if she had heard of him. She told him she hadn't, becoming irritated by the man who seemed to want to chat.

"Are you sure your husband don't know the Montgomerys?" Todd asked again.

"Look, my husband's not home," Diane responded, annoyed and unaware that those very words were what Todd had been waiting to hear. As Diane tried to close the door, Todd used his burly weight to force his way inside her home. And then his big hands were around her throat, squeezing as he pushed her back against the metal door.

"Take me to your bedroom," he commanded. "I have

a knife." Impatient, he pulled Diane to the floor. "Take your panties off."

"I can't. Your hand's on my throat," Diane croaked, fear setting in as she realized Todd's intention.

"Shut up. Shut up," Todd said, dragging her farther into the living room and raising her blue denim dress. "I've been watching you."

He set his knife on the floor, trying desperately to get an erection. Diane tried to reach for the knife, but Todd took it from her, angry now.

"Bitch!" he gritted out.

Todd stood up, looking around until he spotted the phone cord that led to the computer. He cut a section with the knife. Although she was terrified, Diane knew that she must try to stall the man whose eyes glinted fiercely as he looked at her. "You're not a bad-looking guy," she said, trying to appease him.

"No, I'm not," he said as he pulled off his shirt, and then wrapped the cord around her neck. He was sweating profusely. Diane wedged a finger between the cord and her throat, struggling for air. Todd straddled her shoulders, making it impossible for her to fight back. Then he hit her in the head and in her eyes, the blows flying with rapid fury. Diane screamed, her vision going blurry.

And still no erection. Todd tried to rape her and failed. Diane's leg, which had been propped on the couch, fell to the floor. He picked it up and put it back, determined to complete the act. Then he stopped. Diane saw her attacker look up, listening intently for a moment.

He jumped up, then looked down at her, his gaze hardened into a mask of anger, of frustration. He viciously stomped her in the stomach before he ran out the back door of the mobile home. Herman walked in the front.

He had stopped at the mailbox before entering the driveway, his usual parking place blocked by a gold car with the front license plate bearing the words "Hampton Motors." He went to get the cordless phone, usually kept on the top of the microwave, but it wasn't there. It was then he heard the cries.

"Help! Get a knife!" He hurried into the living room to discover his mother lying in a bloody pool, her dress raised. She was barely conscious. Herman noticed the back door swinging open, and he ran outside to see the gold car speeding south down Highway 31. He noticed a cord hanging from the window, flying in the wind. In his distress, his first thought was to catch whoever had done this to his mother, so he ran back in the house to get his keys. His tires spun as he sped from the driveway and gave chase, but to no avail. Todd was gone. Herman rushed back home to find his mother lying unconscious in the bedroom.

Diane wondered why her son hadn't called 911, but in a state of semiconsciousness, she realized where he had gone. She gathered her strength and crawled to her bedroom, leaving a trail of blood behind her. She could barely see, her eyes already swollen from the beating. Reaching for the phone, Diane called 911 and her husband before a welcoming darkness released her from the pain.

Sammy Inzerella had been with the St. Martin Parish Sheriff's Office (SMSO) for fourteen years, ten of those spent as a detective. He was the first deputy dispatched to the Alexander home, although he was unaware that he was about to enter a crime scene. He was expecting a medical emergency and arrived just behind Unit 26 of Acadian Ambulance. Herman was pacing up and down anxiously, yelling that he was going to "get that nigger!"

The detective found the paramedics bent over a woman lying on the floor in the bedroom. He noticed that her face and upper body were covered with blood, as was the floor. One of the paramedics informed him that Diane had suffered severe trauma to her head. Detective

Inzerella immediately notified dispatch and asked that detectives be sent to investigate.

He then questioned Herman, who told him about the car that had been parked in the driveway. "There was damage to the front between both headlights," Herman said. "It was a gold Mitsubishi Mirage. I walked in and found my mom laying on the floor, bleeding. She told me he tried to rape her and was leaving out the back door. I ran out of the house and went almost all the way to Breaux Bridge, but I couldn't find the car."

A helicopter airlifted Diane to Lafayette General Medical Center, where she was diagnosed with a hairline fracture, head lacerations, and other injuries to the back of her head. She would spend five days recovering, reliving the horror of her attack, looking in the mirror at the large black circles etched around her eyes, at the swelling caused by those big hands bent on destroying her.

The other detectives arrived shortly after Diane was transported to the hospital, including lead detective Arthur Boyd, who brought Herman to the sheriff's substation to remove him from the scene. Boyd knew that Herman needed to calm down to be able to provide authorities with leads to the suspect. Inzerella stayed behind to collect evidence.

As he began investigating, Inzerella noticed no signs of forced entry, but a broken ceramic vase, an overturned wicker table, and the victim's blood in the living room told him that this was the site of the crime. He also noticed sections of a phone cord lying on the floor.

Following the trail of evidence into the master bedroom, Inzerella began to photograph anything that looked out of place—Diane's blood on the wall to the left of the phone she had used to place the calls that would save her life, blood in the hallway, the kitchen, the living room. He then dusted the front door for prints. He entered into evidence Diane's underwear, a faceplate, the door handle, the dead bolt, the phone book, and a cordless phone. Diane's purse was nowhere to be found.

Inzerella returned to the phone cord that led to a computer located in the middle bedroom. Because a section was missing, the detective collected a reference sample, cutting a piece from each severed end and tying a control knot on each end he cut. He did not know it, but that reference sample would later tie Diane's attack to the killings that were happening with increasing frequency in Baton Rouge.

Diane drifted in and out of consciousness as the doctors and nurses cleaned the blood from her wounds and ran tests to discover the extent of her injuries.

Although she knew she was safe, Diane's fear had not yet subsided. She knew she did not want to go home—ever. Home was where she used to feel safe, where she had lived and loved her husband and son, where a seemingly harmless man had cruelly taken her sense of security from her. As she moved from X-ray to CAT scan, she wondered why the man had picked her.

She tried to remember his face.

She tried to forget his face.

Detective Boyd needed Diane to remember. He could tell by her injuries how traumatic the attack had been for her. He gently asked her questions, using his experience as an investigator to pull from her the facts, the description of the man who had brutalized her. Diane's memory was surprisingly clear. She described the solid build, the brown eyes, the light black skin. She told the detective how the man had tried to strangle her, to rape her, how her son had saved her life. She recalled how her assailant had said his name was Anthony and that he had been watching her. She said that she would assist the detective with making a composite drawing of her attacker.

She was good to her word. The composite drawn by

FACES Laboratory from Diane's description was only a little off: the hairline was a bit too high, the eyebrows too thin, the jawline too sharp. Police in the quiet town of Breaux Bridge now had in their possession a face that resembled the man who had killed Connie Warner, Randi Mebruer, Geralyn DeSoto, Gina Green, and Murray Pace. But they could not know it.

Frustrated by his inability to sate his lust, the killer would return to Baton Rouge to strike again, in only three days.

Pamela Piglia Kinamore

While Diane Alexander lay on the floor of her living room fighting for her life, the Baton Rouge police announced to the public that the murders of Gina Wilson Green and Charlotte Murray Pace had been linked by DNA—that matching DNA had been discovered at both crime scenes. The city was effectively put on alert. Someone was raping and killing women who lived close to LSU. Students were urged to take extra precautions, told not to walk alone at night, reminded to lock their doors. Anxious parents called daughters who attended the university, fearful that they would be next.

LSU seemed to be the connection to the killer. Was he a student? Did he work there? No one had the answer. And no one suspected that the killer was not especially focused on LSU, but everyone would learn in just a few days that the entire city was a target. No woman was safe.

Especially not Pam Kinamore, who on the night of July 12, 2002, was closing her antiques shop, Comforts and Joys, a little late. The shop was located in Denham Springs, a small community just a few miles east of Baton Rouge. Pam was in no hurry to get home that night. She had talked to her husband of twenty years, Byron, about 6:00 P.M., and he had told her he would be home late. He was enjoying a night at Argosy Casino on the river. Pam

finally left the shop a little after 9:30 P.M., looking forward
to getting to her home off Airline Highway in Baton
Rouge and relaxing in a warm bath.

Pam didn't realize that she had forgotten the keys in
the back door when she entered her home. She had a
bad habit of leaving them there. She walked through the
house, filled with the beautiful antiques and whimsical
decorations that reflected her flair for designing, until
she got to the bathroom, where she would run the water
for her bath.

As she disrobed, the mirror reflected her beauty. At
forty-four, she looked much younger, with a slender body,
shoulder-length brown hair, and eyes that beamed along
with her lips. Those who knew Pam always said that she
did not smile, she beamed. The mirror could not reflect
her personality, though, which was even sunnier than her
smile. Pam climbed into the tub, leaned back to relax, and
smiled as she thought of Byron enjoying himself at the
casino. She hoped he would be home soon. She wanted
to tell him about her day. She loved talking to Byron. After
twenty years, she still loved everything about him.

The two had met at a friend's house when Pam was in
her early twenties. She had never had a shortage of dates
or boyfriends, as men were attracted to her vivacious-
ness. She was adventurous and fun and had even dated
a senator for a while. But that relationship had been over
long before the night she glanced across a room and saw
Byron enter. She thought he was beautiful.

As the two were introduced, Byron reached up from
his wheelchair to shake her hand and say hello. That was
it. Before long, he asked her for a date, and they fell in
love. Pam did not care that Byron's legs had been para-
lyzed in a car accident when he was a teenager. All she
saw was his handsome face and his kind heart.

The couple married in 1982 and soon began considering having a family. They had been unable to conceive,
and after trying in vitro fertilization unsuccessfully, Pam

and Byron decided to adopt, knowing that they could give so much love to a child.

> *Dear Byron:*
>
> *I can remember the day I met you and Pam. I was alone in the office. You had a late afternoon appointment with me and came in separate cars. You both drove into the parking lot simultaneously. Pam, stylish as ever, got out of her car and walked over to where you had parked. Through the open window she greeted you playfully. You flashed her an ear-to-ear smile. While you maneuvered yourself out of the car, she was chatting, laughing, and seemed to be peppering you with a funny story. She casually waited, as though it was the most natural thing in the world for a husband to be handicapped and to have to take a little longer than most to get out of his automobile. At that intimate moment, when I observed the two of you interacting in the parking lot, in my mind's eye, Jacob was born. Before you even entered the office, I had decided that I was going to place a baby with you as soon as possible.*
>
> *—Lillie Gallagher, St. Elizabeth Foundation*

In 1989, Jacob completed the Kinamore family. Pam and Byron couldn't have been happier. Pam enjoyed being a mother and caring for the two men in her life. She was crazy about them and loved watching Byron ride the baby around in his wheelchair. But when Jacob started school, Pam began to want to do something more with her days, something creative, something that she could enjoy. In 1995, she opened Comforts and Joys, choosing Denham Springs because of the row of quaint antiques shops that lined the old downtown area on Range Avenue. Pam was happy to finally be doing what she loved—shopping for antiques, arranging the store, helping others design their homes.

Pam, always a go-getter, had worked in many fields in her life. She had attended LSU and earned a degree in fine arts. She had been a real estate agent, a page in the state senate, vice president of a mortgage company. But the little shop on Range Avenue gave her fulfillment. She would travel occasionally with her mother, Lynne Marino, to New York on buying sprees for the store. Together, the mother and daughter would let the excitement of the Big Apple take hold of their spirits as they traveled from market to market, deciding on this eighteenth-century armoire or that antique English linen press. The two were best friends, and Pam had inherited Lynne's feistiness.

Pam loved her life. She had a husband, who adored her; a baby, whom they both adored; a wonderful home; and a mother, sisters, and a brother, who were her best friends. She thought about how lucky she had been, how blessed, as she lay relaxing in her tub and waiting for Byron. When she heard the sound of someone coming into the bedroom, she smiled. Her Byron was home.

Perhaps Todd first spotted her when he had brought a load of concrete into Briarwood Estates a few days earlier. Perhaps he had seen her at LSU, where she had sung with a choir the previous week. Perhaps it was at her shop in Denham Springs or maybe at the casino. Pam went there sometimes with Byron. She didn't like to gamble, but the couple sometimes enjoyed dining at the buffet together.

Todd liked to go to the casino, spending the money he received from his unemployment check there, hoping to hit the big time. He missed all the money he used to have. Life was much harder without it, and he got tired of going through job after job, trying to feed his family. He was tired of all of the stress. And then that boy had come home before he'd been finished with that black woman the other day. That had made him angry. She had been pretty and had told him he was good-looking. He liked that.

A lot of things had made him angry lately. He had lost control with that other woman, the white one in the town house. That was a wild one. She had not been easy. He hadn't meant to stab her so many times, but she wouldn't stop fighting. She wouldn't die easily, like the other ones, and just let him have his pleasure. Things definitely weren't going his way. But he had a new one in mind. She was so beautiful. He licked his lips as he thought of what he would do to her.

Todd was hiding, watching, as Pam drove into the driveway. He snuck up to her back door and couldn't believe his luck. The keys were in the door. This would be easy.

Pam waited for Byron to come through the door. Then she heard the footsteps. They were heavy, too heavy to be Jacob, who was at a church camp, and it couldn't be Byron. Her eyes widened in fear as she saw the husky black man coming toward her.

She screamed.

She tried to cover her nakedness.

She fought as the man dragged her from the tub and through her bedroom.

He hit her. They knocked over a footstool as they fought. Blood dribbled onto a rug. Todd dragged her from the house and put her into the white work truck he had borrowed from his uncle. Pam was woozy from the blows, too woozy to try to jump out. The man had a knife. He had threatened to cut her.

As the truck made its way north on Airline Highway toward Interstate 12, Todd drove erratically, trying to keep the woman in place. He stopped at a red light. A woman drove up behind them. She had noticed that the vehicle was weaving. Her headlights reflected two people in the truck.

Just before the light turned green, Pam turned to look back through the window, pleading with her eyes.

The woman thought it was strange, but she had no way of knowing what was happening. Still, she jotted down as

much of the license plate as she could remember—
JT341. She had only caught a glimpse of the driver and
thought that he may have been a white male. She would
remember the incident when Pam's face appeared on
the news. Pam had been the woman she had seen in the
truck. She hurriedly called the police.

Pam would be spotted again about thirty minutes later
by the driver of an eighteen-wheeler riding down Interstate
10, headed toward Lafayette by Whiskey Bay. As a white
Chevrolet work truck passed him, he looked down and saw
a female slumped over in the cab. She was naked. He sped
up to look again. Todd slowed down and let the eighteen-
wheeler go by. Todd exited toward Whiskey Bay. The driver
got on his radio and called to report what he had seen.

No one came.

Byron got home about 11:30 P.M. He saw that Pam's vehicle was in the driveway and that she had once again
left her keys in the back door. He called out to her as
he wheeled through the house. When he got to the bathroom, he saw that her bathwater had been run.

"Pam?" he called.

No answer.

He went through every room in the house, then went
outside to look for her. He went back into the bedroom.
Byron noticed that the footstool was knocked over, and
pictures on the dresser were disturbed. The dresser was
slightly out of its usual place. Then he saw what looked
like a little blood on the rug. Byron called the police.

It would not be long before a missing persons bulletin
was released to the media. It soon became obvious to
police that Pam had not simply decided to go somewhere
for the night. Byron called the Piglia and Kinamore families. They began to hold a vigil—Pam's mother; her sisters,
Nancy and Ellen; her brother, Eddie; nieces, nephews, and
in-laws. They waited fearfully, each knowing that Pam

would not just leave. She loved her life too much, her family. They lit candles. They prayed. They hoped. They waited. They would keep waiting for four long days.

Pam's body was discovered around 10:00 A.M. on July 16. Iberville Parish sheriff's deputies responded to the call from a survey company reporting that a white female had been discovered nude by Whiskey Bay. She was lying on an embankment in an inlet, hidden under Whiskey Bay Bridge, with leaves and brush covering parts of her badly decomposed body. A piece of a phone cord that had been severed from a computer was found not far from where she lay.

The area around Whiskey Bay is mostly desolate swampland. Interstate 10, built over the Atchafalaya Swamp, which is home to herons and alligators and lonely cypress trees, which rise up from the murky water, provides a route from Baton Rouge to the west. The interstate leads through small towns surrounded by swamp, like Whiskey Bay and Maringouin and Butte La Rose, before reaching Breaux Bridge and the larger city of Lafayette. The isolation is beautifully expressed through the haunting cast of the cypress. Exit 127 leads travelers to the bay, which empties into the Atchafalaya Basin.

The isolation was also attractive to Todd, who needed privacy for what he intended to do—a place where no one could hear screaming in case Pam came awake, like she had on Airline Highway. Under the bridge, with the cars and trucks rumbling as they sped by overhead, was perfect. The area directly under the bridge was cleared on both sides of the road, but woods on the edge of the clearing offered cover. No one would be there at night. No one but Todd and the lovely white woman he had been watching.

He pulled her from the truck and dragged her to an embankment. Todd raped the beautiful Pam as the bridge shook from the traffic passing overhead. Then he pulled out his knife, raking it across her throat three times, almost beheading her. Each cut covered four to five and a half inches across her neck. Todd covered Pam carefully with available brush before he got back into the truck and headed home to Jackie with a thin silver toe ring in his possession—a trophy to remind him of his conquest.

When police found the woman, whose throat had been cut and who had sustained defensive injuries to her knees and thighs, they immediately suspected that she could be the missing lady from Briarwood Estates.

Byron was informed that a woman had been found and asked if he would try to identify the body. Pam was unrecognizable. Nothing about her appearance resembled the woman who had filled his life with such joy. Only a gold ring on the left hand of the unfamiliar woman, who lay there dead, gave a clue to her identity. It was the symbol of the promise they had made to each other to share an eternal love. It was engraved with the date of their marriage. Byron's heart broke as he viewed the mutilated body of his once-lovely wife.

Byron hung his head and cried, holding tightly to Jacob's hand, as the love of his life was buried on July 21. The beautiful lady with the sunny personality was gone. Discarded by a serial killer under the Whiskey Bay Bridge. The innocence of a city would be discarded with her.

Police knew that Pam had still been alive when her throat was cut because pathologist Paul McGarry had found blood in her lungs. Sperm had also been found in her body, but a full DNA profile could not be obtained from the sample. They added Pam to their growing list of unsolved homicides.

One woman would soon make it her personal mission to see to it that whoever had done this to her beloved daughter would be caught. Lynne Marino was about to become a force with which to be reckoned.

In moments of grief and separation, the human heart knows that the love which unites the members of a family is a lasting reality beyond the world; that love, if it is real love, cannot die. —Lillie Gallagher

Lynne Marino

Do you know what it's like to wake up every morning and know that you will never see your child again?
—Lynne Marino

Pam Kinamore would be the third victim linked by DNA to the South Louisiana Serial Killer. The blood on the rug, evidence that Pam had struggled fiercely with her captor, matched the killer's DNA found at the other crime scenes. Lynne Marino was devastated, haunted by what had happened to her daughter. She could not control the tears that ran unabated down her face at awkward times. She could not understand the hate and rage she felt for the person who had raped and murdered her daughter so callously. Lynne had never hated anyone. But now, anguish and rage threatened to consume her. She knew that she could not sit idly by while police looked for the killer. She had to do something, anything, that would make Baton Rouge residents aware that this killer needed to be caught, and soon, before someone else died. Lynne had no doubt that he would strike again. She did not want another family to experience what she and the rest of Pam's family were going through.

Lynne had never been one to sit idly by for anything. She had married Edward Piglia in 1954 and divorced him ten years later when he refused to stop drinking the beer he liked on occasion. The problem was, Lynne said, that beer made him mean, and she was not going to raise her children in that environment.

She divorced Edward in 1964, before most women had the courage to stand up for themselves and brave the world on their own. Before the Beatles "invasion" began, before the first man landed on the moon, before Women's Lib. With four children in tow, Lynne set out on her own. There were no day care centers at that time. Women could not obtain credit or get the higher-paying jobs reserved for men. But Lynne was determined to give Eddie, Nancy, Pam, and Ellen a good life.

Pam was Lynne's third born, with eyes that were almost black and curly brown hair. She had always run one step ahead of other children her age and began talking at only thirteen months. She used to tell everyone, "Hello, my name is Peggy." Peggy was her cousin, and Pam just liked the name. She liked to sit in her high chair and rub spinach in her hair. She liked to do things her way.

She got that behavior from Lynne. While Lynne was married, the children attended public school in New Orleans where they lived, but Lynne wanted a better education for them. After she divorced, Lynne approached her priest and told him that she wanted her children to attend Mater Dolorosa, a good Catholic school. She explained that she could not afford the tuition for four children. The kindly priest allowed them to attend the school for the price of one child.

"It takes a lot to beg," Lynne said. "But I was never too proud to ask for the best I could for my children."

Do you know what it's like to relive the memories the two of you created and know there will be no more new memories?
                                                              —Lynne Marino

Lynne worked hard as a secretary and later in management to provide for the children. They were a close family, and Eddie helped his mother as much as he could with the younger kids, having been thrust into the role of the man of the family at an early age. Nancy was smart and popular and would be voted homecoming queen in her senior year of high school. Pam was the entrepreneur. She had street smarts. Ellen was the baby and spoiled by everyone. She was close to all of her siblings, but she felt a special bond to Pam, who was nearest to her in age. "I sometimes wondered where Pam ended and I began," Ellen has said many times.

Lynne had always been proud of the way she had raised her children—to be strong, to go after what they wanted in life. It had been a struggle for her, but life had been good. Her children were healthy and happy, and at sixty-six, Lynne was still working, now as an accountant for her son-in-law's real estate firm. Life had settled into a pleasant routine, filled with grandchildren and shopping and the love she shared with her family. Lynne's struggles were over . . . until she got the call that Pam was missing.

Lynne suddenly was faced with the biggest struggle of her life—the struggle to overcome overwhelming grief, the struggle to bring attention to her daughter's murder. She began the day after the funeral.

Do you know what it's like to see a husband grieve for his soul mate of more than twenty years, to see him going to the movies alone when this was such a fun and happy time they shared?
—Lynne Marino

Lynne organized a rally on the steps of the state capitol building in Baton Rouge. She invited the media and family members of the other victims. Before DNA connected Pam's murder to the serial killer, Lynne knew that the same man who had killed Murray Pace and Gina Green had killed Pam. She was certain of it.

The rallies on the capitol steps were held every third Sunday of each month and would soon become controversial as families of the victims gathered together to mourn, to hand out flyers, to inform the public of what the police were doing to catch the killer.

"I started doing it for Pam, but then I met Ann Pace, and suddenly we were doing this for all the families. How would I have felt knowing that I didn't do anything? I wouldn't have been able to forgive myself," Lynne explained. "I was determined. I had no fear in me of the serial killer. I went against the governor, the chief of police, the mayor. My daughter's killer would be found and punished. That's all I knew. It's what kept me going."

> *Do you know what it's like for Byron to come home every night and not be greeted by that beautiful smile and happy banter—no good smells coming from the kitchen because there is no wife here any more, no mother?*
>
> —Lynne Marino

As the days and months passed by, and more women disappeared and died, new groups of families would appear on those steps. Lynne offered to help police. She offered to man the hotline that had been set up so that citizens could report tips. Ike Vavasseur, a detective on the police force and member of the task force that would be formed, was assigned to Lynne. His job was to keep her informed, to help her with what she could and couldn't say to the media. Soon he just tried to keep her under control. That was impossible.

Lynne became a familiar sight on television, sometimes crying as she remembered times she had shared with her daughter, sometimes slamming Baton Rouge police chief Pat Englade, Mayor-President Bobby Simpson, and Governor Mike Foster.

Lynne went to the governor, along with Ann Pace; Dr. Peter Scharf, a criminologist; and Gene Fields, the investigator in the Eugenie Boisfontaine murder. They suggested that Englade did not have the experience to head up the investigation. The group asked that the governor seek outside help. Foster asked them to give him a prototype of what had worked in serial killer cases in other cities. Scharf created the document, but when they brought it to the governor, Foster explained, "We're talking about egos here."

"Are we talking about egos, or are we talking about lives?" Lynne shot back.

Lynne suggested that Foster should have police search databases for anyone with histories of Peeping Tom charges, stalking, burglary, or battery. Foster said, "We can't check every parish in Louisiana."

"I think they thought I was a lunatic," Lynne said. "I gave them tips but never learned if they followed up on them. I understand that there are times when families can get in the way of an investigation, but the solution is to let the families help. Give them chores. Have them make flyers. Let them go door-to-door. We needed to do something. We are responsible for what happens to us. We needed to know what was going on. Consequently, we were riled up."

Do you know what it's like to see a twelve-year-old boy finish the remainder of grammar school without the love and support of his mom, who was always there to encourage him and to witness every accomplishment?
                                                        —Lynne Marino

As Lynne became more and more focused on keeping the murders on the front pages of the newspapers, the need to learn who had killed Pam became all-consuming to her. The public soon gained respect for this sixty-six-year-old whippersnapper who had the nerve to suggest that everything that could be done was not being done. The public rallied behind her, while police officers and detectives worked hour after hour through long days and nights on the cases that were turning the capital city upside down. They strove, through daily press conferences, to assure citizens that they were working diligently to find the killer. And they were.

But they were looking in the wrong direction. All of the witnesses in Pam's case had described a white man driving away in a white truck, and white men would be the only focus of the investigation.

From August of 2002 to March of 2003, all was quiet in "Red Stick." But in November of 2002, on the other side of the Atchafalaya Swamp in Lafayette, another young girl would be raped and murdered. And in the small town of Port Allen, just across the river from Baton Rouge, the wife of the former commissioner of elections would be abducted on Christmas Eve. In Zachary, the attorney general's office continued to assist the local police with their investigation into the killings in Oak Shadows subdivision. Other detectives in Iberville Parish, St. Martin Parish, Lafayette Parish, and West Baton Rouge Parish would continue their investigations, each unaware that their case was connected to the killings of beautiful Baton Rouge women.

The Baton Rouge police had no clue yet what they were dealing with. But they knew one thing. Lynne Marino was right. They needed help. By August of 2002, a multiagency homicide task force would be formed. It would try to allay the panic spreading through the city. It would try to catch the killer. It would be unsuccessful on both counts.

And Lynne Marino refused to be silenced. "I could

just see this man maybe walking up to Pam in the store when she was struggling with a piece of furniture and asking if he could help. She would have smiled and thanked him, but said, 'Oh, I'm used to doing this. My husband's in a wheelchair.' I pictured all sorts of scenarios about how he had found her. It was horrible. I thought about how he must have raped these women after they were dead. It was a nightmare that I couldn't wake up from."

Do you know what it's like to bury your child? I do—and I hope you never have to know what it's like.
                                        —Lynne Marino

Multiagency Homicide Task Force

The dog days of summer arrived hot and humid in South Louisiana—the air thick and sticky, encouraging residents to relax, to take life a little more slowly. But the summer of 2002 was different. This summer, there was an added tension palpable in the air. A nervousness. Husbands feared for their wives, mothers for their daughters. And for themselves. The killer could be watching.

Reports filtered out about an exorbitant amount of unsolved cases involving missing and murdered women in the Baton Rouge area during the last ten years. That number would be touted as in the thirties, but later the public would discover that since 1985, more than sixty cases of missing and murdered women remained unsolved. Rumors began flying.

The killer was a white male in a white Chevy pickup truck.

The killer liked dark hair.

The killer attended LSU.

The killer was a professor at LSU.

The killer had sought out all of the victims at The Caterie, a college bar at the intersection of Stanford Avenue and Acadian Thruway.

The killer was a police officer.

The killer played a tape recording of a baby crying outside of his victims' doors. That's how he got in.

The killer worked at the local BMW dealership.

Everyone knew someone who had seen a man peeping into their windows.

The East Baton Rouge Parish Sheriff's Office began hosting classes for women, teaching them how to defend themselves against attacks. Sales of pepper spray skyrocketed; storeowners couldn't keep it on their shelves.

The Advocate, Baton Rouge's newspaper, began dividing its headlines between reports on the victims and the investigation and reports on the West Nile virus, which had begun taking numerous lives in the area. Bumper stickers appeared on the backs of vehicles: *Baton Rouge Women, Packing Heat and Wearing Deet.*

Men in white trucks no longer smiled at pretty girls while stopped at red lights. Women loaded their guns and learned how to use them. There were no more late-night shopping trips to Wal-Mart, no more leaving doors unlocked, no more sitting on porches after dark.

One man had taken control of a city.

By August 7, a multiagency homicide task force had been formed among the Baton Rouge Police Department, the East Baton Rouge Parish Sheriff's Office, the Louisiana State Police (LSP), and the FBI. Other entities would soon come on board—the Iberville Parish Sheriff's Office, the Lafayette Parish Sheriff's Office (LPSO), the United States Attorney's Office, the East Baton Rouge Parish District Attorney's Office, the United States Marshals Service, the United States Secret Service, Louisiana Probation and Parole, and the LSU Police Department.

Baton Rouge Chief of Police Pat Englade headed the force.

Englade had a long and distinguished history in law enforcement. His militaristic haircut, broad shoulders, and stern demeanor belied the man who lived beneath. Englade cared. He cared about victims. He cared about catching criminals. He cared about his reputation. It had taken him thirty years to work his way up through the department, from uniform patrol to detective to chief of staff and chief of detectives. In all of those years, the reserved officer never received even a reprimand. And in all those years, he had never been responsible for catching a serial killer.

Many in the Baton Rouge area felt that Englade was not the right person to head up this investigation, but Mayor-President Bobby Simpson was confident that Englade could get the job done. Simpson, from the small town of Baker, just a few miles north of Baton Rouge, had been elected to his position in November of 2000. A former certified public accountant, Simpson had proved his value as the former mayor of Baker through his finesse with budgeting, and many hoped he would do the same for Baton Rouge. But Simpson, too, had no experience with killers, with calming a spreading panic, with controlling what would become a media frenzy. He relied on Englade to keep the public informed.

Immediately the task force began giving daily public briefings—briefings that included, for the most part, no new information. Englade did not handle being on camera well. He was too blunt at times and at other times seemed uncommunicative. Public opinion of his abilities soon plummeted. Aware that he wasn't a good spokesperson, Englade appointed Mary Ann Godawa to take his place with the media. She, too, experienced difficulty through day after day of nothing new to report. No new leads. No capture. Simply more warnings that women should be careful, that citizens should report any leads, no matter how unimportant they might seem.

What Godawa, Englade, and Simpson didn't know was that they already had the lead they needed. They had the name of the killer in their possession. They also had clues that their cases weren't the only ones that involved their serial killer.

At 3:00 P.M. on July 3, detectives from West Baton Rouge Parish met with Baton Rouge detectives at the BRPD homicide office to discuss the case of Geralyn DeSoto. Through the exchange of information, it was determined that her killing was not related to the murders in Baton Rouge. Geralyn had been stabbed, but not to the degree that Murray Pace had. She had not been raped, and Murray had. Her murder had not happened in Baton Rouge. West Baton Rouge detectives went home to take another look at Darren DeSoto.

On July 24, just before the task force was formed, David "Mac" McDavid and Dannie Mixon met with the BRPD, the attorney general's office, and the Iberville Parish Sheriff's Office. "I began suspecting Derrick Todd Lee was the serial killer when Gina Wilson Green's cell phone was found so close to where Connie Warner's body had been discovered. There were no signs of forced entry in their cases, and tokens were taken. It just added up for me," Mac said.

Mac and Dannie had gathered up all of the information they had on Todd—his criminal record, the investigation into Connie's and Randi's deaths, reports about the incident in the cemetery. They brought it to Baton Rouge with them and laid it all out for the Baton Rouge police. "Y'all need to look at this guy," they told them.

No one looked. Todd was black. All of the witnesses in Pam Kinamore's case had described a white man.

The FBI soon created a profile of the killer. Profilers estimated his age to be between twenty-five and thirty-five. He would be strong, between 155 and 175 pounds. His shoe size would be between ten and eleven. He would have an average or below-average income. His job would not involve dealing with the public. He would not be very mobile.

The killer would follow his victims. He liked attractive women. The killer might try to interact with his victims prior to the attack. He didn't handle rejection well. He was attracted to excitement, to high-risk situations. The killer was impulsive. He would have become noticeably agitated after Murray Pace's murder because he lost control. The killer was cool under pressure. He might have returned to Whiskey Bay, as he didn't expect for Pam's body to be found. He was moody and volatile in relationships. He might give unexpected gifts to the women in his life. He would become increasingly paranoid. The killer had no empathy.

While the profile did not specifically state that the killer was white, white men would be the only focus of the investigation. Soon a person of interest would appear on billboards along interstates in Baton Rouge—a white man—and more than twelve hundred white men would be asked to submit DNA samples.

Some refused, and subpoenas were drawn up to force the men to comply. Some lost their jobs as panicked coworkers became suspicious of them. Some were pulled over at red lights and swabbed on the side of the road. Any white man in a white pickup truck was suspect. Before it was all over, some of these men would file a lawsuit asking that their DNA be disposed of.

Friction soon developed in the task force meetings, not between detectives who worked the cases, but between the higher-ups. There was much shouting and difference of opinion about how to proceed.

More than 27,000 tips were logged into the task force hotline. Detectives spent grueling hours following leads, searching for new evidence, praying that they would catch

the killer so the insanity would stop. DNA was their main
lead, and they hoped that soon they would get a match.

"An investigation is like a river. It flows and has cur-
rents," explained Sid Newman, executive director of
Baton Rouge Crime Stoppers, who sat in on many of the
meetings and prayed that a tip would come in to stop the
carnage. "In an investigation, you jump into that current.
When you have an investigation that has so many outside
sources that impact a community, the outside sources dis-
rupt the flow. The investigator must stay inside the initial
current. It's a murder. You still have some basic principles
that apply. When you have other agencies stepping into
your crime scene, it's going to break."

New agencies were soon brought in, others excluded.
Outside parishes would report tips, but they would be
overlooked or ignored. The composite of Todd that
Diane Alexander had helped to create was sent to the
task force. No one paid attention. Diane's attacker was
black. Diane was black.

On September 4, Collette Walker, the woman Todd
had been sent to prison for stalking, would call in a tip
to the hotline, informing police that she knew the serial
killer was Derrick Todd Lee. She reported that he was a
stalker and a suspect in the Zachary murders. She told
police that Todd drove a gold car.

The task force followed up on the lead by going to the
house in Starhill. When investigators got there, they noticed that Todd's truck was a show truck, and not the
work truck that had been described by witnesses. They
also noticed that Todd was a heavyset black man. He was
dismissed as a suspect. The lead was cleared.

As more murders occurred, and more witnesses
stepped forward, the task force would again be pointed in
the direction of a white male as their suspect. But, eventually, a new form of DNA testing—Y-STR (meaning Y-short

tandem repeat)—would clear up the matter, and investigators would learn that they had spent the better part of a year looking in the wrong direction.

Meanwhile, Lynne Marino and Ann Pace hosted their rallies on the steps of the capitol. Lynne became more and more vociferous in her criticism of police efforts to catch her daughter's murderer, and while Ann agreed with her, she took a more conservative approach in the media by cushioning her criticisms with understanding that the police were putting in long hours and working hard to try to find Murray's killer.

As August turned into September, and then October pulled the humidity from the air, the task force still had not captured the killer. But investigators soon would be faced with an eerie truth. This serial killer was not the only one terrorizing the women of Baton Rouge. For years, murders of prostitutes had been taking place around the areas of Acadian Thruway and North Boulevard. And other women, who didn't fit the patterns of this killer, had disappeared or were found raped, killed, and their body parts dismembered. Baton Rouge had three serial killers loose in the city.

The public wasn't aware of the prostitute killer or the fact that another killer was attacking average, everyday women, but as they learned about the unusual number of murders that had occurred, the panic grew. As more information came to light, the once-friendly town withdrew. Any white man was a suspect.

Gone were the normal pleasantries at the grocery store. Gone were the innocent smiles between strangers, the chatting in lines.

Women stayed indoors more, stayed away from bars, actually took self-defense classes offered by police. They whispered about what they would do if the serial killer invaded their homes. That was the scary part. The killer could just enter a home and rape and kill at will. All sense of security was lost.

Around the country, jokes appeared on the Internet. "What's in the water in Baton Rouge?" was the common theme.

The city was living a nightmare, and no one had the answer.

In Liz's Lounge, Todd's second cousin Betty and her friend Nita were talking about the serial killer too. Todd, out on the town, happened to walk by and overhear the conversation.

"Whacha gonna do, cuz?" he said. "Whacha gonna do if the serial killer comes after you? I'm the serial killer. Now, whacha gonna do?"

"I didn't believe him," Betty would later say during another night at Liz's. "I thought he was kiddin', but sho' 'nuff, that nigger was talking true."

But the task force couldn't know that Todd had claimed to be the serial killer that night at Liz's. Pat Englade continued to try to catch the killer and to appease an angry public. And at night, he tossed and turned and was unable to sleep, the responsibility weighing heavily on him. Lines that had not previously been noticeable appeared on his face. He was accountable to everyone—the governor, the mayor, the public, the families of the victims. And he had no answers. He had nothing. The serial killer was running and ruining his life.

"It's tough to run a police department and a task force, and that's what Englade had to do," Mac said. "I always wondered why we weren't a part of the task force, but to be fair, I think they were just being cautious. We were all in this for a common goal, but there were so many egos involved. It was a tough situation for everyone."

The task force soon stopped briefing the public so frequently, aware that the lack of leads was frustrating to its audience. For two months, the briefings had been held daily; then it was decided to have them twice weekly; finally briefings were only held when there was something new to report. The public had heard about shoe prints, about white trucks, about missing items from the homes of the victims. They wanted news of a suspect. They wanted an arrest. They wanted their lives to return to normal.

Englade just wanted to be able to sleep at night. So did every woman in Baton Rouge. Lynne Marino gave up on sleep and spent her nights crying.

Todd began looking for his next victim.

Serial Killers

Task forces typically have a great deal of difficulty catching serial killers for a variety of reasons. Almost any time several jurisdictions are brought together to solve a high-profile case, egos become involved. Vital information may be withheld in the hope that one specific group or another will be able to take credit for the capture of the killer. Many times, the task force will focus its efforts on finding someone similar to the profile it has created, forgetting that the way to catch a killer is by good old-fashioned detective work—assembling clues and pounding the pavement. With so many entities involved, the investigation can become confused by differing opinions and approaches. The hunt for Todd was a prime example of the ways in which the task force exemplified these errors.

Historically, serial killers have always been difficult to catch. Some are caught by a fluke, as in the case of the cannibalistic Jeffrey Dahmer, who was caught when Tracy Edwards escaped his clutches and ran to local police, handcuffs still attached to one wrist.

Ted Bundy was pulled over for erratic driving and charged with suspicion of burglary before police realized they had the man in custody who may have been responsible for as many as one hundred deaths. Bundy later escaped and killed three more women and attacked two others.

Some serial killers simply tire of their game and turn themselves in. Edmund Kemper, who had made friends with officers in the Santa Cruz area, called police to confess, but they wouldn't believe him. After several attempts to convince them that he was indeed the man they were looking for, Kemper was finally arrested.

Although the United States consists of less than 5 percent of the world's population, approximately 84 percent of all known serial killers since 1980 have roamed about from sea to shining sea killing for their own perverted pleasure.

Interestingly, serial killing is not a recent phenomenon. In the 1500s, Erzsebet Bathory hired peasants to work in her castle, then tortured, sexually assaulted, and killed them for the pure pleasure of it. She was a member of the royal family, and because of her status, royals simply looked the other way until peasants became scarce and she turned to the daughters of lesser nobility for her sadistic pleasure. She was thought to have bathed in their blood in an effort to retain her youthful beauty. It is thought that she may have killed as many as 650 women, making Bathory one of the most prolific serial killers in history.

With Derrick Todd Lee, the task force in Baton Rouge had its work cut out for it from the start. Todd did not fit much of the profile the FBI had created, nor did his characteristics, history, or patterns resemble the majority of other serial killers. Only about 16 percent of all known serial killers are black. Wayne Williams, of the Atlanta Child Murders, stands out as the most notorious. The son of schoolteachers, Williams terrorized Atlanta during the late 1970s and early 1980s and is thought to have killed at least twenty-three children.

Former Baton Rougean John Allen Muhammad and

his seventeen-year-old comrade, John Lee Malvo, began their killing spree in Alabama and Louisiana, and gained notoriety as the D.C. Snipers through the shooting of innocent motorists around the Washington, D.C., area. The public was shocked to discover that the men were black.

Coral Eugene Watts was another black killer who confessed to thirteen murders that had occurred throughout the 1970s. But typically, black men do not go on killing rampages. Aware of this fact, the task force focused only on white men.

The FBI categorizes serial killers as either organized or disorganized. Todd had characteristics of both, which falls into the "mixed" category, a category that was later added when the FBI discovered that serial killers could not be classified so precisely. Todd resembled the organized killer in that he stalked his victims, planned his attacks, and kept trophies of his conquests. Todd lived with a wife and, at times, with a girlfriend. He could perform sex in a normal manner. He was mobile and followed the investigation in the newspaper. But most organized serial killers are considered to have average or above average intelligence; they do not leave DNA evidence and are usually the oldest or an only child. Todd's IQ was not far above the standard measure of retardation. He did not understand that police could obtain his DNA from his victims. He was the second child. He did not clean up his crime scenes—although he did take items that he had touched. And at times he did act on opportunity, such as in the Buhler Plains Cemetery when he attacked the teenagers.

Disorganized serial killers are impulsive. They kill on a whim. These killers usually possess low to average intelligence and are sometimes mentally retarded. They do not handle themselves well in social situations. These killers usually live alone and do not function well sexually. Victims are rarely tied up or tortured, and the disorganized killer does not try to hide the bodies. They cannot keep employment and go through job after job. Stress does not play a role in their attacks.

Todd displayed characteristics of the disorganized killer in that his intelligence level was low; he did not tie up his victims, nor did he take an inordinate amount of time to enjoy the kill, like the organized killer would do. He tried to hide Pam Kinamore and Connie Warner's bodies, and had successfully hidden Randi Mebruer's body to this day. Other possible victims, like Eugenie Boisfontaine, Christine Moore, and Melissa Montz, were found weeks or months later. But Geralyn DeSoto, Gina Wilson Green, and Charlotte Murray Pace were left to be discovered in their homes. The organized killer is cold and calculating, which Todd was, but he was disorganized in his overkill tactics. When he followed through on his fantasy, he sometimes lost control. Like the disorganized killer, Todd moved from job to job regularly.

Todd did not have distinctive patterns, like many serial killers either, although he was territorial, returning over and over to familiar neighborhoods to stalk and kill his victims. His territory, however, spread over more than a hundred miles. He also used a variety of methods to murder the women he chose—sometimes by strangulation, sometimes by stabbing, sometimes using blunt force. He raped some, but not others. His weapons of choice were knives, screwdrivers, phone cords, or his bare hands. His patterns were too undefined to provide police with valuable information about him that could have helped them connect some of the murders, like Geralyn DeSoto and Randi Mebruer, sooner.

Another interesting detail is that Todd crossed racial barriers, killing both white and black women, although each resembled the other by having dark hair, light skin, and high cheekbones. The women he chose were educated, what he considered to be "high society," and each was motivated to make the most of themselves—the women who would not be attracted to him.

The final and most intriguing way in which Todd is different from many serial killers lies in his background. Many psychologists argue the "nature vs. nurture" theory in which pathological killers must possess *both* a gene of mental illness and an abusive childhood in order to develop the lack of empathy necessary for repeated brutality against other human beings. It is possible that Todd carried the gene from his biological father, but his childhood was a relatively happy one. He did not experience sexual abuse, physical abuse, or the mental abuse that is suffered by most serial killers, like Charles Manson, who was dressed in girl's clothing and sent off to school by a religious aunt and her boyfriend. Todd was raised in the manner of all the children in Lee's Quarters, yet he began his Peeping Tom activities at a very young age.

Todd established long relationships with those he cared about, albeit he occasionally became violent toward them. He enjoyed a normal social life, barbecuing with friends and hanging out in bars with them. He took care of his children, although he did disappear on them occasionally. Because of the confusing traits he possessed and patterns he exhibited, Todd made it very difficult for police to pigeonhole him.

The recent capture of Dennis Rader, otherwise known as BTK, stunned the nation, but Rader displayed similarly confusing traits as Todd, perhaps a reason why it took seventeen years to catch him. Rader also lived a normal life, even more normal than Todd's in that he was president of his church council for a time and a Boy Scout leader. He was a husband and father. Like Todd, Rader was a sexual predator, but unlike Todd, he enjoyed torturing his victims before killing them. Todd always killed and raped in a hurry. However, both displayed a decided lack of empathy for their victims.

It would take good old-fashioned police work to capture

Todd, along with meticulous attention to detail. Investigators would have to think outside of the serial killer profile box. Serial killers are difficult to apprehend because they are so varied in their motivations and patterns, so there can never be a definite approach to hunting for these types of killers. Each comes equipped with his or her own peculiarities, which is why profiling almost never results in their capture. Whether they are women or men, homosexual or heterosexual, black or white, serial killers pose a unique challenge for police.

Although the task force dedicated endless hours and month after month of worry and anxiety to the capture of Derrick Todd Lee, ultimately his arrest would come about as a result of pounding the pavement by an aging investigator with the attorney general's office—but not before several more beautiful women felt the force of Todd's unnatural hunger.

Sean Vincent Gillis

During the summer of 2002, Sean Gillis was taking a break at his home on Burgin Avenue in Baton Rouge, about a mile from Lee Drive, where, in 1994, eighty-one-year-old Ann Bryan had been raped and slashed to death in the retirement community of St. James Place. Sean was taking a sabbatical from murder and mutilation. He was watching the news, reading newspapers, collecting information for the file he kept on the other serial killer. Sean didn't know his name, but he did know that Todd was stealing his spotlight.

Almost every day, some form of media released information about the Green, Pace, and Kinamore murders. But the women Sean had killed—Bryan in 1994, Katherine Hall, Hardee Moseley Schmidt, and Joyce Williams in 1999, and Lillian Robinson and Marilyn Nevils in 2000—had largely been forgotten, their cases not as urgent as the hunt for the person responsible for the three deaths that had been connected through DNA. His murders had not been connected.

But they were much more gruesome.

Sean was a textbook serial killer—cold and calculating, a sexual predator who enjoyed the added dimension of mutilation after death with some of his victims. Sean Gillis was sick. But no one knew or even suspected that the frumpish white man with the bushy mustache, receding hairline, and blue eyes framed with glasses could be capable of such atrocities—not the police, not his longtime live-in girlfriend, Terri Lemoine, or her children, whom Sean had helped to raise.

Sean was just a normal guy who worked here and there, sometimes at the Circle K on Lee Drive, across from St. James Place, sometimes repairing copy machines for Xerox, sometimes not working at all and relying on his parents for financial support. But he was nice to Terri, and they lived together for almost ten years. During that time, he was slow to anger and rarely yelled. The couple shared hobbies, like collecting trading cards. Terri was happy with Sean, had never seen his dark side. Sean kept that to himself.

But others knew.

Johnnie Mae Williams, a black woman who had been friends with Sean for eight years, would find out in 2003 when Sean resumed his hunt for victims. The forty-five-year-old Williams had taken up the use of crack cocaine, and Sean didn't approve of that. Williams was found stabbed to death, her body mutilated in October.

Joyce Williams also knew that Sean had a dark side. She discovered it in 1999 right before he talked her into removing her hand from beneath the long zip tie he had wrapped around her neck, assuring her that if she moved it, he would remove the tie. As soon as she did, Sean pulled tight. The sounds of her dying didn't satisfy him. He sawed her leg off at the hip, then had sex with the severed end of it.

Other victims' bodies would reveal other horror stories. Eight women would die at the hands of Sean Gillis over a ten-year span, eight murders to which he has confessed. There could be more.

Some of Sean's victims lived what the media coined "high-risk lifestyles." Others didn't. Hardee Moseley

Schmidt could have easily been a victim of Derrick Todd Lee's. This fifty-two-year-old white woman was out jogging in the Pollard Estates subdivision near LSU when she disappeared in 1999. Schmidt, a well-known Baton Rouge resident, was found a few days later in a bayou along Airline Highway in St. James Parish. Her death was widely publicized, but no killer was found until Sean confessed in April of 2004.

Police had difficulty distinguishing between the murders committed by Sean Gillis and Derrick Todd Lee, with good reason. Both black and white women were being killed. Both killers used knives and strangulation. Both killers left their victims in or near water. Sean left Lilian Robinson's body in the Atchafalaya Basin, between Butte La Rose and Whiskey Bay, not far from where Todd had disposed of Pam Kinamore. Both men were killing during the same years, although Todd's rampage actually lasted far longer than Sean's if some of his possible victims are counted.

Sean's spree ended in 2004 with the death of Donna Bennett Johnston, who was found in a canal on Ben Hur Road in February. This forty-three-year-old white woman, whom police classified as having a high-risk lifestyle, had been strangled to death. An unusual tire track found by the canal would lead police to Sean's door to collect a DNA sample. He would be taken in for questioning that same day.

Sean would return home to spend a cozy evening with Terri, acting as if nothing had happened. He wanted to spend one last romantic evening with his longtime love before he confessed to Johnston's murder the next day.

Fifteen deaths would be connected by confession or DNA to Sean and Todd, with Sean being responsible for eight and Todd seven. It is possible that both men could have murdered many more, as police reported more than sixty missing or murdered women in the area since 1985. And during the same period, another killer, who is still at large, was killing prostitutes with regularity.

In the summer of 2002, police did not yet know what they were dealing with. They had three murders that had been connected by DNA. They assumed their killer was a white male. As police began to dig deeper, they began to realize that there was more than one serial killer threatening the lives of Baton Rouge citizens. That was a chilling discovery for police who, with the eyes of a nation watching, were having difficulty catching only one.

They prayed they would crack the case.

They prayed the killer would not strike again.

They prayed that the community would remain calm.

Their prayers went unanswered.

In September, Todd was again found guilty of violating his parole. For the third time, the parole board only reprimanded him, releasing him back into society. But aside from that, things were going badly for Todd. He had been released from his job at JE Merit on September 30. On November 17, he would be involved in an automobile accident. With no money and the looming possibility of losing his home, Todd and Jackie filed for bankruptcy on November 19.

With so much publicity surrounding the serial killings, Todd had laid low since July. But by November 21, he could wait no longer. He headed to Grand Coteau, a small town outside of Lafayette, where a young girl sat beside a lonely grave and grieved for her mother. Todd had found his next victim.

Sean was about to add another clipping to his file.

Trineisha Dené Colomb

Trineisha Dené Colomb was not concerned with serial killers. They were attacking women in Baton Rouge. The one they talked about on the news only went after white women. She was black. She didn't know about Diane Alexander in Breaux Bridge, only a few miles from her home. She was safe, more than an hour's drive over the Atchafalaya Swamp from Baton Rouge. And though the killer had left Pam Kinamore's body in Whiskey Bay, that was a world away from the Cajun college town of Lafayette. Dené, as her friends and family called her, had no cause for alarm. Besides, she was much too immersed in grief to dwell upon it. The worst had already happened.

After a long bout with cancer, her mother had died in April. Verna Colomb had adopted Dené at birth and had given her daughter a happy childhood. The two were very close, spending a lot of time with her father, Sterling, and her older brother, Sterling Jr. Although Dené sometimes wondered about her real paternity, once even registering with a Web site that finds parents of adopted children, she was happy with her family. She often thought she was half white, because she had heard the whispers—the light coloring of her skin seeming to bear that out. A beautiful girl with long, dark hair and lush, full lips, which created lovely dimples when she smiled, she had a preference for

white men, and those were the boys she would bring
home to meet her dad.

Dené loved to learn, although she flitted from interest
to interest. She taught herself four foreign languages. She
spent two years in the army, two years in college. She read
anything she could about travel and planned to see the
world one day. She hungered for new direction and began
looking at joining the marines, attracted by the idea of
experiencing new places. Dené was searching for anything
that would fill the void left by her mother's death.

Since April, Dené had distanced herself from her
family, spending much of her time in her room, watching
movie after movie rented from the local Blockbuster. At
other times, she could be found at the Lafayette Parish
Library, surfing the Web and talking to friends she met
online. Occasionally she dated men from the personals.

Sterling Sr. was concerned. He felt that his daughter
was locking herself away from the world. She was quiet,
withdrawn. While Dené had never been particularly outgoing, she had been friendly, curious, interested. Now
she kept to herself, grieving for the woman who had
given her a family, who had loved her and nurtured her
through life. Sterling had good cause to be concerned.
He knew Dené was visiting Verna's grave site regularly,
sometimes finding Tweety birds placed beside the stone
that marked her passing. Dené loved Tweety birds.

In September, Dené had tried to commit suicide.

The pills she took did not kill her, but she was hospitalized and later began making regular visits to her social
worker, Jeanne Sonnier. Dené knew she had a problem,
but she could not seem to emerge from the cloud of grief
that threatened to destroy her. She did not know how. She
missed her mom.

In the early part of November, Dené did not report for
work at Helping Hands, Inc., where she was employed
part-time. She didn't call to let them know she was
quitting. She just didn't show up. Sterling asked her

each day if she would be working. She always said yes. She went to the library instead. And to Grand Coteau, where her mother was buried. The twenty-three-year-old girl was reaching out to her mother for help.

It is not difficult to imagine the conversations she had.

"I miss you so much, Mom. I don't know how to cope with this. I don't know what to do. Why did you have to leave me? I love you, Mom. How do I go on? I need to talk to you, to hug you, to kiss your face. I don't want to be here without you."

Every day for two weeks, Dené visited the cemetery behind St. Charles Church.

Interstate 49 runs alongside small towns leading one into another on its way north from Lafayette to Opelousas and beyond. The residents of the area enjoy the slow and easy quiet of small-town life. Dené traveled this road on her way to Grand Coteau each afternoon to the beautiful old graveyard with its aboveground tombs reminiscent of those found near the New Orleans French Quarter. Flanked by the old St. Charles Church, with its crowning steeple, the Jesuit Novitiate and Spirituality Center, and Our Lady of the Oaks Jesuit Retreat House, adorned with a breathtaking oak alley, the atmosphere is one of devout holiness. Visitors to the large cemetery commune with their loved ones—crying, talking, praying for their souls.

A gravel road to the left of the cemetery's entrance leads to a dead end under a Spanish moss–laden oak. Verna Colomb's tomb lies just yards from that spot, a gray marble resting place adorned with flowers and a candle burning eternal light.

It was at that site on November 21, 2002, as a young girl sat grieving, that Todd found his next victim. It had been four months since he had quenched his thirst for power. Faced with losing everything he owned, Todd went on the prowl.

* * *

There were no signs of struggle near the Mazda MX3 parked close to the dead end on Robbie Road, near St. Charles Church. The car was reported abandoned to the Grand Coteau Police Department (GCPD) by local resident Robert Barry, who had noticed the car at 3:30 P.M. on November 21, and then that it was still there the morning of November 22. Dené's keys were in the car, as was her wallet and identification. Sterling was notified.

"She may have committed suicide," Sterling worriedly explained to the police. "She's been very upset since her mother died."

On the morning of her disappearance, Dené had made a phone call at nine fifty-eight to the Lafayette Parish Library. Records later subpoenaed from Yahoo.com would show that she had been on the Internet at the library at 11:00 A.M. She had spoken with her father briefly around midday on November 21, telling him she would be going to work. She did not return home that day.

Sterling Sr. and Junior, and other friends and family, along with police, gathered to search the area. For two days they searched, through woods and down country roads, asking questions in the quaint shops that lined Lloyd Lewis Road, near the church. Fearing the worst, hoping for the best.

"Have you seen this girl? Does she look familiar? Has she come in here before?"

They had no luck. At noon, on November 24, the search was called off. Dené had simply disappeared, leaving her car, her purse, and her keys. If she had fought with her captor, there was no sign.

For almost twenty miles, to the small town of Scott, Louisiana, Dené rode with her abductor, back down Interstate 49 to Lafayette, to the Ambassador Caffery

Parkway exit, north, then west, down roads twisting and turning through the rural farmland.

Perhaps Todd had approached her before in the cemetery. It was his habit. To stalk his victims. To approach them with idle chatter. He had done so with Murray and Gina, with Pam, with Diane and Geralyn. He had done so with Collette Walker. He liked to introduce himself as Anthony, to become acquainted before he struck. He was an attractive man, confident of his power to appeal, but it is not reasonable to assume that Dené went willingly. No woman would leave her purse and keys behind.

The 1600 block of Renaud Drive was sparsely populated—only one inhabited dwelling, one business, and two abandoned houses interrupted the wooded landscape. Todd brought Dené to an almost hidden pathway through the woods that only someone familiar with the area would notice. The tree line that ran parallel to the road masked a clearing. A muddy path through the trees on the other side led to another clearing made for heavy power lines, which were barely visible from the roadway. Beyond the right of way, the woods grew dense again.

It was in those woods that terror and helplessness overshadowed grief as Todd beat Dené with his fists. Over and over.

In her face.

To the back of her head.

His blows growing harder and harder. The rage inside of him fueled his punches, the blood fed his lust.

He slammed her head into a tree, causing Dené's blood to streak the trunk in cast-off patterns. A pool of blood gathered at her feet. But nine open head wounds did not satisfy Todd.

He ripped off her pants, her panties. And then he violated her, raping her viciously before he dragged her thirty feet through the mud to her place of rest.

Replete, Todd left her there, facedown, for the

scavengers, who would nibble at her right hand, her left cheek, her left earlobe.

At about eleven o'clock on the morning of November 24, Detective Sonny Stutes was notified that a female body had been discovered by a hunter off Renaud Drive. He grabbed his jacket and headed for his car. He knew it was not going to be a good day. It never was when a body was found, especially a female. He knew his mind would soon become obsessed—following clues, talking to witnesses, anguishing late at night over who could have killed the young girl. What he did not know was that his victim would soon become part of a much larger investigation, a part of the horror that lurked quietly in the neighborhoods of Baton Rouge.

Dené had been missing for three days. Patrol units from the Lafayette Parish Sheriff's Office and the Scott Police Department (SPD) were already on the scene when Stutes arrived. Near the edge of a briar patch, a woman, obviously deceased, lay naked from the waist down. Her gray shirt bore the army logo. Her tennis shoes were muddied.

Stutes ordered everyone to stay away from the body.

"I was out hunting with some friends this morning in Arnaudville," a rattled Reginald Holman told Stutes. "We didn't have any luck, so I decided to stop here on my way back. I was hunting over there," he said, pointing toward the east. "I saw her when I came back. I didn't go too close. I just left and called the police."

Stutes called Detective Kristen Bayard, a forensics expert with the Lafayette Parish Metro Forensics Unit. Bayard informed him that a girl had been reported missing from St. Landry Parish. Bayard mentioned that the missing girl had several tattoos. Stutes walked toward Dené carefully, searching for the identifying marks. He noticed two—one a yin yang with Oriental writing, and the other a heart and flower embellished with the word "Dené."

Trineisha Dené Colomb was pronounced dead at 12:32 P.M.

A dried pool of blood thirty feet away flagged the spot of her murder. Two sets of shoe prints were discovered, and the soft ground yielded drag marks from the blood to her body. These clues would not matter.

DNA would lead investigators to Dené's killer—a rare DNA with three unusual markers, belonging to a man whom the multiagency homicide task force had already rejected as a suspect.

The police were searching for a white man.

It didn't matter that Collette Walker had called the task force hotline to report that she knew who the serial killer was.

It didn't matter that Dannie Mixon and David McDavid had repeatedly brought Todd's name to the attention of the task force.

No one would listen. Todd was black. The killer was white. And with the discovery of Dené's body, police would have even more reason to believe their suspect was white.

A sketch of the suspect would be obtained from a woman who had seen something suspicious on November 21. As Angela Boutin and her sister rode along Mills Highway on their way home from Michaels arts and crafts store, they observed a vehicle parked on the other side of the road, with its front tires in the roadway. They had to stop alongside it to allow a vehicle coming from the opposite direction to go by.

As they waited, Angela, who was in the passenger seat, watched a man in the vehicle suddenly sit up in the driver's seat. He appeared startled to see her there.

Angela saw a black female, who appeared to be slumped over against the passenger door. Angela thought they might have been having sex right there on the side of the road. The man smiled at Angela as her sister drove away. When she heard about the missing girl, Angela called the police.

She would describe the vehicle she had seen as a white pickup truck. "The man was in his late thirties to early forties," she told police. "He had dark hair, with spots of white or gray. His hair was well-groomed and cut like a little boy's style. He wasn't tall or muscular. He had a very large nose. He was tanned, but not overly dark, more like someone who does roofing work."

Angela was asked to undergo hypnosis in order to produce an accurate sketch of the man in the pickup. Stutes and Sergeant Dirk Bergeron, who was with the LSP, explained the procedure to her before they started. Lieutenant Debbie Brasseaux drew the composite from Angela's description.

Twenty-four days after Dené's body was discovered, Detective Stutes again called the LSP. He had interviewed many witnesses, but his leads were going nowhere. He had suspicions that Dené's murder was related to the serial killer. He described his case to Lynn Averette, the state police coordinator for the task force.

"The serial killer in Baton Rouge has struck three times to date," Averette told him. "All of his victims have been white women, and all have been stabbed. The victims were all attacked in their homes. The method of operation is different with your case. I don't believe the incidents are related."

Averette gave Stutes the number for the task force and hung up.

* * *

In late December, Carolyn Booker, an analyst with the Acadiana Crime Lab, called Stutes to inform him that her tests had revealed that the DNA profile gathered from Dené's sexual assault kit matched the profile of the serial killer.

Two days before Christmas, Dené became the fourth victim linked to the South Louisiana Serial Killer.

But it did not make sense. Serial killers do not usually cross racial barriers. They kill within one race. Serial killers use a repeated method of operation. Serial killers look for identical victims.

Derrick Todd Lee once again proved that the task force needed to revise its preconceived notions about serial killers.

A composite sketch of a person of interest, a white man with a large nose, was released to the media—the sketch Angela Boutin had helped to create under hypnosis.

And on Christmas Eve, outside of a Subway restaurant in the small town of Port Allen, just across the Mississippi River Bridge, the wife of a jailed former commissioner of elections for Louisiana would disappear.

In the cemetery of the St. Charles Church, the stone placed over a young girl's gray marble tomb read: *I lay next to my mother, joining her as an angel in heaven.*

Mari Ann Fowler

Early-morning thunderstorms welcomed Christmas Eve to the Baton Rouge area, casting a gloom over an already gloomy city. The news had spread quickly that Dené had been linked to the serial killer. Citizens had hoped her murder was unrelated to the ones in Baton Rouge. With this latest discovery, women in an ever-widening area of Louisiana were put on alert as everyone finally realized that Baton Rouge was not the sole target.

As shoppers hurried to make last-minute purchases, they were even more vigilant than usual as they walked through crowded parking lots. Mari Ann Fowler was at home, thoughts of a serial killer far from her mind, as she wrapped the last of the Christmas gifts she would take on her trip to Beaumont, Texas. The sixty-five-year-old woman had no cause to think the killer would come after her—he liked younger women. But Mari Ann was beautiful. She bore a startling resemblance to Lynne Marino, with her high cheekbones, brown hair that flipped attractively away from her face, and easy smile. She was smart and friendly, and people were drawn to her spirit. But the last few years had been difficult.

Mari Ann's husband, Jerry Fowler, had been the commissioner of elections for the state of Louisiana for twenty years. Life had been good then, happy. As assistant superintendent of research and development for the Louisiana Department of Education, Mari Ann had enjoyed much prestige in her position, as did her husband in his. Together, they enjoyed the culture of Louisiana and the privilege that comes with money and power. Mari Ann loved her husband and did not abandon him, as some wives would, when he got a little too caught up in Louisiana politics.

In fact, she had celebrated Christmas early that year with her son, John Pritchett, and her friends, and was looking forward to visiting with her husband on Christmas Day. She would be making the familiar pilgrimage to the prison that had housed him for the last two years.

In late November of 2000, Jerry had pled guilty to three counts of willfully filing false tax returns in a kickback scheme, which had ruined his long career in politics and brought shame to the family. He had originally been charged with four counts of malfeasance in office, four counts of money laundering, and one count of filing false public records. In order to spare his wife the embarrassment of a very public trial, Fowler accepted a plea bargain. He did not want the public to hear the sordid details of how he had made millions through purchasing voting machines for the state of Louisiana.

As her world came crashing down, Mari Ann stood strong. That was her way. She held her head high as she faced the media, her friends, her coworkers. She visited her husband often, though it saddened her greatly to see him like that, caged in a prison. But she always had a smile ready for Jerry.

By the time Mari Ann got on her way, the rain had cleared. She was hungry, so before she got on the interstate, she stopped at a strip mall next to Cash's Casino in Port Allen to get a bite. It was just after 5:30 P.M. Brandi Collie and Paula Villarreal were cleaning the Subway sandwich shop, anxious to get home to celebrate Christmas with their families, when Mari Ann walked inside, shivering from the dampness. As they prepared the sandwich Mari Ann would take with her on her long drive, the three ladies chatted. Even after Mari Ann had paid for her meal, Brandi and Paula continued talking with her, warmed by her friendliness. Mari Ann wished them a merry Christmas as she left the restaurant with a wave. Brandi and Paula went back to their cleaning.

Unlike Mari Ann, Jackie Lee had not finished her Christmas shopping. She had worked late at the post office and then went to fight the last-minute shopping crowds with the little bit of money she had saved from her paycheck. She finally finished around six o'clock. She hid the presents in her trunk before picking Doris and Derrick Jr. up from Tarshia's house. Jackie visited with her sister-in-law for a while and then headed home. She noticed Todd's truck wasn't in the driveway. As she ushered the kids into the house, she wondered where he was. He never called to let her know where he was. She waited for him for a while, and then rushed the kids to bed so she could wrap their presents. Todd didn't come home. Finally, around eleven, Jackie went to sleep.

Consandra Green would spend that night alone as well.

Todd was very careful as he drove through the darkness in his burgundy pickup. He had gotten a ticket for driving ninety-five miles per hour in a 65 mph zone just a few days before. He was upset about the ticket. The last thing he needed was something else to pay for. He had not even been able to give Jackie money to get the kids anything for Christmas.

Todd didn't think about the money he had lost that year gambling at Casino Rouge—a little over $5,000. That would have bought Doris and Derrick some nice presents. He didn't think about the times he had stopped at Cash's

Casino to have a few drinks and play video poker. He was thinking about the pretty white cashier at the gas station in Grosse Tête as he drove.

Todd had been hustling her, and she had even met him once at the Waffle House in Port Allen, just up from the Subway. He had told her he was divorced, that he had an operator job and an apartment in Baton Rouge. He had thought everything was going well, but that was before her husband had interrupted his phone call to her and had threatened to blow his brains out. Now she wouldn't talk to him. Another white bitch was rejecting him. Todd wasn't happy that Christmas Eve.

Angrily he called some numbers on his cell phone. His phone hit the Grosse Tête tower at 5:20 P.M. He was around fourteen miles west of Port Allen.

Mari Ann didn't see the man sneaking up behind her as she hurried to her car. When he grabbed her, she dropped her food. Her perfectly manicured acrylic nails ripped from her fingers and fell to the ground as she fought for her life in the parking lot of Subway that Christmas Eve. Mari Ann Fowler would never be seen again.

A few minutes later, Paula noticed that Mari Ann's car was still where it had been parked. She and Brandi walked outside and saw a vehicle leaving the parking lot. Paula looked down and noticed the food by the car. Contents of Mari Ann's purse were scattered on the ground. They didn't see the lady anywhere. Worried, Paula called the police.

News of Mari Ann's disappearance cast an even greater pall over the Christmas of 2002. Everyone just knew the serial killer had struck again, this time an elderly woman. That meant that absolutely no woman was safe. Age, race, location—it didn't matter. The only requirement was beauty. As residents looked at the pictures of the friendly lady, who was known and loved by so many, some couldn't help but notice her resemblance to Pam Kinamore's mother.

Todd has never been positively linked to Mari Ann's disappearance. But a video camera at a discount cigarette business next to Subway had been scanning the parking lot in fifty-five-second cycles on that Christmas Eve night. Its range of vision was partially obscured by the awning of the building. Police would later watch Mari Ann walk to her car. They would see the lower half of a man's body come up behind her. They would watch as Mari Ann dropped her food. Fifty-five seconds later, the camera cycled back around, and police could see a man's body, from the chest down, calmly getting into the driver's side of a burgundy truck. They watched as the truck turned onto Highway 415.

Police would find no conclusive DNA evidence from Mari Ann's purse or under her fingernails. Sheriff Mike Cazes and his deputies would spend over a year investigating, before another clue connecting Mari Ann's disappearance to Todd would emerge.

In February of 2004, Todd's cell phone records would finally reveal that he had placed the call just miles from Port Allen at five-twenty that evening. And at 11:20 P.M., he placed another. It was picked up by a tower in St. Gabriel, close to the Ebenezer Baptist Church on River Road, where Christine Moore's body had been discovered in June of 2002. WBRSO deputies, IPSO deputies, and Louisiana Attorney General's Office investigators searched the entire area to no avail. Mari Ann was simply gone. Her body has never been found.

Jackie would later report that she woke up between four and five that morning, and Todd was sleeping soundly in bed beside her. She had no idea what time he had come home. The couple got up Christmas morning and prepared to spend the day with Todd's family. Christmas dinner was scheduled for noon. Jackie didn't notice anything unusual about Todd's behavior. He laughed and joked, as he always had, that Christmas Day, while Mari Ann's family cried and prayed that police would find her. Their prayers would go unanswered.

Mari Ann was declared dead in 2004, more than two years after her disappearance. On August 27, 2005, Jerry, who had been released from a halfway house two months earlier, would hold a memorial service for his lovely wife. He wanted his friends and family to honor the lady who had loved him, who had stood tall beside him through thick and thin. Even as Jerry tried to give his family closure, he knew that they would always wonder where she was, what had happened to her, and if it was really Derrick Todd Lee who had killed her.

And as that heartbreaking year that had brought so much pain to South Louisiana came to a close, everyone prayed the terror was over.

It wasn't.

Carrie Lynn Yoder

The crawfisherman used a blue ribbon to mark the spot where he had seen the body, then maneuvered his boat into the landing. He had come to Whiskey Bay to scout for the numerous crawfish that live in mud holes along its banks. He had been stunned by the sight of the young woman floating in the water. He had to call the police.

Todd was becoming more and more arrogant, taunting the task force. He had pulled over on the side of Interstate 10 near the Whiskey Bay exit that night in March of 2003. No cars were in sight, but the thought that one would come excited him, made him hurry. He pulled the young woman, with the curly brown hair, from his truck, then dragged her to the side of the bridge. Todd picked her up, held her over the concrete barrier, then dropped her into the murky swamp below. He heard a splash as she hit the water, then peered into the darkness to see where she had landed. He couldn't see anything.

Fearful that he would be spotted by oncoming traffic, Todd jumped into his truck and headed back the way he had come. No one saw him.

It was Lundi Gras in the Capital City of Baton Rouge, the third of March, the day before Mardi Gras.

Carrie Lynn Yoder sat on the sofa in her Dodson

Avenue home, munching on a piece of cheese and reviewing the photos she and Lee Stanton, her boyfriend, had taken on Saturday in New Orleans. The streets had been filled with revelers from around the world vying for beads and cups and doubloons. Carrie and Lee had checked into the Holiday Inn in Metairie before joining friends for a parade. After hours of fighting crowds and yelling "Throw me something, mister!" they collected their treasures and returned to the hotel. The couple drove back to Baton Rouge on Sunday, laughing and reliving their adventure. Carrie spent the night with Lee before returning to her house, Monday morning.

It was back to work for Carrie after her exciting weekend, and she headed to LSU, where she worked at the Life Sciences Building. Carrie was working on her Ph.D. and had moved to Baton Rouge for that specific purpose. She had grown up in Tampa, Florida, and had attended the University of Florida. After graduation, she had worked on her master's degree at the University of Central Florida. Carrie was very intelligent. With an IQ of 135 and excellent grades, she had easily breezed through the interview process that would lead her to LSU. She had met Lee during her initial visits, and the two dated off and on for two years before becoming more serious during their third year together.

She soon fell in love with Louisiana, with its slower pace and air of endless gaiety. She had been a vegetarian for many years, but after she tasted her first crawfish, she was hooked. That led her to try other Louisiana seafood specialties, and Carrie soon found herself eating meat again. She had always been against drinking as well, but amidst the party atmosphere at LSU, Carrie soon found herself joining in the fun every now and then.

She had always been adventurous, but Carrie blossomed throughout her college life. She liked to jump into things with both feet and out of things, like airplanes. She had gone skydiving sixty-one times in her twenty-six years. She had traveled to Switzerland to see the family crest of her father, David. She loved ballroom dancing. She was learning to play the violin, though she hadn't told anyone. She kept it hidden under her bed. And she loved the wetlands.

In school, she studied coastal wetland plant life and how it was affected by flooding, fire, and the numerous hurricanes that swept through, disturbing the ecological system. She had developed a hypothesis that global warming, which, she stated, caused rising sea levels and flooding, was even more destructive than nature's handiwork. Humans and their disregard for their environment were damaging her beloved wetlands. Carrie wanted to change all of that.

The bungalow she had chosen on Dodson Avenue was just two blocks from the South Gates of LSU. A small street, consisting of only four houses and two apartments located to the back and sides of Carrie's house, Dodson Avenue provided easy access to school and a countrylike atmosphere, tucked away as it was. Carrie's cozy raised bungalow was trimmed in deep green. A sidewalk led to the gate of the privacy fence, and brick steps led up to the porch.

Carrie had heard all of the warnings; every student at LSU had. The university had taken special care to educate its students about safety, had installed new lighting upon previously darkened pathways, had hired extra security personnel to keep an eye on students. Chancellor Mark Emmert cared about his students and was worried about the killings that had happened so close to the university he was charged to protect. He worried that the killer would strike again.

But in early March, LSU students were enjoying the spirit of Mardi Gras. They had spent many months fearing for their safety. It was time to throw off the doom and gloom and have some fun. As many took off for New Orleans that Monday, ready to enjoy the Krewe of Endymion Parade, Carrie helped a professor remove a table from the third floor of the science building.

She got home from LSU around 12:30 P.M. A little over

an hour later, Carrie signed for a UPS delivery. She
excitedly unwrapped it, eager to read the book *Louisiana
Dayride: 52 Short Trips from New Orleans*, which she had
ordered from Amazon.com. At about 4:30 P.M., she called
Lee to ask him if he wanted to come over for dinner. Lee
was doing some work around his house and didn't want
to leave it unfinished, so Carrie headed off to the Winn-
Dixie on Highland Road to buy a steak to cook for herself
for dinner. Her receipt for the purchase was printed at
4:58 P.M.

Carrie didn't mind spending the evening alone after the
excitement of the weekend. She unloaded her groceries
from her car, forgetting about the gallon of Arizona tea on
the front passenger seat. Carrie smiled as she sprinkled
mushrooms over her steak, thinking she would look at the
pictures from Mardi Gras, then relax with her new book.
She enjoyed her meal before uploading the memory card
from her digital camera onto her IBM laptop. Her computer would last be used at 7:42 P.M., the pictures Carrie
had uploaded still on her screen.

Around 10:00 P.M., calls from Todd's Cingular Wireless
cell phone hit the Ramah tower twice from Interstate 10
near Whiskey Bay, and six minutes later, a call hit the
Grosse Tête tower. Todd had Carrie with him for two
hours.

Lee called Carrie later that evening. He got no answer,
so he left a message and went to bed. On Fat Tuesday, he
got up early to work on a school project and then puttered
in his yard for a while. He called Carrie again that afternoon about five, thinking it was a little strange that she
hadn't returned his call from the night before. Around ten
o'clock, when he still had not heard from her, Lee became
concerned and drove over to her house. Her car was in the
driveway and lights in the house were on, but she didn't

answer his knock. He thought she might have gone out with friends, so he left.

Around 1:00 A.M., Lee called again, and again Carrie didn't answer. By Wednesday morning, his concern was growing. At nine o'clock, he drove to her house. After knocking repeatedly on the front door, Lee walked around to the back of the bungalow and saw that the bedroom window was ajar. He pushed it open and climbed in.

"Carrie," he called. She didn't answer. He searched the house but could not find her. He saw groceries still in their bag on the counter. He checked the front door and realized that it had not been locked. He knew something was very wrong. Mindful of the serial killings, Carrie always locked her doors. Lee called 911.

Carrie had been missing for two days.

Detective Ike Vavasseur called Detective John Colter immediately. He wanted his lead investigators from the task force working on this missing persons case. Carrie's keys had been found on the living-room table. Her purse was still on the floor by the sofa. Her cell phone was on the table beside it. There was a half-eaten wedge of cheese on the arm of the sofa, and her laptop was still open to her pictures. Her new book lay unread on the sofa. Vavasseur knew that foul play was involved. Carrie's house was too close to LSU. Carrie's boyfriend was too worried.

Colter waited until crime-scene personnel photographed and videotaped the home; then he began to look for evidence. He started outside by checking her vehicle, noticing the gallon jug of tea still on the front seat. He found nothing unusual, no signs of blood, so he went into the front yard. A For Rent sign decorated the sidewalk in front of the apartment to the left. He noticed that the shade covering the front window of Carrie's home left a gap of about eight inches.

Todd had been watching.

Although there were no obvious signs of a struggle,

Colter discovered a necklace lying on the floor near the dining-room table. It was unclasped, not broken. A wooden mail and key ring holder on the wall just inside the front door was hanging askew, the only real sign that things were not as they should have been. Stains on the carpet by the door were tested. No blood. Nothing else seemed out of place. Carrie was simply missing, her home left in nearly perfect order. Forty-four dollars were found in the wallet of her purse, along with her driver's license and credit cards. Nothing was missing.

Neighbors were interviewed, but most had been in New Orleans catching beads while Carrie sat on her couch reliving her own Mardi Gras experience. No one had seen anything.

Police would return with luminol but would find no blood in the house. Carrie's parents Linda and David Yoder were notified, and a missing persons bulletin was released to the public. The air of merriment surrounding Mardi Gras blew away in the cool March breeze as the word spread like wildfire that another LSU student was missing. Panic that had been calmed by Carnival resurfaced on campus and throughout the entire city.

Linda and David Yoder, along with Carrie's younger brother, Greg, and his girlfriend, Lauren, made the long journey to Louisiana, fearful of what they would find when they arrived. They would wait eight days to get the answer that would forever change their lives.

Linda and David had been married thirty-four years, and theirs was a happy family. David had worked for IBM for many years, and the family had moved to Tampa in 1983. The couple had raised their children in a loving environment and had worked hard to live the American dream. Life had been good to the Yoders, until the day they got the call from Louisiana. Their precious Carrie was missing—Carrie, who had really just begun to spread her wings; Carrie, who, before she came to Louisiana, had been somewhat reserved. Their Carrie, who so loved the people and the food of Louisiana. Carrie was missing, and Linda and David did not know what to think. South Florida was a long way from the locked doors and loaded guns of Louisiana.

Police would later give Carrie's purse, which they had retrieved from her home, to the Yoders. Greg's girlfriend would notice a spot that looked like blood on the side of it. After testing, it was discovered that the spot was indeed blood. But police would know who it was they were dealing with before they got a match on the blood. They knew as soon as the call came in on March 13, ten days after Carrie had been taken from her home.

A female body had been discovered under the Whiskey Bay Bridge.

Todd was flexing his muscles to the task force. Carrie's body was found not far from where Pam Kinamore had been found, eight months earlier. But whereas Pam's body had been carefully placed and covered with brush, Carrie had been thrown from the top of the bridge. She was found floating facedown, nude from the waist down. Mud and debris covered her legs, from thigh to foot. Vegetation had adhered to her skin, was entwined in her long, curly hair. She still wore the blue halter, covered by a black sweater and gray-and-black fleece jacket, which she had put on to go to Winn-Dixie, so many days before. Three interlocking bands of silver were still on the ring finger of her left hand. A contact lens was in her hair.

Carrie would go back to LSU one more time. Her body was transferred to LSU's FACES Laboratory, where Mary Manhein would try to identify another of Todd's victims. The Yoders had told police that Carrie had a tattoo, a Celtic weave on her lower back, but police wanted to be sure. Mary took X-rays of Carrie's upper and lower jaws to compare to dental records. The X-rays were a match. The young woman, whose decomposing body bore the marks of an enraged beast, was indeed Carrie Lynn Yoder.

Connie Warner's usually tidy bedroom reveals that she struggled for her life. *(Photo supplied by the Zachary Police Department)*

Three spots of blood were found in Warner's laundry room, where Derrick Todd Lee fought with her before pulling her from her home. *(Photo supplied by the Zachary Police Department)*

Derrick Todd Lee used the Azalea Rest Cemetery as a haven where he would spy on unsuspecting women. On numerous occasions, he evaded police by running behind tombstones. *(Photo by Susan D. Mustafa)*

A mug shot of Lee after he was arrested by the Zachary Police Department in 1997. *(Photo supplied by the Zachary Police Department)*

Bloodstains on the living room floor indicate that Lee dragged Mebruer's body through her home. *(Photo supplied by the Zachary Police Department)*

This trash can liner left on Randi Mebruer's porch contained DNA that would later link Derrick Todd Lee to her murder, although her body has never been found. *(Photo supplied by the Zachary Police Department)*

NOTICE TO HUNTERS!

Friends and family of Randi Mebruer, the 28-year-old mother who has been missing since April 18, 1998, are pleading to all hunters in the area to take extra steps when hunting, in search of Mebruer. Please report any unusual sightings to the Zachary Police Department Detective Division at **(225) 654-6841**

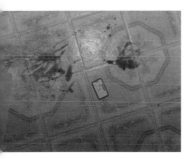

Mebruer's kitchen floor reveals the brutality of the attack. *(Photo supplied by the Zachary Police Department)*

This poster was released by the Zachary Police Department, asking hunters for help with finding Mebruer's body. *(Photo supplied by the Zachary Police Department)*

The home in Lee's Quarters in St. Francisville where Derrick Todd Lee grew up. *(Photo by Susan D. Mustafa)*

The home where Lee lived with his wife and children on a well-traveled highway in St. Francisville. *(Photo by Susan D. Mustafa)*

Lieutenant David McDavid of the Zachary Police Department holds a composite sketch of the killer. *(Photo by Susan D. Mustafa)*

Sergeant Ray Day worked with Lt. McDavid and Dannie Mixon to catch the killer. *(Photo by Susan D. Mustafa)*

Dannie Mixon, an investigator with the Louisiana Attorney General's Office, was assigned the cold cases of Connie Warner and Randi Mebruer. He would eventually catch the South Louisiana Serial Killer using old-fashioned detective work. *(Photograph by Leatus Still, Still's Photography, Inc.)*

Collette Walker lived in St. Francisville Square, a complex of town homes, where Derrick Todd Lee stalked her. *(Photo by Susan D. Mustafa)*

Archer Lee was the detective who investigated the stalking and arrested Derrick Todd Lee. *(Photo by Susan D. Mustafa)*

Gina Wilson Green's home on Stanford Avenue, where Derrick Todd Lee killed her. *(Photo by Susan D. Mustafa)*

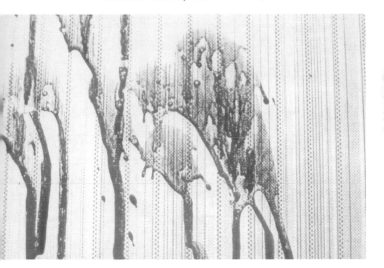

The walls of Geralyn Barr DeSoto's home indicate the killer's rage. *(Photo supplied by West Baton Rouge Parish Sheriff's Office)*

Christine Moore was jogging along River Road when she disappeared. *(Louisiana State University yearbook photo)*

Moore's body was found beside the Ebenezer Baptist Church on River Road. *(Photo by Susan D. Mustafa)*

The ravine next to the church where Moore was found June 16, 2002. *(Photo by Susan D. Mustafa)*

Charlotte Murray Pace had just graduated from Louisiana State University when Derrick Todd Lee performed his most sadistic act of murder and rape. *(Louisiana State University yearbook photo)*

The home on Stanford Avenue where Murray lived just before her murder. Her home was just a few doors down from Gina Wilson Green's home. *(Photo by Susan D. Mustafa)*

The townhouse on Sharlo Avenue where Murray had moved the weekend she was killed. *(Photo by Susan D. Mustafa)*

Eugenie Boisfontaine's body lay just feet from the Alligator Bayou Bar for months. *(Photo by Susan D. Mustafa)*

Boisfontaine's body was found in these reeds near Bayou Manchac. *(Photo by Susan D. Mustafa)*

Diane Alexander's home in Breaux Bridge was covered in blood after Derrick Todd Lee viciously attacked her. *(Photo supplied by West Baton Rouge Parish Sheriff's Office)*

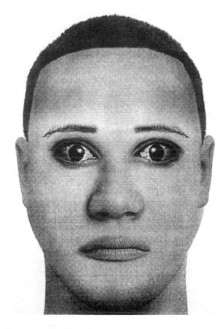

Police released this drawing of Derrick Todd Lee based on Alexander's description of her attacker. *(Photo supplied by the Zachary Police Department)*

Pam Kinamore was the beautiful owner of an antique shop called Comforts and Joys when she was kidnapped, raped, and murdered. *(Photo by Vincent J. Marino)*

The remains of a cross mark the spot where Derrick Todd Lee disposed of Kinamore's body under Whiskey Bay Bridge. *(Photo by Susan D. Mustafa)*

Kinamore's mother, Lynne Marino, a voice for the victims in the media, with her beloved dog, Lily. *(Photo by Susan D. Mustafa)*

Trineisha Dené Colomb was taken from her mother's gravesite and murdered seven months from the date of her mother's death. *(Lafayette High School graduation photo)*

Colomb's tombstone reads, "I lay next to my mother joining her as an angel in heaven." *(Photo by Susan D. Mustafa)*

Carrie Lynn Yoder was just settling in after a weekend at Mardi Gras when Derrick Todd Lee invaded her home and took her life. *(Louisiana State University yearbook photo)*

The home where Yoder lived near the gates of LSU. She was the killer's last victim. *(Photo by Susan D. Mustafa)*

Yoder's body was found under Whiskey Bay Bridge near the spot where Pam Kinamore's body was found the previous summer.
(Photo by Susan D. Mustafa)

Suspect is wanted for the ***SERIAL MURDERS*** of at least five south Louisiana Women. Suspect is to be considered Armed and Dangerous. Anyone with information on the whereabouts of this suspect is encouraged to contact their local law enforcement immediately or the

Multi Agency Homicide Task Force
1-866-389-3310

The task force released this poster when Derrick Todd Lee was finally arrested in Atlanta. *(Poster released by East Baton Rouge Parish to media)*

Special Prosecutor Tony Clayton won a life sentence for Derrick Todd Lee for the murder of Geralyn DeSoto in this courthouse in Port Allen. *(Photograph by Will O'Halloran)*

Assistant District Attorney John Sinquefield put the nail in Derrick Todd Lee's coffin by prosecuting him for the murder of Charlotte Murray Pace. Lee was sentenced to death. *(Photo supplied by the Louisiana Attorney General's Office)*

* * *

Carrie had been raped. She had been punched so severely in the stomach that ribs two through ten were broken away from her spinal column. Ribs had punctured her lung and liver. Her eyes were bruised. Her wrists were bruised. Her face was swollen from the blows. A contusion covered part of her forehead. There were scratches on her lower abdomen.

Carrie's neck was ringed with bruises, but no ligature marks were found. Petechia was discovered in both her eyes. The official cause of death was listed as asphyxiation due to strangulation. Like he had with Gina Green and Dené Colomb, Todd had killed Carrie with his bare hands.

It is not known exactly where Todd raped and killed Carrie, as there were no signs that he had done it in her home. But for two hours before they got to Whiskey Bay, the young woman had been in Todd's possession—two horrible hours during which Todd vented his rage and frustration upon the beautiful girl. She had traveled around the world and had come to her beloved Louisiana wetlands to die.

Carrie would become the fifth official victim of the South Louisiana Serial Killer. David and Linda Yoder would soon join the other families on the steps of the state capitol.

Lee Stanton mourned the loss of his beautiful girlfriend. The wetlands lost a determined and valuable ally.

Dannie Mixon had another name to add to the timeline he was creating on the life of Derrick Todd Lee. Carrie Lynn Yoder would be the last name he would have to add.

Soon, the terror would be over.

An Unexpected Twist

Morale at task force headquarters had already been low, and with Carrie's murder, that low morale sank to new depths. Members of the task force were taking a beating in the press, and the criticism from some of the families wasn't helping matters. The public wanted answers, and the task force had none. With the discovery of Carrie's body at Whiskey Bay, now it seemed like the serial killer was taunting investigators as well. By this time, more than $500,000 had been paid in overtime to the officers who worked weekends and nights to catch the killer. And all they had was a billboard of a person of interest to offer the public. Tensions were running high, not only at the Emergency Operations Center, on Harding Boulevard, but on the streets of Baton Rouge as well.

Women became even more frightened as they viewed photos of the beautiful, smiling girl, with the long, curly hair, on their televisions. They watched report after report about how Carrie's body had been found at Whiskey Bay, so close to where Pam Kinamore's body had been discovered. They wondered why that area had not been under surveillance. They slept with their guns by their beds. They clung to their husbands. Parents made LSU students move away from the university. *The Advocate* reported that shortly after Murray's death, Pat Englade had advised a friend that it wasn't safe for his daughter to live close to LSU. With Carrie's murder, that statement had been confirmed. It wasn't safe there or anywhere else—not in Grand Coteau or in Port Allen or around LSU or in quiet neighborhoods in Baton Rouge and Zachary.

Single, married, black, white, young, old—it didn't make a difference. This serial killer struck randomly, and anyone could be next. Everyone had read the profile. Everyone knew what kind of person they should watch out for, what his habits would be. Everyone knew the killer was a white man in a white pickup truck. Everyone knew the killer could be watching them.

Investigators lived in as much fear as the women and men of South Louisiana. They all wondered when and where he would strike next. With each additional murder, their job got harder—the investigating, the explaining why they were unable to catch him. The competition to apprehend the killer and end this nightmare became even fiercer. The national media had gotten involved, and the task force was not looking good. Pat Englade's job now mostly consisted of figuring out what to say to the media.

The pressure was intense, and everyone lost faith in the ability of the police to protect them. "The average experience of task force members—I was shocked to discover how young the homicide detectives were and inexperienced," Sid Newman recalled. "They had a lot of loners. Some agencies sent their best. Some didn't. When you're going after a serial killer, you don't use forgery guys."

But the task force had reasons to be going after the wrong guy. Witnesses at four of the murder scenes had described a white male in the vicinity. But there were clues that their guy could be black. The area on Choctaw Drive where Gina's cell phone had been found was a predominantly black, seedy area of Baton Rouge. The shoe print found at the scene of Dené's murder was an Adidas brand—the Give-N-Go model—worn mostly by black men. Witnesses in Murray's case had described a black man.

By the middle of January, task force members began to think that maybe they had made a mistake in telling citizens that the killer would be driving a white truck. If it was the serial killer who had taken Mari Ann Fowler, then he could be driving a burgundy truck. In a press release on its Web site, the task force began to urge citizens not to screen information about possible suspects.

"While a white truck is of interest to investigators, people are urged to keep an open mind with information called into the task force regarding suspects' vehicles. A vehicle description has often proven to be way off the mark, and we must consider that this offender may or may not own a white truck or has moved on to a different vehicle."

Englade knew that the situation was becoming desperate and issued his own statement. "This is a very difficult time for all of us in South Louisiana. Our citizens are feeling frightened, angry, and helpless, but no person, no evil should divide us—the people of Louisiana. . . . We live by our commitment. Louisiana, standing together, standing strong."

But Englade's relationship with the public, and with Lynne Marino, was deteriorating. "When I asked Englade what he thought about Carrie and Pam's bodies being found so close together, he said, 'Nothing.' Now, how could he not see they were related? I was shocked," Lynne said.

Englade was not without his supporters, though. Governor Mike Foster and Mayor-President Bobby Simpson were firmly in his corner, and some of the victims' families respected the big man and understood the severity of his task. However, Lynne had been quoted in the *Advocate* as saying that she had nothing personal against him, but that he made mistakes out of arrogance and inexperience.

* * *

In late February, one week before Carrie's murder, the task force finally made a very smart move. It had been contacting outside agencies, including Scotland Yard, to find anyone who could racially profile the killer through his DNA. On February 25, members of the task force called a company in Sarasota, Florida—DNAPrint Genomics, Inc. This company, founded by scientist Tony Frudakis, claimed it could determine the serial killer's racial makeup. The Louisiana State Police Crime lab sent Todd's DNA to Frudakis, along with twenty other DNA samples to be used as tests of the company's accuracy.

DNA racial profiling was a relatively new science, not yet proved to the extent of other DNA testing methods, but Frudakis assured the task force his results would be accurate. Carrie was still missing on March 7 when Frudakis called with his results. He advised the task force in a conference call that the offender was 85 percent sub-Saharan African and 15 percent Native American. There was silence on the other end of the phone. No one could believe it. Frudakis was asked to submit his analyses of the other samples—samples whose racial makeups were known to police. Frudakis got every one of them correct. The task force was convinced. The serial killer was black. Everyone had been wrong, and in swabbing only white men, in refusing to consider other alternatives, lives had been lost.

On March 21, the task force issued another statement: "We are asking the community to broaden their thinking about this offender and consider that this person could possibly be a dark-complexioned white male, a man of mixed heritage, or a black male."

The community was stunned. All of this time that they had been frightened of white males, they had opened their doors to black males—delivery men, politicians,

salesmen. Carrie had opened her door for a black man.
The task force had told her the killer was white. This information had come too late to save her life.

The task force began reviewing all of its old leads—
those black men who had been cleared simply because
of their skin color. On March 24, Captain Spence Dil-
worth, of the West Feliciana Parish Sheriff's Office, called
the task force to supply it with the names of several black
men in the area who had a history of sexual misconduct
and arrests. One of the names he gave them was Derrick
Todd Lee. That was a name that had been heard before.
Investigators had been to his house in the fall of 2002 and
had cleared him because his truck was a show truck and
not old, like the one that had been described by witnesses.

Research analysts dug up the old lead that Collette
Walker had called the task force hotline with the previ-
ous September. The lead was reassigned to Detective Lee
Alfred.

On April 7, Detective Alfred went to Todd's home in
Starhill, but no one answered the door. He returned the
next day, along with Detective Mike Lockwood. Again,
no one was home, so Alfred left his business card on the
door and another with a lieutenant from West Feliciana
Parish, according to a report filed in June by Detectives
John Colter and Chris Johnson: *Detective Alfred was
assured by the lieutenant that his department would contact
Detective Alfred if they had any knowledge of Lee's whereabouts.
This lieutenant advised task force investigators that they saw
Derrick Todd Lee on a regular basis, and they would call the
task force investigators the next time they saw him.*

No one called.

Todd was left to roam freely for another seven weeks.
His routine didn't change. On the very day Alfred first
went to his home, Todd was in a pawnshop in St. Francisville pawning a ten-karat nugget ring, a ten-karat
chain with a cross attached—and a knife. He would be
released from his job at JE Merit on April 25, and he and

Jackie would appear in bankruptcy court on April 29. As his pattern exhibits, Todd usually searched for victims just after losing a job. And with the additional stress of filing bankruptcy and losing his home, surely his tension was mounting. In late April of 2003, no woman was safe.

Dannie Mixon, who had brought Todd to the attention of the police in Baton Rouge in 2001, and to the attention of the task force in the summer of 2002, decided to step in—to save the day and to save some lives.

Dannie Mixon: The Swabbing

It was cold—late February in Atlanta—and Dannie had just walked into the Hampton Inn at the Atlanta Airport. At his age, he felt the cold go right through him, and he rubbed his hands together to get warm. Dannie's cheeks, already pink from the frigid air, turned red as they usually did when he was upset about something. He and J.B. Cormier, the retired chief of detectives for the Lafayette Parish Sheriff's Office, sat down in the warm lobby for a moment to discuss the serial killings.

"J.B., I'm convinced Derrick Todd Lee is the serial killer, but no one will listen to me. They think I'm a crazy old man. All that crap about a white man in a white truck is crap. It's just like the D.C. snipers. Everybody thought they were white. It'll be just like that—the direct opposite of the profile."

J.B. nodded his agreement.

Upon their return to Louisiana, the two men discussed Dannie's feeling with Ronnie Black at the attorney general's office. Ronnie told them to talk to the LPSO, as they were still investigating the Dené Colomb murder. Sheriff Michael Neustrom told J.B. to talk to Major Wendell Rayburn, the Lafayette contingent on the task force.

"I work with this old man at the attorney general's

office, and he knows homicide," J.B. said to Rayburn. "He swears Derrick Todd Lee is the serial killer."

Rayburn said he would get back with J.B. He never did. Carrie Lynn Yoder disappeared on March 3.

Dannie was frustrated. He sat in his office surrounded by maps and charts, each with pins and flags stuck in them to denote locations and times and dates. He had collected so much information that it was impossible to keep it all organized. He had requested Todd's incarceration records from the Louisiana Department of Corrections (DOC). He had a list of all of the vehicles Todd had ever owned from the Louisiana Department of Motor Vehicles (DMV). He had Todd's arrest record, which dated back to 1981 when Todd was just thirteen. He had spent years piecing it together. And his desk was covered with everything he had collected. While he worked on his timeline of Todd's life, his thoughts were fearful.

He worried that someone else would die before Todd was arrested.

He worried that he was getting too old for this. That's what everyone else seemed to think. He could tell by the way everyone ignored him when he talked about his theory of the case. But he had that feeling—the one that never let him down. And he knew he was right.

Dannie began with Connie Warner. At one time, he knew that Connie's daughter, Tracy, and her boyfriend, Andre Burgas, had been suspects, simply because Tracy had not told her mother the truth about where she was the weekend Connie had died. But Dannie had never believed that Tracy would have killed her mother. A witness had reported seeing a man taking a bundle out of Connie's house and putting it into the backseat of a Buick. Todd owned a red Buick Electra at the time. Andre would later identify Todd in a lineup. He had seen Todd standing in the vacant lot next to Connie's home in the days before her disappearance. In November of that year, almost two months after Connie's death, Todd would be issued a traffic citation by the Zachary Police Department in that car, but no one made the connection.

Eugenie Boisfontaine was next on his list. Dannie knew that Todd was not in jail at the time of her murder. He didn't have anything concrete to link Todd to Eugenie other than the fact that she had lived on Stanford Avenue and had disappeared while walking around the LSU lakes. That was enough for him. He felt that Eugenie's death was connected to Gina and Murray's. Dannie was well aware that Todd often returned to the same places to find his victims or to dump their bodies.

He moved on to Randi Mebruer. He had long since decided that her husband, Michael, wasn't the culprit in that murder. Dannie wished he hadn't spent so much time chasing after Michael. Considering Todd's history with Oak Shadows and the close proximity of Randi's and Connie's homes, Dannie had no doubt now that Todd had killed Randi. There had to be some evidence somewhere.

"DNA was not requested originally," Dannie recalled. "The Zachary police screwed that murder scene up terribly. Connie Warner's crime scene was even worse. They walked through the blood. They made coffee. These guys had never worked a murder scene, and there were too many people messing around. They've got a lot to cover up, let me tell you."

Dannie made a note to tell Sergeant Ray Day to resubmit all of the evidence in the Mebruer case to the lab for retesting. Dannie liked Ray, was impressed by him, so much so that he had asked Zachary police chief Joey Watson to let Ray work with him on the cases. Little did Dannie know that evidence that could have been used to put Todd in prison was locked away in an evidence room in Zachary, and it had been there since 1998, waiting to be discovered. The overlooked detail—semen on a trash can liner—would have saved the lives of so many women. But in 1998, the use of DNA to catch killers was costly, and the ZPD had not even considered that option, even though many in the department thought that Todd had killed Randi.

Dannie picked up Todd's work history and began matching it against his list of victims. As he dug through report after report, he began noticing that the murders always seemed to happen at times of crisis for Todd—some just after he had lost jobs, others when he got into trouble for violating probation, others when he was experiencing money troubles. Dannie looked for patterns and noticed that most of the murders had occurred on days that Todd hadn't worked. He thought about bringing what he had discovered to the attention of the task force. But he knew they wouldn't listen. They hadn't listened before, hadn't invited the attorney general's office to become part of the team, even though its investigators had years and years of experience breaking cases.

"The task force refused to talk to us. We had already given them everything we had on Todd in 2001 and again in 2002—his history of Peeping Tom incidents, the stalking incidents, the Zachary murders—it was all there for them. But they didn't want to hear it," Dannie said.

It was time for Dannie to take action. He decided to draft a motion for a subpoena duces tecum, a motion stating probable cause that he would put before a judge to enable him to swab Todd for DNA. Although this kind of a subpoena was not the normal procedure for obtaining DNA from a suspect, Dannie had used this writ commanding a person to produce certain designated evidence many times before to obtain fingerprints and blood samples. "If you asked me now, I would have used a body search warrant to get the saliva sample, but that was the way our office did things. We've used them for years."

Dannie called for his longtime secretary, Penny Jones, who had typed up all of his thoughts about Todd for years. "I need you to type up a subpoena for me, Penny. It has to be perfect," he said as he started dictating his thoughts. Penny was used to Dannie rambling his thoughts to her. His handwriting was horrible, and in the time they had worked together, he had never written anything down. She began to take notes.

Dannie mentioned Connie Warner's homicide, then launched into the details of the Mebruer case. He knew the facts by heart. He talked about the times Todd had been arrested for Peeping Tom incidents. He went into what Consandra Green had said about Todd's whereabouts that night. He showed how Todd's route would have taken him by the entrance to Randi's subdivision. He mentioned Todd's criminal history, especially the stalking incident with Collette Walker and Todd's subsequent conviction. Dannie talked about how Todd was not incarcerated during the times when Gina, Murray, Pam, Dené, and Carrie had been killed. Finally he mentioned the confidential source who had reported that Todd had mentioned a missing woman to him before it was on the news. He then asked that a subpoena duces tecum be issued directing Todd to submit a DNA specimen to Dannie Mixon or Ray Day.

Penny realized the significance of what she was doing and got down every word. She hurried to her desk and drafted the six-page motion.

Dannie and Investigator Christopher Ribera contacted Judge George H. Ware, of the Twentieth Judicial District Court in Clinton, Louisiana. That same day, May 5, 2003, Judge Ware signed the motion.

* * *

Dannie sprang into action, his heart pumping fast and hard as he realized he was about to catch the serial killer. He just knew it.

"I told Ray to run down David McDavid," Dannie said. "Mac called Ray back and said he was following Lee to the truck stop. Then they lost him. Me and Todd Morris and Chris Ribera, who was my new partner, were busting ass to get over there. We sat on his house and saw his daughter, Doris, get dropped off. We waited for Lee and watched him pull into the yard by his front door. I asked Todd Morris to go in with me."

Morris gave Todd a certified copy of the subpoena and asked him to go inside, but Todd wanted to do it in the front yard. "Where's the order?" he asked.

"It's filed under seal at the East Feliciana Clerk of Court's Office," Morris told him.

"Let's do it right here," Todd said.

"No, not in front of your kids," Dannie interjected.

Dannie, Morris, and Todd went inside. Todd sat down on the love seat in his living room. Dannie put on gloves and got the buccal swab he would use for the sample. "He was as calm as a pussycat," Dannie said. "I knew how brutal he was, so I expected him to resist." Todd didn't, just sat there calmly as Dannie took the plastic nipple off the swab and placed it in the left side of Todd's mouth.

"I swabbed his jaws. I poked the hell out of him, swabbed him as good as a human being could be swabbed," Dannie said.

After Dannie collected the first sample, he sealed the cotton tip with a plastic container that is attached to the swab and handed it to Morris. *L 4:00 PM,* Morris wrote on the swab package. Dannie repeated the process on the right side of Todd's mouth. *R 4:01 PM,* Morris wrote. The men gave the sealed packages to Ray Day, who inventoried them and filled out the crime

l   a   b
receipt. He called the Louisiana State Police Crime Lab and was asked to bring them in at 1:00 P.M. the next day because the swabs had to dry overnight.

On May 6, the swabs were submitted for analysis.

The wait began.

Derrick Todd Lee—On the Run

Todd knew he was busted. He may not have completely understood how DNA could implicate him in the serial killings, but he knew one thing—the swabbing meant that police would come to arrest him soon. It was time to run.

Jackie understood why they had to leave. She had watched the police harass Todd for years, had listened to him complain about that harassment. She was convinced that they were out to get him, and had once warned Todd that they might try to pin the serial killings on him. "Watch your name come up," she told him. And though she knew Todd could be violent when he was angry, Jackie did not believe that he was capable of murder. He was the father of her children.

Things had not been going well for the couple. They had filed for bankruptcy in November and were about to be evicted from their home. They had reported debts equaling $84,742, which they could not pay on their $3,400-per-month income. The Lees were more than $4,500 behind with the mortgage, which they had not made a payment on since September. With nothing left to lose, Todd and Jackie began to make their plans.

"There's too much stuff going on around Baton Rouge—people being killed, the truck stop being robbed, and drugs," Todd told Derrick Jr. "It's time to go."

Todd decided that he would get a bus ticket to Chicago, where he would try to find a job. Jackie was to see if she could take the children to Detroit to stay with her aunt, Joann Chandler, for a while, until the family got back on its feet. It was agreed that the couple would reunite when Jackie or Todd got a job, either in Chicago or Detroit.

Jackie called her aunt. "Would it be okay if we come stay with you? Something big is about to blow up here, and the media is going to be a madhouse with it. I don't want to subject the kids to [it]," she explained.

"Is Todd on the run?" Joann queried.

"No."

"Is he in trouble?"

"Sort of."

Joann didn't ask any more questions; she simply agreed that Jackie could come.

The day before his departure, Todd gathered the family. "It's time for me to go," he said. "I'll miss y'all. Take care of you'selves."

Derrick Jr. watched as Todd packed his belongings into a purple-and-black book sack, a black leather bag, and a large garbage bag: tennis shoes, black-and-white house slippers, work boots, a blanket, shirts, slacks, socks, work gloves, underwear, toothpaste, and a toothbrush. Todd packed his wedding ring, a gold watch, and several gold chains, one with a crucifix attached. He placed some letters and mail into the garbage bag, as well as a list of telephone numbers and some work-related papers. Todd also filled a second garbage bag with old clothing to be given to his cousins.

The day after the swabbing, Jackie dropped the kids off at Todd's mother's house, then drove Todd in the family's gold Hyundai Accent to the Greyhound bus station in Baton Rouge. Dressed in black jeans, a short-sleeved red shirt, and Adidas tennis shoes, Todd boarded the bus and headed to Chicago. He would be unsuccessful at finding a job and would return to Baton Rouge several days later. Jackie and the kids picked him up around three in the afternoon on May 8. The family went home to clean out their house.

A big-screen television, along with three other TVs, and several bikes were taken to Tarshia's mobile home, just down the gravel road from mother Florence's house. Kitchen items, chairs, and lamps were taken to Todd's sister Tinita. Beds, pillows, sheets, the refrigerator, and dressers were taken to the Barrows' home. Todd threw their couch into the Dumpster by the Chevron Truck Stop, just down the street from their home. All of their old clothing that would not be taken with them was donated to the Salvation Army.

Derrick Jr. and Doris spent the night at their aunt Tarshia's house, while Jackie and Todd shared what would be their final night together at a local motel. The next morning, the couple gathered with the Barrows to say good-bye.

"I love you," a worried Florence told Todd. "Don't be gettin' yourself into anything."

Todd hugged her, then turned to Derrick Jr. "Be the man. Take care of your mama and sister. Be good and don't get into no trouble. I'm gonna go make enough money to come to Detroit and see y'all, maybe spend the night."

Jackie took Todd once again to the bus station, only this time his destination was Atlanta. It was the last time she would see her husband as a free man. Jackie's life was about to be turned upside down, but she didn't know this as she hugged him good-bye. She returned to St. Francisville, oblivious, and spent her last night in Louisiana with her children at Tarshia's. On May 10, Jackie, Derrick Jr., and Doris boarded a bus to Detroit to

start their lives over. They arrived the next day—
Mother's Day.

It wasn't long before Todd began to feel at home in Atlanta. He rented a room at the Lakewood Motor Lodge and began making friends with the other occupants of the motel. He landed a job with a construction company and used his first paycheck to party with his new friends. He barbecued ribs and chicken for them, hosted a Bible study, and entertained several women in his room. The guests at the motel loved him.

A Wanted Man

Natasha Poe, forensic DNA analyst for the Louisiana State Police Crime Lab, couldn't believe her eyes. It was a Sunday, May 25, and she had stopped at work to check on a test that had been sent to the lab nineteen days earlier. With more than one thousand DNA samples taken by the task force in the last month, the lab had been overwhelmed. This one had been sent by Ray Day, of the Zachary Police Department, and investigators there were getting antsy for the results.

As she looked at the test, Natasha mentally matched it to the sample she had become so familiar with in the past year. She recognized the pattern the minute she saw it. She knew those markers by heart, but to double-check, she ran it through her computer software program. It was a conclusive match. Natasha Poe knew the identity of the serial killer. She hurriedly called her supervisor.

Word spread quickly throughout the task force. The serial killer had a name. Telephone lines around the city were burning up. "Derrick Todd Lee is the serial killer. The DNA matched!"

"I was cutting grass that evening when Ray Day called and told me to get in touch with the task force," David McDavid said. "They told me to come down to task force headquarters. There were a lot of people there. Someone said, 'Congratulations. Y'all just solved the serial killings.' I was overcome with joy. I had tears in my eyes. I wanted to say, 'I told you so,' but I've got a lot of respect for those guys. They worked so hard and were under so much pressure."

Investigator Todd Morris contacted Dannie Mixon and told him the news. The men grabbed Dannie's files and went to meet the task force. It was almost midnight, and the headquarters was bustling with activity. More than one hundred men and women were there to discuss how to proceed. Dannie informed everyone about the swabbing.

"What's he driving?" Detective Paul Maranto asked.

Someone said Todd's car was a Mitsubishi.

"It ain't no Mitsubishi," Dannie said. "It's a Hyundai." He had seen the car at the Barrows' home just weeks before when he was tracking Todd.

"It was bought at Hampton Motors. They sell Mitsubishi," another investigator said.

"I'm telling you, it's a Hyundai," Dannie responded, becoming agitated.

"You're wrong. It's a Mitsubishi, you crazy old man."

Dannie argued his point, but no one would listen.

Dannie met with FBI profilers for much of the night, discussing Todd's behavior during the swabbing, as members of the task force wrote search warrants for the Barrow home, Todd and Jackie's home, and Todd and Consandra's home.

Captain Archer Lee knew the minute he got the call. "We're getting ready to move on the serial killer."

"Derrick Lee?" Archer immediately responded. "That was my first thought. I knew if they were calling me, it was someone from St. Francisville."

But Archer had a dilemma. He had known the Lee family all of his life. He worried that if the state police and

SWAT teams converged on the home, it was possible that things might get out of hand, especially if Todd was there. He knew that children might be in the home. He asked the task force to wait until the morning after the children left for school to execute the search warrant. The police formed a perimeter around the house and waited.

The next morning, after the kids had boarded the bus, Archer called Coleman Barrow and asked him to come outside and talk with him. Curious neighbors and relatives peeped out of windows and doors to see what was happening.

"The police are here to search your home," Archer said. "We're looking at Derrick for the serial killings."

"What? No way, man," Coleman said.

"Is he here?"

"No. He left town."

"I knew you would tell me the truth, man," Archer said, patting Coleman on the back.

"You know me. You know me, man, all your life," Coleman said, looking a bit dazed.

Archer and the other detectives placed chairs outside for the family to sit on while they searched the house. Todd's grandmother was there, obviously shaken, and his mother and stepfather. They sat quietly, not quite believing what was happening as they watched the police go through their home and Todd's Hyundai Accent, which was parked in the yard.

"I understood the severity of the situation, but had it gone any other way, had Todd been there, it might have been bad. This is a small community, and I have to deal with these people," Archer explained. "If we had laid them out and cuffed everyone, which is procedure, and the grandmother had a heart attack, that would have been the focus of the media. I've been doing this for fifteen years. You have to give people respect to get it."

Meanwhile, police were already at the house in Starhill. Their battering ram left a large hole in the front door as they forced their way in. They were not being as considerate here. The place was a mess, and obviously abandoned. The furniture was gone, and aside from a few unimportant items left carelessly strewn about, the home offered no solid leads for police. It did, however, tell the story of what life in that house must have been like.

As they made their way from the living room to the kitchen, they noticed that the cabinets and walls behind the stove were covered in thick layers of grease. The walls throughout the home, especially in the hallway and three small bedrooms, were riddled with holes, the kind that indicate that some sort of violence had taken place there. Some of the walls looked like objects had been thrown through them. Other holes looked like they had been made by a fist.

After a thorough search, police cordoned off the house and headed to Consandra's. Her home would offer up valuable clues—namely, a Wolverine boot, a boot that had left a bloody footprint at the Geralyn Desoto crime scene along Highway 1—but police did not realize what they had discovered as they bagged up anything that looked like it could be evidence. They brought Consandra to headquarters for questioning, as they had Todd's family just a short time before.

The only information they could obtain was that Todd had left town two weeks earlier to go to Chicago. That's what he had told them. No one knew where Jackie and the children were, and nobody in Todd's family would believe that he was the serial killer. To their minds, it just wasn't possible. By the end of the day, the whole world would know that it was possible.

WANTED, read the headline of the *Advocate.* An enlarged mug shot of Todd covered much of the front page. Local television stations broke into regular programming with

Todd's name and photograph. Stunned viewers were glued to their sets, not quite believing what they were seeing. After years of living in fear, years spent learning about victim after victim, the killer had a face and a name.

And he was still out there. Somewhere.

And his victim list was about to grow larger, only this time he would not take his victims' lives through murdering them. These victims were his family, the ones who loved him. As surely as Todd took away the lives of so many beautiful women, he also took away the lives of his family members—his mother, his stepfather, his sisters, his wife, and his children—who would never know normalcy again.

It was Memorial Day weekend, and Jerome Chandler was at home waiting for his wife and Jackie when the phone rang. Jerome's niece Angela was calling from New Orleans. "I just heard on the news that they think Derrick Todd Lee is the serial killer," she said, holding out the telephone so that Jerome could hear the news report. Jerome had been suspicious about why Jackie had come to Detroit, but he didn't want to pry, so he hadn't asked her any questions. Suddenly he knew why.

When Jackie and Joann drove up, Jerome sent the children out of the room. "How much do you know about your husband?" he asked Jackie. "Do you know that he is wanted for the serial killings?"

"I don't know anything about him being involved in any murders, but the police did take a DNA sample from him," Jackie replied.

Jerome told her what Angela had said.

"He's not guilty. He's being set up," Jackie said, defending her husband. Tears began pouring down her face as the realization of what was happening sank in.

Captured!

Jerome Chandler suggested that it might be a good idea to call the FBI. Jackie agreed, took some time to collect herself, and then called the Detroit office, around seven o'clock on the night of May 26. Agents asked her to come in.

Jackie told them she saw on the news that Todd was wanted for the serial killings. She said that she had come to Detroit after she had lost her home, and that she had been married to Todd for thirteen years. FBI agents questioned her vigorously.

"Where is Derrick Todd Lee right now?"

Jackie hesitated for a moment, battling with herself, wondering if she should reveal Todd's whereabouts. She took a deep breath. "He's staying in Atlanta, Georgia. I don't know where, but he got a job working construction and finally got a room to stay in."

"Do you have a number where he can be reached?"

"At my aunt's house, in my suitcase. If I can leave with my aunt, I can get it for you."

Jackie told agents that Todd had a burgundy vehicle, which was owned by his girlfriend, Consandra. "Todd returned the vehicle to her before we left town."

The FBI let her go on the condition that she contact

them immediately with the phone number. When Jackie returned to her aunt's, she was unable to find the number.

The next day, Jackie, Joann, and Jerome headed back to the Patrick V. McNamara Federal Building for further interrogation. Joann and Jerome were asked to wait while Jackie was interviewed in private—this time by Prince Earl Ross, Robert Bulgarelli, Cheryle King, Michael J. Mozer, and John W. Piatanesi. They asked her again why she had left Louisiana, and again she told them about losing the house. Jackie informed them that she had no knowledge that Todd had murdered anyone.

"He never talked to me about the serial killer," she said.

"Did he have any unusual reactions to news releases that referenced the serial killer?"

"No."

"Is he violent?"

"No."

"Did he ever lose his temper with you?"

"Well, he did slap me once, but most of the time, he just yelled at me. Called me fat. Told me I was ugly. Called me a bitch and told me that nobody else would want me."

"Do you still love him?"

"Yes, I still do."

Sergeant Bulgarelli, who was with the Detroit Police Department (DPD), asked Jackie to explain again what had happened the week of May 4 through 11. He pressed her further about why she had left town.

"Because they took the swab of Derrick's mouth, and he told me something was going to blow up on us, that they were going to try to pin something on him."

"Has your husband called you since you've been here?"

"Yes. He called this morning about ten-thirty. It was a three-way call his sister Tinita placed."

"What did he say?"

"He wanted to know how I was and what was going on. He asked if I had seen the news, if I knew he was wanted for killing five women. I told him I had. He said he didn't do it. He said he wasn't where he was before and couldn't call me anymore 'cause the phones are tapped. He told me to take care of the kids. He said he loved me and them."

Special Agent Piatanesi left the room to question Joann and Jerome.

Joann told him that she thought Todd was in Chicago because she had heard Derrick Jr. ask Jackie how his dad liked Chicago. "He was a ladies' man, smooth talking and very convincing," she said. "Jackie told me that women were always calling their house. It got so bad that she had to put a privacy manager on her telephone to stop them from calling. And Todd has another child, named Dedrick, with another woman. Jackie said her name is Cat [Consandra]. They used to work together at the Jetson Youth Center, but Cat was fired because she and Jackie had a confrontation at work."

Jerome didn't say much, but he did recall a time when Todd walked into a conversation he was having about the Bible at a family gathering. "He walked up and quoted the Bible, [chapter] and verse. He carried on a conversation that really impressed the family, but I never thought he was a sincere man, certainly not in his feelings for Jackie. He was a player of women."

Neither Joann nor Jerome believed that Jackie knew anything about Todd's involvement in the serial killings. The FBI let them go.

Back in Louisiana, West Baton Rouge Parish sheriff's deputies were busy interrogating Consandra Green.

They were at her home when she received a phone call from Todd. Consandra's caller ID device recorded a number with a 404 area code.

"I'm in Atlanta. What's going on?" Todd asked Consandra.

"The police are looking for you. They say you're the serial killer," Consandra replied, somewhat dazed and disbelieving.

Todd hung up.

He had placed the call from the cell phone of the hotel's manger, Bubukutty Idicalla. Police called the number, and Idicalla told them Todd was staying there. Immediately Sergeant David Smith, Detective Chris Johnson, and Investigators Ricky Murphy and Brant Thompson left for Atlanta. They arrived the next morning, but Todd had already left the motel.

The investigators then met with the U.S. Marshals Service. The group decided to ask the media for help in apprehending the serial killer, knowing that getting his photograph to the public might provide leads to his whereabouts. The FBI agreed to man the phone line the media would provide. Soon the Atlanta Police Fugitive Squad had joined the chase. Police narrowed down the area where Todd had last been seen through the help of local citizens.

They pounded the pavement. They drove police cars down dark alleys shining their spotlights. They showed Todd's picture to everyone they saw. Their vigilance paid off. Within two days of matching Todd's DNA to that of the serial killer's, Todd was spotted in the parking lot of Green's Tire Shop, about 8:45 P.M.

"Let us see some identification," officers from the Atlanta Police Department (APD) ordered.

Todd handed over his driver's license. He did not try to run, did not resist as officers handcuffed him and put him into the backseat of their vehicle. After more than a decade of killing, the South Louisiana Serial Killer had been apprehended without incident.

Smith and Johnson read Todd his Miranda warning at the APD on Ponce de Leon Avenue. Then all of the investigators from Baton Rouge interrogated him, but Todd wasn't feeling especially talkative.

"Y'all might as well go ahead and give me the needle," he said, neither confirming nor denying his guilt throughout the process. At one point, he told Thompson, "I'm closing the book." That was all they got. Todd was booked, fingerprinted, and taken to Fulton County Prison.

The next morning, he waived extradition before Atlanta judicial authorities and was transported to the airport. Todd was escorted home in an FBI jet, accompanied by Thompson and Johnson.

Jackie couldn't believe it. This couldn't be happening. Todd had been arrested in Atlanta. But her husband just couldn't be the serial killer. She didn't know how she was going to tell the children. She asked Jerome to help her.

Jerome called for Derrick Jr. to come talk to his mom. Together, his uncle and mother sat him down and told him his father was in jail. "You should pray for him. Pray that everything will be all right," Jackie said. They didn't explain what Todd had been charged with.

A few minutes later, Derrick was watching television alone when a news bulletin interrupted his program. "The serial killer has been captured," the announcer said, and a picture of the young boy's father flashed before him.

Man, they're spreading my name all over the news, Derrick thought as he watched a scene of his father being led away in handcuffs replay over and over. He called to his mom so she could see. "People think your dad is the serial killer, but don't worry about it," she consoled him.

But Derrick was worried and left the room, going to a computer to search on the Internet for stories about the murders that had happened in Louisiana—stories about horrific murders his dad was accused of committing. He did not believe what he read. His dad was a nice man.

The Interrogation

Todd knew that he was a dead man walking before he was caught. He had it all figured out and had made his peace with it. Todd wanted to die. He sat in the chair quietly fidgeting as Detective Chris Johnson and Department of Justice Investigator Brant Thompson began the interrogation, answering "yes" as each of his rights was read to him. Todd's only restraints were the chains wrapped loosely around his legs. His big hands rubbed his shaved head, sometimes obsessively, as he stared down at his feet. Muscles bulged from beneath the sleeves of his prison-issue shirt. Todd was not comfortable with the white investigator, Thompson. However, Todd had established a rapport with Chris on the plane ride back to Louisiana.

"I don't want my family getting drug through all this shit," Todd told him. "Just leave them alone, because my mom, she got, uh, high blood pressure, bad heart, and my dad, he got high blood pressure and bad heart. And, yeah, they been harassed, you know."

Chris was sympathetic, his strategy to be Todd's friend. Throughout this interview, there would be no crime-scene photos slapped on the table in front of Todd. He would not see the hideousness of his deeds staring back at him. Instead, he would listen as Chris tried to explain what DNA was and how it linked him to the murders.

"Let me tell you something about taking someone's DNA, okay," Chris said politely. "DNA is definite, you know. Like I told you last night, I'm not gonna bullshit you. I'm not gonna lie to you, and I haven't lied to you since I met you, okay? I'm not gonna start today. DNA is some definite signs. It's like no two fingerprints are alike; no other person's DNA, you know, is the same as someone else's. So that's a definite sign somebody is telling me DNA is not correct, I'm gonna call him a liar, you understand?"

Todd fidgeted with his chains while Chris went on.

"Just like you and I discussed about you being on an airplane, you know you was there, right? And you know you're in that chair, and I can't convince you otherwise, okay? Nor can you convince me that the DNA, which we collected and matched with yours, is not correct. You know we got DNA evidence. It's positive."

Todd sat with his arms folded, shoulders hunched over, and head hung. He was shaking his leg as he listened.

Chris went on discussing DNA, how it could convict or exonerate a person. He discussed how people make mistakes and how others can be understanding of those mistakes. "What we want you to know is that everybody has a story to tell. Everybody has a picture to tell. We all know a story and what picture you want somebody to paint of you is . . . depends on you, Derrick, okay? The kind of person you want somebody to see and tell about Derrick Todd Lee is gonna be on you. And I think you owe it to your family and stuff, you know, that you paint the—the best picture you can. Nobody is gonna blame you for making mistakes, okay? Because we all . . . we all fall short. Just like you and I discussed last night. We all fall short."

Todd simply agreed.

"You believe in God, man?"

"Yeah," Todd said.

"You believe in the Bible?"

"Somewhat."

Chris knew that Todd was known for preaching the

Bible to his friends on occasion and tried to use his knowledge of the Bible to persuade Todd to confess. "I'm not here to judge anybody. The Bible also says 'Judge not lest ye be judged,' you know. It's not for me to sit here and judge you. We all have a story, Derrick, and yours can be fascinating. It really is fascinating, you know. I mean, uh, I . . . I guess I shouldn't use that term. There's a lot of answers. And only you can provide. Only you."

Chris went on and on. Todd looked bored at times, nervous at others, as Chris explained again that everyone makes mistakes, but that sometimes a person just has to surrender and tell the truth.

"Yeah, uh-huh, I hear you" were Todd's responses as Chris tried to persuade him to trust him. Todd asked to talk to a lawyer. Feeling Todd's discomfort with Brant, Chris asked the investigator to let him talk to his suspect alone. Todd relaxed a bit.

"You want something to eat?" Chris offered.

"No, uh-uh."

"You straight?"

"Yeah" was Todd's response.

Chris immediately returned to the subject of DNA. "You know what DNA is, right?"

"No, I don't," Todd said.

"Okay, touch this table right here. We could swab that table right there, and DNA profile is in there."

"Uh-huh."

"There's no way you can plant somebody's DNA, this place, that place, that place, and that place. Okay, do you understand that?"

"I hear you."

"Now, we can't—we can't begin to understand a lot of the pieces in that puzzle unless you provide it to me do you understand, really? What I'm saying is that you understand that you were—you were swabbed on May fifth, right?"

Chris touched a nerve.

"Yeah," Todd said before launching into a tirade about the Zachary police. "I was coming from my mama's house, and, uh, I picked up my dog, and I was, I picked up my dog and get ready to go and, uh, pulled in my driveway, and they come from everywhere and blocked me in my driveway 'cause I had to take a DNA test, and I asked them why."

"You took one, right?"

"Yeah, and I asked them why."

"What did they say?" Chris pushed. He had Todd talking.

"And, uh, they didn't say nothing, and, uh, the guy from Zachary, uh . . ."

"Who's that?"

"Ray Day. Um, he come there, and, uh, he was, like, you know, past my house and stuff. Somebody was cutting my grass, my cousin was cutting my grass and stuff. They just walked, told me I had to take a DNA, and I asked them why, and I ain't signed nothin' or nothin'. That what I can't understand. They had a court order, but I ain't . . . they ain't let me sign nothin'."

Todd was just warming up. "And that guy got stuff belongs to me over eight or nine years old. Ray Day. He come and got stuff . . . investigating somethin' about some woman in Zachary. And he had all my stuff and, uh, he came and took some pantses and a couple more items from my house. And then, all a sudden, he getting back involved with this here, and then they coming up telling me about my DNA. That's what got me puzzled."

Chris again tried to explain DNA. "Okay, so they test just, like, a fingerprint, your fingerprint, you know. If it wasn't, let's say your fingerprint was left at a crime scene, any crime scene, anyplace, okay?"

"I understand what you're saying."

"Okay, you understand. They can match it against what was found at the crime scene, as to what you have—"

"But my thing is this here. This what I'm saying," Todd interrupted. "They gave me a court order for my DNA in which I felt, like, I should have signed something and had, you know, because the man here bothering me for eight or nine years. I believe he set me up. How I know what they . . . he lied and told me he took some pantses and some more personal stuff from me, you know, with my stuff, and how I know he ain't just set me up? That's what I'm saying."

"What we know is that, uh, well, first of all, he's not a part of this investigation," Chris said of Ray Day, who had spent so many years investigating the Zachary murders.

Todd reiterated that Ray had come to his house, but Chris refused to debate it, informing him that the Zachary investigation was a separate investigation and not part of the task force. Todd sputtered on about how police had taken his wife's car and had been harassing him for years. The interview went on and on—Chris trying to explain that DNA was irrefutable evidence and Todd complaining about the police. For hours, they sparred. Todd began to enjoy the game. Chris pled with him, for the sake of his family, to confess. Todd came close on a few occasions.

"Y'all got my DNA, what you know, like I told you last night, man, if you got my DNA, you know, hey, you know. Y'all already, you know, you know I'm already convicted, Chris."

Chris decided to use a new tactic, to mention the murders specifically.

Todd denied any knowledge. "It's like this here, I'd rather go ahead and talk to a lawyer. Like I told you, and I'll tell him the same thing. I—I don't want my family drugged through nothin' 'cause like you say, you got five murders there. You said the DNA don't, I mean, the DNA don't lie, and I told you how I felt about it. You understand what I'm saying? I don't know nothin'. I ain't got nothin'

I can tell you. Now, [as] far as you want me to tell you that 'hey, I did it,' I can't tell you that. You see what I'm sayin'?"

And then Todd, this man who had held the lives of so many women in his own hands before stabbing and beating and squeezing the life out of them, apologized for being rude. "I don't mean to be ugly. I don't mean to be rude, but, uh, I'd rather, you know. Y'all gonna take me to court in the morning, if you take me to court in the morning, and the judge appoints me a lawyer 'cause I told him my mama poor. I ain't got nothin'. You say you a black man, you know where they comin' from, so I rather for to go ahead, whoever the judge appoints me, to a lawyer or whatever, and let me and him get together. You know what I'm sayin'?"

Chris knew what Todd was saying and just let him ramble, hoping that something would accidentally spill from his mouth, something damning.

"But I'm just tellin' you I don't want to drag my family into none of this here. Whatever. We go to trial, the jury find me guilty, I take my lick, death row or life or whatever. I done made up my mind, you know, because I've been sittin' back. I ain't tried to run from the law. If I wanted to hide in—in—in Atlanta, I wouldn't even went to work, you know what I'm sayin'? I was associating with everybody, you know, that I ran across. I ain't tried to hide from nobody, but like I say, uh, if that's what y'all got or whatever, let's take it on to court. You know what I'm sayin'? Cause I ain't got no story to tell."

Then Todd began to tell his stories, the ones about how he had lost jobs because of "that mess in Zachary," how he had been dealing with this "the last eight or nine years of my life. Every mornin'. Every day. I woke up, and it's been in me. I don't have no story to tell nobody. This shit been on my mind, this shit. These are things that have been poppin' up, die down, pop up. I get tired of people came in the street, people tellin' the club I go to, people telling, 'Man, the police been here, the FBI, the attorney general been here askin' questions about you.' If I had something to run from, I'da ran years ago when they came out. Like I told, me and my wife, we just say, 'Look, we tired of all this mess.' Now this done come up about the serial killer, and my wife say, 'Watch, you name come up. Watch.' Just like this, she said."

But as he complained about being harassed, Todd knew. Todd knew they had him, but he wasn't about to confess, to give the police the satisfaction of hearing him say it. He just liked to hear himself talk. The roles between him and Chris had reversed. Now it was Chris who sat back and said, "Yeah, right, I understand." And then Todd started talking about his favorite subject, the subject that had entertained friends at work and in the clubs he frequented.

"You know, I done walked around, you just don't know, man. I'm here to tell you, I done walked around, man, with, uh, a lot on my mind, a lot in my heart, bro, a lot of sleepless nights because there were some things I got accused of I know I ain't had nothin' to do with it. I done been in the wrong place at the wrong time, you know, dealing with women. I been dealing with women or done slept with some women. You, uh, you're probably say I'm gonna tell you a lie about [them]. I can bring some women name up, you know, right now, and you probably go and ask them. Say, 'You ever been with Derrick?' They'll tell you no. But I know and that person know, you know what I'm sayin'? I've been with women where I didn't want to get seen, be seen with me in a date, but, like, you know what I'm sayin', I done been there. I remember women, like they high society, and then when they was around they friends, they didn't want their friends to know they were dealing. You know, everybody got their little skeletons in their closet. You know what I'm sayin'? I done been through all that, Chris. I done been with—I done been through all that. You know what I'm sayin'? I done been with some women, where some women tell me, say, 'Lord, if somebody see you here, they'll—they'll ask me what's wrong with me.' I done been through all that in my life."

It was the closest we will probably ever get to an explanation of why Todd did the things he did and chose the women he chose—"high society" women who didn't want to be seen with him. Perhaps it had been only one in his distant past, that one rejection that hurt his ego, fueled his rage. Perhaps it had been the cousins whom he had violated by peeping into their windows; perhaps a girl at school, one who wouldn't give him a second look. But whatever the trigger, rejection had been a sickness that ate at him and stirred him to seek out and destroy those who did not want him. And all of the money that he once had, the gold chains and fancy clothes he had worn, the expensive vehicles that he drove, couldn't buy him their approval, couldn't make him acceptable. And so Todd hated with a passion that drove him to rape, to kill. And now he wanted only to die.

Chris asked Todd if he still wanted to talk to an attorney or if he wanted to continue. Todd kept talking.

"Either way it go, when I'm dead asleep in my grave, buried up there in St. Francisville, it's gonna be on a lot of people's minds. 'I wonder, did this man . . . I wonder, did he do this? I wonder, did he do that?' People always gonna a'wonder for the rest of they lives about me, you know what I'm sayin'? But I don't want nobody bustin' my cherry. It's just like I told my wife, uh, you know, like my son, like I told her, all I want her to do, just get his name changed, you know. Ain't gotta change his last name, just get it changed, his first name. You know, like Dedrick."

Todd rambled on. "I ain't got the puzzle, the pieces of

the puzzle to unwonder they mind. You know what I'm sayin'? And I ain't gonna come in here, and the DA can come in here right now and say 'Lee, we'll cut a deal with you.' I'm not takin' no deal because I don't know nothin'. Do you understand what I'm sayin'? I'd rather the DA come here right now [and say], 'Would you rather go on death, you rather be on death, you rather go ahead and die, huh?' That's the way I'm feeling, just like that, just like that."

Hours passed during which Chris discussed the FBI profile and the murders. He told Todd there were other missing women, that his family would want him to do the right thing.

Soon Mary Ellen O'Toole, the FBI profiler, entered the room. Todd immediately perked up, his demeanor changing to that of a polite young man, a man to whom any woman would respond. O'Toole explained that she felt like she knew him and tried to get him to talk to her. Sticking to his guns, Todd repeatedly told her that he had no story to tell. He explained that he had made his peace with God.

"I'm gonna be honest with you. I ain't even gonna, I won't have no fear in my, I won't have no fear. I'm gonna be honest with you. Wherever they, the day we go to court, they come back, they say, 'Lee, we give you the death penalty, for, what you say, five, five murders.' You give me the death penalty. They can electrocute me up. They can electrocute me up the same day. Like I told, I done dealed with God, my heart and my mind is made up. Media all that, the . . . you know, I ain't gonna get no fair crack, you know. The only thing I ask is that, uh, like you say, you know, about my children. Me and you talked about that earlier," Todd said, looking at Chris. "About my three kids. You know what I'm sayin'? You know, that they have a better life, and maybe they can keep they nose cleaner than I kept mine. You know, I pray to God on that. You know, don't nobody judge them because of what they daddy may have done."

"What did he do?" Chris seized the opportunity that statement provided, but Todd wasn't biting.

"You know what I'm sayin'."

"What did you do?"

"I'm talkin' about you say you got my, uh, what—that DNA? You know, being judged by DNA, right or wrong."

"Right, but what—"

"And what I'm sayin' is this here. Maybe nobody, maybe, you know, my children, maybe, I just pray to God that they can have a better life than I had."

"Right, I understand," Chris said.

"That's what I'm sayin'. Just pray to God about that. You know what I'm sayin'? I don't have no story. I ain't gonna come here and tell you and say, 'Chris, I got five different stories to tell you.' I don't have the closed book. I don't have it. The book closed. The chapter closed."

"You know, you know someone's gonna tell that story, huh, Todd?"

"Can't nobody. How can somebody tell the story when they don't know the story? You can't go and check from here to Egypt. Can't nobody tell a story when they don't know—know the story. Can't nobody tell the story, if there's a story. Only me can tell it, and the good Lord. You see what I'm sayin'?"

Chris knew that he would get no more out of Todd. Mary Ellen knew it too, but they tried for a while longer. Todd had said what he wanted to say. He knew it was over. He knew that he would die for what he had done, and he was convinced that his God had forgiven him. He was at peace.

"When Chris ain't around, when all this trial, all this publicity die out, the media gone, where God gonna be? Still right there. You know what I mean. Just like I told you, man. They decide they want to give me death row, you know, and I'm layin' down, bro, all I see is they looking through me at the curtain, looking through me, you know what I'm sayin'? Looking at me, if it turn out that way, and they looking at me, Lord God know my heart, you know what I'm sayin'? I ain't worried about it no more. My mind, I hope you'll respect that. My mind made up."

And though the interrogation went on until everyone in the room was tired of hearing the same things over and over, no progress was made. Todd's mind was made up. At one point, he did ask Mary Ellen what white woman would let a black man into her house, emphasizing that would not happen in the South, but that was the only real effort he made to defend himself.

As Chris and Mary Ellen rose to leave the room, Todd gave a small glimpse into how he had achieved just that very thing.

As he rose to tell Mary Ellen good-bye, a slight swagger appeared in Todd's walk. He smiled broadly and shook her hand. "Ms. Mary Ellen, it was a pleasure to meet you."

"You're an interesting man, Todd. It's an interesting case."

"I been told that a lot in my life." The smile got bigger, the swagger more pronounced, the friendliness almost eerie. Todd was once again in his element—trying to charm the ladies—only this time, he had no way to follow the lady home.

Many police officers wished that Baton Rouge homicide detective Keith Bates and East Baton Rouge Parish sheriff's detective David "Wolf" Denicola had been sent to Atlanta to pick up Todd. Bates was considered to be the best homicide detective Baton Rouge had on its police force, and Denicola, known for his toughness, had recently cracked a major murder case in only two days. Yet neither detective had been assigned to the task force.

It was politics as usual. Bates was planning to make a run for chief of police, and Denicola had been let go from the Baton Rouge Police Department for his sometimes questionable tactics. The sheriff's office had snapped him up. Just about everyone in law enforcement believed that had these two detectives been sent to escort Todd on the plane ride back to Louisiana, they would have come back with not only a confession, but with the location of the missing bodies.

Others thought West Baton Rouge sheriff's detective Richard Johnson should have made that trip. He was known to be a top-notch interrogator, and in his career had traveled as far away as Bangkok to teach police officers his successful methods. However, it wasn't to be.

As Chris Johnson pussyfooted around with Todd in the interrogation, the families of the missing victims found themselves waiting once again, wondering if their loved ones would finally be found. Their answer would not come from Todd.

The Aftermath

Like a cool breeze on a sunny spring day, a wave of relief swept down the bayou. The darkness had lifted. The South Louisiana Serial Killer was in custody. It seemed that it was safe once again to smile at strangers. It was safe to open windows and doors to feel the last remnants of spring before the searing heat of summer set in. Women no longer had to worry about being followed. They did not have to peer this way and that before getting into their cars. They no longer needed a male escort to walk them through the darkness. Residents in Louisiana could once again let their natural friendliness guide their actions.

But for many, healing did not come so easily. Todd had taught the women of Louisiana a harsh lesson—you are never safe, not in your homes, not on your walks, not in your cars, not anywhere. At any time, a man could grab you, rape you, kill you. Pepper spray stayed attached to key chains. Small handguns stayed in purses. Doors remained locked. Fear had become ingrained.

Members of the task force assured residents that all was well and everyone could relax. They did not warn them that two other serial killers were still lurking in the shadows. They wanted to alleviate the fear that had been so palpable for so long.

At a huge press conference held at Louisiana State

Police Headquarters on May 28, Mayor-President Bobby Simpson congratulated sixty-five agencies, which had participated in the investigation, on a job well done. An obviously relieved Pat Englade bowed his head as tears overcame the big man. Simpson defended the task force, saying that everyone owed them a debt of gratitude. He called the task force "cutting-edge." No one mentioned the attorney general's office. No one mentioned Dannie Mixon.

"The task force was purely political and media-driven. I will go to my deathbed saying that," Dannie said. "When Bobby Simpson was asked why he didn't mention the attorney general's office, he said, 'I forgot.' They had always refused our offers of help. Bobby Simpson put everything on the chief of police and rolled the dice. He rolled craps."

Within two weeks, Dannie would present the task force with his victim homicide analysis, which would be used to create a timeline of Todd's life. All of the information he had gathered through years of old-fashioned detective work would help to build the case against Todd.

Police, meanwhile, began digging, searching for Randi Mebruer's body. They dug up a five-by-five-foot area of concrete at an old farmhouse where Consandra once lived. Near Jackson, where Todd and Consandra lived together, a concrete parking area was also dug up. Eventually they would drain a creek where Todd liked to fish. They had no luck. To date, Randi's body is still missing. Her family is still waiting for the day they can give her a proper burial.

The families of the other victims, who had long since buried their loved ones, experienced a plethora of emotions upon hearing the news that the man who had brought such sadness to their lives was in custody. All were relieved, but mixed with that relief were anger and bitterness that he wasn't caught sooner, perhaps in time to save some lives. The public celebrated Todd's capture with the families. Through the media, everyone in South Louisiana had come to know the victims, to care about them. They knew the faces of their families. They had watched Ann Pace cry. They had followed Lynne Marino's fight with the task force. They had attended the sometimes heated, sometimes heart-wrenching rallies on the capitol steps. They were angry about what had happened to these innocent people. And as information about Todd's criminal history began to emerge, that anger accelerated. Everyone wanted to know *why.*

Why did the task force focus only on white men for so long? Why hadn't this career criminal been behind bars, instead of out killing women? How many of his victims died needlessly? Many felt that Dené Colomb, Mari Ann Fowler, and Carrie Lynn Yoder's deaths could have been prevented had the task force followed up on the information they had received about Todd throughout the investigation. They had swabbed about twelve hundred white men, many solely on the basis of owning a white pickup truck. Todd's name and criminal record had been repeatedly brought to the attention of the police. Why hadn't he been swabbed?

And then there was the biggest question of all: how many more women had Todd killed? At the time of his arrest, he had been linked by DNA to five: Gina, Murray, Pam, Dené, and Carrie. Police around the South began to test Todd's DNA against their unsolved murders, in Atlanta, in Mississippi, in Alabama, in Arkansas. In the Baton Rouge area alone, more than sixty unsolved murders had occurred in the past two decades. Two of them were about to be solved.

On May 30, just days after Todd's arrest, fingernail clippings from Geralyn DeSoto were hand-delivered to ReliaGene Technologies in New Orleans. ReliaGene received a sample of Todd's DNA on June 11. His DNA could not be excluded as the DNA under Geralyn's fingernails.

The victim count went to six.

Dannie Mixon waited anxiously for the results of the lab tests on the evidence in the Randi Mebruer case. But it would be February 2004 before he got those results. Semen on the trash can liner came back a match to Todd. On February 11, another warrant was issued for Todd's arrest for first-degree murder.

Seven.

David McDavid was ecstatic. After all the years he had spent chasing Todd, he finally had something concrete to link him to Randi's murder. But he had possessed that evidence all along. A simple DNA test in 1998 could have saved the lives of all the victims killed after that date.

"In the late 1990s, DNA testing cost around five or six thousand dollars, and it was best-guess results back then," said Sid Newman, of Baton Rouge Crime Stoppers. "Now it's a couple hundred bucks."

That does explain why DNA testing wasn't done on the evidence in Randi's case, but it is little consolation to those who lost loved ones to Todd's brutality. In retrospect, any one of those families would have happily paid for that test in 1998.

That wasn't the only time that cost factored into the Derrick Todd Lee equation. In 1997, a new law was passed by the Louisiana Legislature that required that DNA profiles be taken when suspects are arrested for a crime. In September 2001, just days after Gina Green was killed, Jackie filed a complaint with the West Feliciana Parish Sheriff's Office stating that Todd had hit her in the head and twisted her arms. He was arrested for simple battery. By law, his DNA profile should have been taken and put into a database.

But in September 2001, funding was not yet available to enforce that law, so Todd's profile wasn't taken and the database wasn't operational until August 2002. Again, the opportunity to stop Todd from killing was ignored due to financial concerns.

"When Lynne Marino came into the picture, she wasn't going to let it go. Through her persistence, we got the task force, new DNA legislations, and now convicted felons get tested for DNA," Sid said. "She slammed law enforcement. Did they need slamming? Well, I don't know, but some of her stuff was accurate. She forced everyone to work toward a solution."

Lynne would continue to slam the task force, and the more she learned about the investigation and the number of times Todd could have been caught or should have been in prison, the angrier she got. She wasn't the only one.

"This thing took its toll," explained Sid. "There were so many unknowns. The community had a lack of trust. Everybody died—the victims, their families, the whole community, the police. Everybody died."

Dannie Mixon felt like he was among the dead. At the end of his long career in law enforcement, when he should have been relishing his greatest accomplishment, he was being overlooked for aesthetic reasons. Simply put, Dannie was not the most beautiful of men. He was stout, wore large wire-rimmed glasses, and had hearing difficulties. Because of that, Dannie talked loudly at times, especially when he was trying to make a point or when he was upset. And Dannie was always trying to make a point.

"I do rant and rave sometimes, I know." He shrugged. "I got my man, though. But after his capture, the public relations people at the AG's office gave me a quiz. They told me what I could and couldn't say. They thought I was too old to talk to the media. It was political. My boss, Richard Ieyoub, was running for governor and didn't want to run his campaign based on this case, so they kept me away from the media. I should have been on a high, but I was very depressed. I went into a shell. I didn't know which way to turn."

Task force members also didn't know which way to turn. They were asked questions they couldn't answer. They were swept up in a media circus, from which there was no escape. Police officers who had been friends for many years no longer spoke to each other. The competition to catch the killer, to get the glory, had been fierce, and the investigation had brought out the worst in many officers. Heated arguments over which leads to follow, what could be said to the media, who should be doing what, had caused feelings to be hurt beyond repair. But the ordeal had brought out the best in others. Many men and women had dedicated themselves solely to this investigation for more than a year, and though they had been unsuccessful, they were to be commended for their service to the community. Each had learned hard lessons that would never be forgotten.

The task force's inability to adequately defend itself resulted in a collective silence, a refusal to talk about what had happened. So the questions remained unanswered, and mistrust of law enforcement grew.

It would take years to heal the wounds Todd had inflicted upon a whole community, a culture whose love of making merry with strangers had been erased. And for the families of the victims, the hardest part of it all was about to commence—not one, but two trials, where they would have to relive every detail, every photograph, every horrifying moment of what Todd had done to their loved ones. For them, the tragedy just went on and on.

Tony Clayton

It was September 2003, and Special Prosecutor Antonio (Tony) Tony Clayton, West Baton Rouge Parish sheriff Mike Cazes, and Detective Brian Doucet gathered in a daiquiri shop in Port Allen to discuss Derrick Todd Lee. Mike and Brian wanted Tony to prosecute Geralyn De-Soto's case in West Baton Rouge Parish, but Tony wasn't so sure. From what he knew, Y-STR had never been tested before a jury, and much of the evidence was circumstantial. He knew they had a boot and a knife. But that was all he knew.

"Just look over the file," Mike persuaded.

"Nobody wants to try this, but we know Lee did it," Brian added. "Will you take a look at it?"

Tony committed. The next day, another detective called and said that he had heard Tony had agreed to try the case. "I was drinking, man," Tony said, laughing. But by December, Todd had been indicted for second-degree murder. Tony was always good to his word, and this case had special meaning for him. He and Todd had grown up similarly, and Geralyn had been murdered in Addis, just down Highway 1 from the home where Tony had been raised.

* * *

Like Todd, Tony had three siblings, Don, Millette, and Arndrill, with whom he was very close. But unlike Todd, Tony was not the fair-haired child. He had been born an ugly baby. His father, Ernest, insisted that he was the ugliest baby alive. But his great-grandmother Clara, whom everyone called Hun, would always defend him. "Bring that baby boy to me. All my grandbabies are beautiful on the inside," she would say indignantly. Hun helped to raise him through the first six years of his life, and when she died, Tony told his first lie to his mother just to have a keepsake of his beloved Hun.

"She had a tin box with a roller on the side. When you turned the roller, a monkey popped out. I loved playing with that monkey, so when Grandma died, I told my mom that she wanted me to have it," Tony recalled. "But every time I looked at that box after that, I was reminded of my lie. It wasn't a good feeling."

Of his siblings, Tony had the darkest skin. Ernest was descended from the Creole people—to his family's way of thinking that meant black mixed with white. Many Creoles in South Louisiana don't acknowledge the common definition for Creole, which is black mixed with French and Spanish. In the hierarchy, if you are Creole, you are still black. The mulattos were the ones who looked whiter and didn't like to acknowledge their black heritage. But in those days in Southern Louisiana, being regular black was at the top of the social hierarchy, and Tony, with his deep brown skin, looked like a regular black.

Like Todd, Tony was raised surrounded by an abundance of extended family—aunts, uncles, and cousins who all participated in the rearing of the younger ones in the family. His father was the disciplinarian and would not hesitate to "beat my butt when I did something wrong," Tony said. "He's a black Archie Bunker and gave me more butt-whippings than Kellogg's has Corn Flakes."

His mother, Clara, was spirited and very intelligent. She was a nurse, and Tony's dad worked on the railroad.

Between them, they made a good living for their family, but back then, Ernest liked to gamble on occasion, sometimes his whole paycheck. Clara, a small, beautiful woman, with long black hair and a mocha-chocolate complexion, was not only intelligent but calculating to a degree. She often anticipated her husband's actions and would go into his wallet on payday and remove what money she would need to care for the family, leaving him to do as he wished with the rest. Clara loved her children and pampered them. She tried to teach them right from wrong and could often be heard saying, "God bless the child who has his own," instilling into her children that it was important to earn one's way through this life. She kept the kids in line by saying, "I'm gonna tell your dad when he gets home." All of the children knew what that meant and had a healthy respect for their father. But they also knew that he loved them.

Born in 1963, Tony started school at the height of integration. He had been taught, like Todd, to stay away from the white women as "they'll scream rape and get you in trouble." But unlike Todd, Tony heeded the warnings. He loved the black girls and began to have sex at an early age. "I remember this one girl my cousins told me I should have sex with. I was scared of her because she had all this hair on her arms," Tony recalled, wrinkling his nose. "It was almost enough to curb my appetite for the ladies. Almost."

But whereas Todd's obsession with women led him to become a Peeping Tom, the girls were always attracted to Tony's booming laughter and flamboyant personality. And he liked the attention, his antics sometimes getting him into trouble. But Tony had the ever-present threat of a whipping when he got home to keep him somewhat in check. That threat forced him to do well in school, even though he wasn't the most dedicated of students.

This unfamiliar world where black and white children were forced to study together, to play together at recess, was a difficult adjustment for Tony. He had grown up near Chuck's Lounge, where blacks had to go to the back window to buy liquor and were not allowed to mingle with the whites. He can remember the stories his mom and dad told him about the time Civil Rights activist James Forman came to town to give a speech at the Plymouth Rock Baptist Church. State troopers soon descended on the church to break up the rally, beating several men in the process. Forman was hidden in a coffin and whisked from the Good Citizens Funeral Home in a hearse, right under the troopers' noses. So this world into which Tony entered school was far from the one in which he had been raised. Suddenly it was okay to mingle with whites, but for most of his early school years, like many blacks, Tony kept his distance, scarred by the stories he had heard.

While many of the black children, like Todd, were placed into special education classes, Tony went into the gifted program and did well throughout his school years. By the time he reached high school in the late 1970s, his vision of the world had changed. Blacks were no longer being treated like second-class citizens, and many of his friends now were white. But still, he would not have dreamed of dating a white girl. That was against the rules. By this time, Todd had begun to follow them, excited by their fair skin and shiny hair, enraged by their rejection of him.

When Tony reached college age, a decision had to be made. Most of the men in his culture did not go to college. They went into fields that required hard labor to feed their families. It was the black women who had the advantage of furthering their education. But Tony was determined, wanting to prove that he could do it, that he was as smart as anyone and could have a good life. He entered Southern University in 1982 and earned his bachelor's degree in political science. By the time he met the lady who would change his life, Tony, the ladies' man, had fathered four children, all of whom he loved, and he knew he must continue his education to be able to support them properly. But he didn't know which field would be best for him to pursue.

Then he met Paula. There is no altruistic reason why Tony decided to become a lawyer. He did it simply to impress a girl and, in the process, found his true calling. "Paula was in undergraduate school, and she liked a guy who was in law school," he explained. "This guy was nice-looking and had a car. He was pushing me out. I knew if I wanted to get her, I had to go to law school."

Tony graduated from Southern with his Juris Doctor in 1991, with dreams of big money dancing in his head. "I thought I would represent some drug dealers and make some cash money. Instead, my mentor, Jesse Stone, told me to go down to the courthouse to the DA's office. I met Doug Moreau there, and we connected on the spot. I just loved him. Doug made me a strong man, and Dr. Stone made me a wise man. I decided to become a prosecutor instead, thinking I could make a name for myself."

And Tony spent the next years doing just that. He worked as an assistant district attorney (ADA) for East Baton Rouge Parish in the early- to mid-1990s before being appointed as a judge for the Nineteenth Judicial District Court. In 1999, Tony became the special prosecutor for East Baton Rouge Parish, where he earned a reputation for being hard core, for taking on the cases no one else wanted—murder cases committed by black men who had grown up like him, but had gone bad. Soon he and Paula, who had earned her law degree, opened their own firm, becoming partners in law and also partners in their journey through life. The two married and had a son, T.J., who helped inspire Tony to greater heights.

* * *

By the summer of 2002, as Todd was spreading terror throughout Baton Rouge, Tony's reputation for prosecuting and winning murder cases was firmly established. After a multitude of trials, his prosecutorial record was unblemished. He had not lost a single case and had placed several men on death row for their hideous crimes. He had learned the art of argument early, from being in a big family where brothers and sisters and cousins squabbled over toys constantly and argued their cases before their parents.

And Pearline Williams, who lived just down the crowded street in Addis, with her seventeen children who would beat Tony up and take his lunch money on the way to school, helped as well. Tony had learned to be a fighter, to argue his point, to be persuasive and charming. Juries loved him. The ugly baby had grown into a handsome man, big and authoritative, with laughing eyes and a flamboyant style. His sense of humor always came across in the way that he loved to taunt his opponents, deliberately upsetting them to cause them to make mistakes. His courtroom antics were theatrical at times, but always with a purpose. Tony was there to win. He was representing the people, the victims whose lives had been taken unfairly from them by men of his skin color, men who made him ashamed. And Derrick Todd Lee upset him more than most.

By the time he had that meeting in the daiquiri shop, Tony was already very familiar with the case. As special prosecutor, he had worked with investigators and prosecutors in the numerous jurisdictions where murders had been committed, and he had prayed along with everyone else that whoever was killing these innocent women would be caught soon. He, too, thought the perpetrator was white. No black man would ever commit so many horrific murders. Black men killed in robberies or drug deals gone bad. They beat their wives when they talked back too much, sometimes to death. They didn't stalk and rape and kill numerous victims. But, like so many others, Tony was wrong.

In the case of Geralyn DeSoto, Tony had agreed with the other detectives. Darren DeSoto was the murderer. He had abused the girl. It made sense. When DNA came back a match to Todd, Tony was shocked. Todd's crimes became even more personal. This murder had taken place just down the road from his mother's home. Todd had driven the same road looking for victims that Tony had ridden his bike on throughout his childhood. This was a beautiful young girl studying hard at LSU to make her dreams come true. It was then that Tony knew if he was asked, he would prosecute Todd, pulling out all the stops to put this evil behind bars forever.

But many wondered why Todd even needed to be prosecuted in West Baton Rouge Parish, as authorities had made it clear that Todd would be prosecuted in East Baton Rouge Parish for the murder of Charlotte Murray Pace. "Insurance," Tony said. "I thought about the possibility that he might get off, due to some technicality or other. It happens all the time. I decided to try him for second-degree murder for Geralyn DeSoto. I could not go for the death penalty because there was no underlying felony, like rape or kidnapping. I told East Baton Rouge, 'I'll get him life. You get him death.' That way, I knew that if he somehow managed to get off in East Baton Rouge, he would still have to spend the rest of his life in prison. It was simply a little insurance."

It was unprecedented to have a murder trial in Louisiana within eight months of an indictment, but that is exactly what happened. The public was eager to see this man punished for the fear he had instilled into a whole population. Judge Robin Free was more than happy to accommodate both the prosecution and defense to ensure that Todd's right to a speedy trial was fulfilled. The supreme court kept the motion for a continuance until the eve of the trial, then came back at five in the afternoon—"Motion denied." Tony was in an airport in North Carolina when he got the call. He got a sudden case of the butterflies as the responsibility he had to the victims' families hit him.

A packed courtroom on a blazing hot August day in Port Allen, Louisiana, marked the significance of the event—the most sensational trial ever to be held in the West Baton Rouge Parish Courthouse. The fight was on—the biggest fight of both Tony's and Todd's lives.

The Trial for Life

The parish courthouse in the Eighteenth Judicial District in Port Allen, Louisiana, was much too small to host the five hundred people who had been summoned, then questioned, as Todd's lead attorney, Tommy Thompson, and Prosecutor Tony Clayton struggled to find an impartial jury in an area that had been so affected by the serial killings. The proceedings were held in the Tourist Information Center, which was surrounded by sheriff's deputies. Judge Robin Free presided over jury selection, and at one point dismissed a fourteen-member panel of potential jurors due to a comment made by a woman concerning media coverage of the other killings of which Todd was accused.

Jury selection took three days, and although defense attorney Tommy Thompson had argued for a change of venue in the second-degree murder trial of Derrick Todd Lee, he had been unsuccessful. Free, a good-looking and friendly state district judge who had been elected to his post in 1996, did not agree that the trial should be moved, opting instead for a gag order. No cameras would be allowed into the trial. Nor would the jury be sequestered.

Todd's demeanor during pretrial motions had fluctuated from laughing at jokes to belligerence. That would be the pattern throughout the trial, as Todd, seemingly unconcerned with his fate at times, moved between extreme politeness and unexpected outbursts. Those in the courtroom watched Todd's moods change from day to day as Free's relaxed courtroom environment allowed for his antics. During breaks, Todd was allowed to walk around the front of the courtroom, accompanied by a guard and equipped with a stun device around his leg.

As the trial commenced at one o'clock in the afternoon on August 5, 2004, Todd was represented by attorneys Tommy Thompson, Paul Pendley, and Yolanda Batiste, an experienced team with the public defender's office.

District Attorney Ricky Ward, Antonio Clayton, Becky Chustz, Dana Larpenteur, and Ali Shields made up the prosecution. Chester Cedars, a prosecutor from St. Martin Parish, would be allowed to question witnesses during the part of the trial in which Diane Alexander would testify. Her case, in a Prieur motion, would be allowed into the trial, as would testimony about Dené Colomb's death. The families of most of Todd's victims sat in the courtroom to watch as he was tried for the murder of Geralyn DeSoto. All were anxious about the outcome.

Tony was nervous. He had stayed up most of the night before, putting the final tweaks on his opening statement. He was famous for being dramatic—and the facts he would present to the jury, which consisted of five white men, five white women, one Hispanic man, and one black man, were more dramatic than usual. He knew he had to win them over in the first few minutes of the trial.

Tony introduced himself and Becky Chustz to the jury and then described Todd as a cold-blooded murderer. He gave the jury a preview of what to expect. He talked about Diane Alexander, about how Todd had come to her door, then rushed her into the house. Tony grabbed himself around the neck to demonstrate what had happened as he told the jury what Todd had said. "'Show me the bedroom.

I'm going to fuck you!' She says, 'Just do it here, right here on the floor.' He throws her on the floor, beats the living daylights out of her, beats her, beats her with the phone, just beating her. She will tell you that she was lackadaisical. Just punching her, beating her. She's going in and out. Nobody is at that house, but him and her. He has his clothes off, and what's he going to do to her? He's going to show her who's the man, but he can't get an erection. He can't get it up. It's July. He's sweating."

Tony told the jury he had the dress with Diane's blood and Todd's sweat to show to them. He explained that DNA had been taken from the sweat on the dress, but that forensics experts had only been able to pull five markers from it, one of which was an unusual marker, a marker Todd possessed.

He moved on to Geralyn. He described her sense of humor. He outlined what she had done that morning on January 14, 2002. He talked about the phone call that had been placed from her home at 11:51 A.M. to an Exxon plant where Todd had worked. He demonstrated how Geralyn had fought, how she had run for the shotgun she knew was in the bedroom.

"Let me tell you, this little woman put up a fight. Wait until you see those pictures. She's fighting. He grabs her. Stand up, Mrs. Chustz—she's still fighting—excuse me for what I'm about to do to you, Mrs. Chustz. I won't hurt you." Tony reenacted what had happened to Geralyn, with him playing the role of Todd and the ADA as Geralyn. "She's fighting him back. And you're going to see from the autopsy photos, the stab wounds, that they're fighting so much. She attempts to run—twice in the back, stabs her in the back, she's still fighting. He grabs her by the left arm."

Tony was still demonstrating the attack as he spoke. The jury was riveted. "Stabs her here, stabs her. When he slides that knife out of her right breast that last time, he takes it from ear to ear, ear to ear, almost decapitates her. He cuts the trachea. He even goes back to the C-seven bone. At that time, they are still fighting."

Tony got an easel and a large pad.

Thompson interrupted. "Excuse me, Judge. I'd appreciate it if he would leave my evidence alone."

"It's not yours," Tony responded.

"Oh, I'm sorry," Thompson said.

"I'm sure you are." There was no love lost between these two attorneys.

Tony continued describing Geralyn's last moments, mimicking Todd's attack, still using Chustz as his model. He showed the jury photographs of where Geralyn had fallen, how her last act was to grab for her throat as it was spewing blood everywhere. "When she dies, she dies right here," he said, pointing. "And he's back here, and he has to leave. When he walks out"—Tony stomped his foot powerfully—"stomps her, and goes on with his life."

Melanie and John Barr sat silently, cringing inside, as they watched and listened to what had happened to their young daughter.

Tony explained that DNA had been discovered under Geralyn's fingernails and that the Y chromosomes had been extracted. Three male DNA profiles had been discovered, he said. One of them was Darren DeSoto's, one was John Barr's. Y-STR had eliminated 99.6 percent of the world's male population. Todd was in the 0.4 percent of the population who could not be excluded.

"And let me tell you about that little small percentage—0.4 percent—it could be any male in his family. It could be his brother. It could be his daddy or it could be his male first cousin—just like Thomas Jefferson when they looked for his DNA. It's the Lees' DNA. It's Derrick Todd Lee's DNA.

"So I said to myself—'Self, I need to bring something else of evidence to this jury.' So we took the markers from Dené Colomb. Do you remember the murder toward Lafayette? We took his Y chromosome to see who that hits. Remember, he has special, peculiar markings that are rarely ever seen. And they will tell you how many millions and billions when you see that. When they did Dené Colomb, guess who it hits on? Matches ol' Derrick Todd Lee, the murderer in this case."

Tony described how Darren DeSoto had phoned Geralyn during the attack. "I'm going to tell you right now, I don't like Darren DeSoto, and I don't think he likes me. Darren DeSoto, you will find, was extremely possessive, jealous, the whole nine yards. I have a whole lot more to tell you about Darren, and I'm going to wrap up with him."

Tony moved on to the boot prints found at the scene. He told the jury that the boots were a Wolverine brand, like the ones that were found at Consandra's house. He explained that they were found a year and a half after the crime and had experienced wear and tear on the sides during that time. He talked about how Todd had gone to Dow Chemical, just up Highway 1 from Geralyn's home, that day. Tony brought up the knife that had been found in Todd's Ford Explorer, which had been repossessed. He mentioned how sharp that knife had been when it was originally found in the vehicle. He told the jury that he would call Todd's son to the stand to identify it.

Tony was ready to wrap it up with Darren. "I suspect you will hear a whole lot of people from the trailer park—'Yeah, Darren was a mean guy, and Darren beat his wife.' He did. And, you know, Darren is going to have to answer to his God for that. But Darren did not kill his wife. If he had done so, I'd be right here, standing up here, proving the case against him. He didn't do it. So prepare yourself for Darren bashing, because I'm going to do a little of it too. Bash him all day long, but the bottom line is do not get deflected from my man over here"—Tony pointed to Todd—"the person who, January the fourteenth, took it upon himself, anointed himself God, to suck the life out of those folks' child— because he could. He cut her throat, stabbed her in the side three times, stabbed her in her back two times, and cut her from [one] ear to the other, because he was Derrick Todd Lee, and he could do it.

"Folks, at the conclusion of the evidence, come back and tell him, 'Mr. Derrick Todd Lee, you're guilty of the murder of Geralyn DeSoto.' And remember one thing— he had to show Geralyn DeSoto that he was the man by hitting her. He had to show Diane Alexander that he was the man by beating her. Show him who the man is. Show him who the man is at the close of this case."

Tony was smart. He had chosen to speak in language to which the jury could relate. Made up of a construction worker, a processor at a chemical plant, a housewife, a man retired from Dow, and a lady who worked for an insurance company, among others, the jury comprised average, everyday people, many blue-collar workers.

It was Thompson's turn. He informed the jury immediately that the prosecution wasn't at the scene, in an effort to counteract Tony's reenactment. "Let's make no mistake about it. A tragedy occurred in this case a little over two and a half years ago when a young girl in the prime of her life, Geralyn DeSoto, was murdered brutally. Nobody disputes that. And my heart goes out to her family. I've got four daughters myself. I want to make sure that we don't expound on that tragedy and create another tragedy. I want to make sure we have all of the evidence and the decision y'all reach is the right one."

Thompson talked about the witnesses who would contradict the state's evidence. He told the jury to remember the number 99.6, to remember the telephone call, the work boots, the date—January 15—that Todd had cashed his check, that Darren slapped his wife. Thompson's opening argument was short, to the point. He reminded jurors that they had promised they would be fair and impartial.

"I ask you to use your good hearts and your good minds and to come to a just and fair conclusion in this trial. Thank you."

Opening arguments did not last an hour. The court recessed before the state called its first witness—Diane Alexander.

Todd smiled at his family as they returned to the courtroom. Sitting at the defense table, wearing gray pants, a white shirt, and a tie, he looked more like an attorney than a serial killer.

Diane approached the stand and sat in the witness chair, where she could easily see the man who had attacked her more than two years before, the man she had tried so hard to forget. Mechanically she described for the jury the events that had transpired that day. Answering Cedars's questions calmly and succinctly, Diane studiously avoided looking at Todd. Cedars introduced pictures of Diane's home into evidence and asked her to identify them while she told her story. She described how Todd had tried to rape her, how he had beat her, and had tried to strangle her.

"It's like he showed no emotion, you know, he was, like, there for—like he had a purpose. He had a mission," Diane said.

Diane told the jury that Todd had told her not to move while he took off his shirt. "'I'm not going to do you anything, just stay where you are. I'm just going to change my shirt.'" Diane described how Todd had looked for something, then tried to strangle her, how she had wedged her finger between the cord and her neck. "I have no idea how many times he hit me. I only remember the first blow," she said.

* * *

Thompson questioned Diane about the composite she had made with Detective Arthur Boyd and how she had asked to make a change a year later.

"The profile analyst, Mary Ellen O'Toole, and the sheriff's department, they all got together, which Detective Boyd came and spoke with me and said the task force and some people that were working on the case wanted to speak to me. And in the process of speaking with Mary Ellen O'Toole, I mentioned to her that the only difference about the first composite is the hairline, because it came a little lower, but the computer did not have one available to make that correction," Diane said.

Thompson asked her what date she had made the change. The answer was May 22, 2003. Diane identified Todd in a lineup, May 26. Thompson hoped the jury would deduce that she had made the change after she had seen a photograph of Todd, that perhaps someone in the task force had shown her one.

Tommy Thompson would later ask Detective Boyd what kind of car Diane's son, Herman, had initially described to police. "He described a Mitsubishi Mirage," Boyd said.

"And what kind of car is that that you just saw?"

"A Hyundai Accent."

"And how many doors does that car have you've just seen?"

"That car has two doors, sir."

"How many doors did he say the car he saw had?"

"Four doors."

Thompson moved on to the composite drawing Boyd had completed with Diane, still trying to cast doubt on how it came to resemble Todd.

When Boyd stepped down, the court recessed for the day.

Tony was pleased with the way everything had gone. He was anxious that his evidence would not be enough to convince jurors of Todd's guilt, but he had watched them all day and could see that they had liked Diane. That was good. Although he may have been too dramatic in opening, they had gotten his point. He wanted them to feel the pain that this helpless girl had felt. He wanted justice for her. He wanted Todd to pay.

Geralyn's Abuser and Her Killer

The second day of the trial would reveal what Geralyn's life had been like before Todd came through her door. Bridget Drumm told jurors about the interview Geralyn had scheduled with her at two-thirty that afternoon. She explained how she had called, and no one had answered the phone. John Martin, a security manager for Bellsouth, discussed the phone call made from Geralyn's phone that morning. Stephen Bradford, Geralyn's neighbor, identified photographs of the crime scene.

Tension in the courtroom elevated as Darren DeSoto took the stand. By the time Tony Clayton and Tommy Thompson finished with him, Darren would admit to the world how he had abused the pretty young girl he had vowed to love forever. Each lawyer had his own agenda. Tony's was to create sympathy for Geralyn and to show that, although Darren had hurt her, he had not killed her. Thompson was trying to create reasonable doubt.

Darren told Tony that on January 14, 2002, he had worked all day and had become concerned because he hadn't heard from Geralyn. Tony asked Darren to establish the timeline of his activities. The jury listened as

Darren relived finding Geralyn in a bloody pool in the doorway of their bedroom.

"I pulled up her shirt to see if, like, she fell on something and it penetrated through the front. I didn't see anything on her abdomen. I lifted up her brassiere a little bit, you know, just a little. I still didn't see anything. And I was just—I didn't know what to do. So, then I went back, I turned around, and I knelt down at her head. And I noticed that's where all the blood was coming from. I noticed her face appeared to be swollen and bruised. And I turned her head a little bit, and at that moment I saw that her throat was cut wide open.

"I didn't realize at that time it was actually a cut. I was still trying to put the shotgun in there somehow because it didn't make sense. Nothing made sense, you know. I was, you know, if she would have shot herself in the throat, it wouldn't have looked like that, and BBs wouldn't have ricocheted out of her back."

"Okay. What did you do next, son, Darren?" Tony asked.

"I—I got up. Well, at that point, I swung my arm, and I hit the door on the side of me because she was in the doorway. And I just started screaming and crying, and I stood back up and I ran out of the house. And on the way, I punched the wall. And then there was a view light in my way on my way out, and I just kicked it out of the way."

Darren told the jury how he had run to his neighbor's house to get him to call 911.

"Darren, I need you to look at this jury. I need you to look them eye to eye. Did you do what you just described, that happened to your wife? Did you do that to your wife? Tell them, did you do that to your wife?"

"The injuries?"

"Did you kill your wife?"

"No, sir, I did not kill my wife. I loved her too much. I wouldn't let her die."

Darren said that he was only in the house for a minute, but that it felt like an eternity.

"Now, let's talk about this, Darren," Tony said. "I'm going to get right to it. You ever slapped your wife?"

"Yes, sir. I slapped her once, and I've regretted it every day since. My wife and I had many struggles during our relationship. There was some shoving between us. We—we had a rough, verbally abusive . . ." Darren did not want to continue.

"Were you emotionally abusive to her?"

"Emotionally? It was very emotional, and it was verbally abusive."

"This relationship—" Tony began.

"But we loved each other very, very much, and I did not murder my wife," Darren interrupted.

"You were the person being verbally abusive to her?"

"Yes, sir."

"You were the person that was emotionally abusive to her?"

"Yes, sir."

"And when you say you all struggled or fought, this happened several times?"

"Yes, sir."

Darren told Tony about a time when he discovered that Geralyn had been smoking. He described how he had seen ashes on the car window, but that Geralyn had denied it.

"I said, 'Come look at the car.' I said, 'I'm telling you, you can't tell me these are not ashes on the driver's side of your car. It's stuck to the window.' So we went outside, and I led her by her back, and I had my hand on her back."

Tony asked Darren to demonstrate on him. Darren put his hand on Tony's back.

"When we got to the car, I grabbed her by her neck, you know, pointed her down, and I said, 'Right here, you know, you cannot tell me that's not what it is.' We started arguing, and we went back inside."

"Darren, do you have any regrets to that?"

"Absolutely. I wish our marriage could have been a lot

happier and been—we could have had the family we always wanted before she passed away."

"Do you know this man here?" Tony asked, pointing to Geralyn's father.

"Yes, sir."

"Who is that?"

"That's John Barr. That's her father."

"Can you look him eye to eye and tell him you didn't kill his daughter?"

"John Barr," Darren said earnestly, "I promise you, I loved your daughter with my whole heart and soul. I did not murder her."

Tony tendered his witness. No one in the courtroom moved. Everyone was shaken by Darren's testimony. Darren had garnered sympathy as he described finding Geralyn dead. He had lost it, word by word, as he described what their relationship had been like. And as Thompson made him go through that day again, Darren became visibly upset. It was difficult for the young man to talk about Geralyn dying, and then have to admit how he had treated her.

Thompson made Darren tell the jury what had happened the Saturday before she died when they were at the Barrs' house and Darren was playing with Geralyn's niece.

"Actually, I was very tired, and I laid down on the couch. And I put my head on her mother's lap."

"And then at some point you got on the floor with Geralyn's little niece, didn't you, to play with her?"

"Yes, sir. We'd often pick at her and play together."

"Tell the jury what you did while you were playing with her," Thompson commanded. "You pulled your knife out of your pocket, didn't you?"

"Yes, sir. I pulled my knife out."

"You opened it up, didn't you?"

"Yes, sir."

"You took her by the back of the head, didn't you?"

"Absolutely not."

"You didn't touch her by the back of the head or the neck?"

"No, I didn't," Darren said, becoming agitated. "I can tell you—do you want me to just go ahead and tell you what happened instead of you trying to lead me into something?"

"I want to know the truth."

"The truth is, we were playing around," Darren explained. "And I've had this done to me numerous times growing up, and, you know, probably a little different than the society that is in here, you know—things that would be considered absolutely unacceptable in other places, just, you know, common, whatever.

"We were playing around on the floor, and somehow she hurt her finger or something. I don't know exactly what the instance was. And I grabbed her finger, and I pulled my knife out, and I opened it, and I grabbed her hand and I said, 'Come on. I can fix that.' I said, 'Let's just cut it off.' I said, 'That way, it won't hurt no more,' and just teasing her, you know. And she was like, 'No, no, no, Darren,' laughing and playing. So I would tease her like that all the time. I, like, you know, play with them on the floor, wrestle with them. They'd jump on my back and, you know, flip them over, and so forth and so on."

"What else did you do with your knife that day?"

"What else did I do with my knife that day?" Darren asked.

"With that little girl."

"Nothing else."

"You didn't play like you were slitting her throat with the knife?"

"T-that's outrageous! You—you—" Darren was stuttering.

"Answer my question. I agree it's outrageous," Thompson said.

"Yeah."

"Answer my question."

"Absolutely not."

But the jury wasn't so sure. Tommy Thompson had done his job well.

Tony called Alejandro Vara, a forensic scientist with the Louisiana State Police Crime Lab, to the stand as he prepared to play a video of the crime scene for the jury. Thompson objected.

"This is a murder trial," Tony argued. "There's a murder victim on here. There's a murder scene on here. And this jury has to determine and see the evidence, and this is the main evidence of the entire case—the body."

"And I understand that, Judge," Thompson said, "but my appreciation is that they've already showed pictures of the crime scene and pictures of the murder victim."

"Judge," Tony said, "also, I might add, there's a trailer door that's been ajar. There's a whole bunch of evidence that this man videotaped, and he's going to tell you what he's looking at on this tape for the sake of the jury. It's the crime scene."

"My concern is just the gruesomeness of it—that the jury will be exposed to—without putting these into evidence."

Judge Free overruled Thompson's objection.

Tony asked Geralyn's family if they would like to leave the courtroom. Mom Melanie Barr and Geralyn's sisters stayed. John Barr couldn't bear to look at it. He left the room.

As Geralyn's mother and sisters watched, Vara and Tony took them through the trailer. They saw the blood splashed onto the walls in the hall, running down. They saw the blood in the bathroom. They saw their beloved Geralyn lying dead on the floor. They saw her stiff, clenched fist extended away from her body. They had to look away. They tried not to listen as Vara talked.

"That appears to me to be what's called arterial spurt. And that's when the throat is cut, you have the artery— as the heart is pumping, blood is shooting out," Vara explained. Some of the jurors had trouble watching and listening as well. No one wanted to see this.

Vara went on to explain what he had seen in every room in the house. He identified pictures of Geralyn and explained that her hands were wrapped in brown bags to preserve any evidence that might be under her nails. Everyone was relieved when Vara finished.

Tony called Brant Thompson, investigator with the Department of Justice, to the stand. He testified that he had recovered a knife belonging to Todd from the Explorer, which had been repossessed. Tony asked him to identify the knife. Although it had been disassembled by the crime lab, Thompson was able to assure the jury that it was the same knife.

Tony called Dr. Alfredo Suarez, who specialized in forensic pathology, to the stand. It had been his job to discover the cause of Geralyn's death, to perform the necropsy, the forensic autopsy.

"Is the television on for a reason?" Thompson interrupted Tony's questioning of the witness.

"I'm going to use it," Tony said.

"Can we turn it off until you're ready to use it?"

"Is it bothering you, or do you want to take the knife off?" Tony had left the photo of the knife on the screen for the jury to view as Suarez described Geralyn's wounds.

"I'm trying. I want to take the knife off so I can get some glare off so I can see sitting here. Thank you,"

Thompson said. He knew the jury didn't need to be staring at that knife.

"The trachea was completely severed," Suarez said. "The thyroid gland was severed. The muscles that move your head like this, that swivel your head, called sternocleidomastoid muscles, were both gone. And the knife went all the way to the seventh cervical vertebrae. That's the bottom part of the neck.

"So the blood vessels, important blood vessels that bring blood to the heart, that's the jugular vein, and blood that comes from the heart up to the brain, called the carotid artery, were both severed on the right side."

"Let me stop you there," Tony said. "Man, there was blood all over this crime scene. I mean, blood up against the wall, and blood and blood and blood. Is that jugular vein or that carotid, which one of the veins, will it continue to pump out blood if she was holding her neck like that? It would still come out?"

"Mainly because the carotid is a major artery coming out of the aorta—with every pulsation of the heart, blood will come out rapidly."

"So when her throat was cut, is it possible that her heart would still be pumping blood out, pumping blood out if her throat was cut?"

"Oh yes."

"Was she—she would still be alive?"

"Bled to death."

"Bled to death?"

"Yeah," Suarez said.

Suarez described the other knife wounds and the defensive wounds on Geralyn's arms. He told the jury that the knife had a three-and-a-half-inch blade. "I think she was trying to avoid the weapon because I found two superficial cuts on the left side of her neck, as well as on the top part of the left shoulder."

Suarez said that Geralyn had been punched in the mouth and nose. He was still talking when Thompson interrupted, asking Judge Free if he and Todd could approach the bench. Thompson and Todd had been holding a quiet debate. Everyone was glad for the interruption.

* * *

"Your Honor," Todd said, "my life is on the line. Like I told you yesterday when we talked. I figured if Tony could put his expert on the stand, mine should be. He's telling me my expert can't take the stand."

"Your expert can take the stand," Free said.

"No. He said that he's not putting him on the stand."

"He can't put him today," Free explained to the increasingly upset killer.

"No," Todd said. "He told me he's not catching the stand."

Thompson tried to explain. "He's waiting right now to catch a flight. I can put him on the stand."

"Like the thing, like, when Tony put the name up there. I asked him to discredit these people," Todd continued.

Judge Free tried to calm him down. "He's coming back, you know."

"Your Honor, I'm getting screwed by—Your Honor, I'm getting screwed by—I ain't—I am not happy with my attorney."

"Let me ask you this—" Free said.

Todd interrupted, getting louder. "He lied to me from day one. And I done asked him, like I told you the other day down the road. Get some help. Like I told him, I got people."

Outside of the presence of the jury, Todd had told Free in preceding days that he was unhappy with having Thompson for his lawyer. He had informed the judge that Thompson had told him he had four daughters. "He told me that in my cell—like he thinks I'm the serial killer. How can he defend me?" Todd had complained during that conversation.

"I thought you were all right with everything," Free reminded Todd.

"No. I asked him about my expert, about my witness with everything, like the knife. I had told them who my witness was when I borrowed the knife. He's just now sending the subpoenas out to them today." Todd was showing unusual understanding of court procedure for a man who would later claim to be mentally retarded in an effort to save his life.

"He ain't subpoenaed them people until I asked him. He told me he did. My life is on the line here. If we ever go to the Bar Association or whatever, tell them I got insufficient counsel."

"Okay," Free agreed.

"Because I'm not happy."

Free decided this conversation needed to go on the record. He asked the jury to leave the room.

"I'm going to caution you not to be too loud," Free told Todd, "because if they hear you, it's on you, okay? That's why I put them out, so they cannot hear what you want to say. Now, if you would, go ahead and make your appearance, please, sir."

"With all due respect." Todd turned toward those in the courtroom. "Everybody in here, the people's family. Everybody in here, my family. My life's on the line in here. I want them to find out the truth what happened to their daughter."

Tony interjected, concerned that Todd was moving closer and closer to the families. "Judge, wait a minute. I don't want him to—"

"Get up here and talk to me," Free ordered.

"My—Tommy, he ain't representing me like he said. He lied to me from go, from day one. And me and him talked about some things. He lied to me. I come to you man to man about this. You found out I told him to his face. He told you he couldn't deny it. I want to fire him because he is insufficient of counseling me. He lied. He lied. Everything I asked him to do, like people I asked him to subpoena where I can prove my innocence, prove to those people that some things were here. But I told Tommy, I asked him to prove my alibis and stuff, he didn't do it. Every time I told him to do this, do that, he's going to tell me, 'Hold up, hold up, hold up, blah, blah, blah this.' So I'm, to me, he's not giving me a fair deal. And my life's on the line."

"Okay" was Free's only response.

"He's not giving me a fair deal. He is, like, 'Understand,' he says, 'I got four daughters.'"

"Uh-huh." Free let Todd rant.

"Everybody in here know what I'm faced with. Everybody in here done heard of me. He got four daughters. If he felt that way, he shouldn't even took the case. That's the way I feel about it. If he feel—I understand if he felt that way. He's steady telling me, 'I got four daughters. I got—I got four daughters.' If you know you felt that way, don't try to play me with my life. Don't try to play me like that. Don't do me that. That's all I have to say."

Thompson decided it was time to defend himself. Everyone in the courtroom stared, fascinated by the events that were unfolding. Many could not believe that Todd was being allowed to go on and on about his attorney like that.

"If you tell me I still have to defend Mr. Lee, I'm right here, ready to do it," Thompson said. "I've been in your courtroom many times, Judge. You've been ready to throw me out and kick my butt outside on many an occasion because of how vigorously I defend my clients. Is that correct?"

"That is correct."

"I've never told Mr. Lee, you know, 'I've got four

daughters, so it's going to be hard for me.' I never said that. I may have told him I have four daughters. I've got four daughters and three granddaughters. I love them very much. My friends ask me all the time, 'How can you defend Derrick Todd Lee?' My standard answer is 'You ask me that when your son's sitting in that chair where he is, and I'll tell you how I can defend him.'

"I've done everything I can possibly do in this case. I've never worked a second-degree murder case the way I've worked this case, nor has the rest of the public defender's office. There are things Mr. Lee has asked me to do, and as a lawyer, I advised him that it would not be in his interest to do. One of those involved me questioning some witnesses that I didn't think I should question at that time in front of the jury. And there was some witnesses he wanted me to question at a particular time when I was trying to get Dr. Suarez on the stand while my expert was still here."

"Uh-huh." Free nodded.

"That witness was going to come back on the stand, and I could ask him and intended to ask him all those questions."

"Uh-huh."

"I understand how Mr. Lee feels. I respect his frustration. I would hate to be in his shoes. But I know in my heart I've gone over and above and beyond the call of duty in this. Because I want to. Because I believe in what I'm doing."

Todd jumped back in. "Your Honor, another thing I want to tell you. Seeing my situation, what he did to me, you see, you whole thing, sooner or later somebody, everybody, wants to be a part of this here—what I'm accused of from here to East Baton Rouge Parish. Everybody wants the fame and fortune. This ain't no fame and fortune to me. You know what I'm saying? My life is on the line. I done heard people holler about, 'Hey, maybe your lawyer or somebody will come back and write a book ten or fifteen years from now.' It's not like that for me. Tommy's sitting up here telling you a lie."

Todd was unrelenting. He did not want Tommy Thompson to be his lawyer. He complained that Thompson did not visit with him in prison for more than fifteen or twenty minutes at a time. "He's just sent, he's just sending stuff out, and I had to, like, constantly beg him. Like when they put up about the knife. I said, 'The people I had just subpoenaed could tell them where—what I was doing to prove myself when I got this here, when this here was bought, who was with me when I bought it.'"

Todd had just made a mistake. Tony, who had been quietly listening to Todd's litany, interrupted.

"He also just admitted that that is his knife," he pointed out.

"No, I did not submit, say that."

"You said where you bought it from, where you got it, and I want to use it." Tony addressed Todd and the judge at once.

"I did not say that," Todd argued.

"That's what you said."

"Whatever you said, you said, and it's on there, whatever it is," Free said, indicating the court record.

"Well, Your Honor, like I said, if I say it, I can prove where it come from."

Tony began to enjoy himself. "That's another thing. If he wants to take the stand, I don't want to deny him. Let him take the stand. Go ahead and take—"

"I don't want to take no stand," Todd said. "But what I'm saying is this. Why did he deny me of mine? When I asked him to get more help and told him about this and told him about that, he didn't do it. Why?"

Free was tiring of the exchange. He informed Todd of

the law—that Todd could not fire his attorney. He did not have that right, as the public defender's office appointed who would represent someone. "In other words, if he is not doing a good job, if he's messing up as an attorney, you have ineffective assistance of counsel. That's built-in reversible error, built into the record. That even if you're convicted, and if the supreme court believes you, they can overturn his conviction and say send him back."

Free said that Todd's only alternative was to represent himself, which the judge cautioned him against. Free said that he could not fire Thompson, that Todd could not fire him either. "If Mr. Thompson wants to get one of the others, I see he has two other public defenders with him here, Paul Pendley and Yolanda Batiste, who have been assisting him in this matter. If he wants to request everyone from the indigent defender's office to come help him, I don't care. That doesn't bother me."

Thompson offered to step down, to let one of the others take over the case.

Judge Free suggested that they bring Suarez back to the stand and finish up for the day. He told the defense that they could visit on the matter with Todd after court adjourned.

Tony Clayton had something to say. "Judge, can we just put on the record in defense of Mr. Tommy Thompson that he has worked this case, that he's thoroughly worked with Mrs. Chustz and I. He's filed motion after motion. I mean, regardless of what Tommy feels about this case, and just for the record, so if any reviewing court were to see, on second-degree murder, he's gone way beyond the call of duty in this case."

Todd disagreed.

"I understand. I understand you don't feel like he's

doing a good job. I understand what you're telling me," Free said.

"I know he's not. I know he's not. Ain't no feel," Todd said. "All due to respect, I know he's not. See, Tony can sit up there. I ain't going to criticize nobody in here. He got a job to do. He's going to have to do his job. That is different. But he ain't going to see what I see."

Todd wasn't finished. "I been asking for help. He's steady telling me I don't want to piss the judge off. I said, 'Let me.' I say, 'Let me have a meeting with the judge, and everything, you know what we said yesterday, it's on the record now.'"

"Hopefully. I heard you the first time," Free said.

"That's his excuse he kept giving me, the runaround, runaround, runaround."

Todd was beating it into the ground, but then, he was good at beating things into the ground, as the families in that courtroom could attest. At one point, he had informed the judge that he had a wife and three kids to worry about. The mothers and fathers of the victims wished that he had had as much concern for their children.

Free called the jury back in and Suarez resumed his testimony, describing every wound on Geralyn's body. Finally Tony finished painting his gruesome picture. The jury got his point. The person who had committed this act was inhuman.

In a sidebar with the judge and the prosecution, Thompson asked that the court recess so that he could find someone in his office to take over. He told the judge that Todd did not want him to cross-examine Suarez, and that Pendley wasn't certified to handle second-degree murder cases.

"Why don't you tell him this?" Free said, telling Thompson to inform Todd that he would cross Suarez, and if

Todd wasn't happy, the court would allow Suarez to come back and testify again.

"He won't talk to me," Thompson replied.

"Why don't you ask him? Let Tommy cross him now," Free said to Pendley.

"All right."

Free told Pendley to tell Todd, "If you're not satisfied with the cross-examination and then we get someone else to take his spot in this case, then, on our case in chief, we can call him back and make him available and you get to benefit from it."

The men discussed it for a few more minutes, trying to come to a solution.

"As Tommy indicated, our client's in a mood," Pendley said.

"He's in a mood? Talk to him like a man, and you'll be okay. You pussyfoot around with him, and he's going to eat your lunch. That's all I can tell you," Free said.

"I agree. Thank you, Your Honor."

Tommy questioned Suarez about the knife, establishing the possibility that the knife that had been collected from Todd's truck may not have been the actual murder weapon, as thousands of knives were consistent with that one. No blood had been found on the knife.

By the end of that Friday afternoon, everyone in the courtroom was ready for a break. Geralyn's family had been through enough for one day. All of the families had. The court recessed for the weekend.

Todd was brought back to his cell.

Darren went home to wrestle with his regret.

The Final Days

Tony Clayton couldn't sleep. Court would resume in the morning, and he knew he needed to get up early to prepare, but he lay there, staring at the ceiling through the darkness and listening to Paula breathing softly beside him. He had tried many black men for murder, and he had thought he was immune to violence, no matter how horrific. But this case was different. Tony had developed an affinity for Geralyn, perhaps because she was so young or because Darren had treated her so poorly. He had read her journal, the description of Geralyn's life in her own words. He knew that she had suffered long before Todd had come through her door with her phone as a weapon. He wondered how long Todd had been watching her.

Maybe I'm getting soft, he thought. *Maybe it's time to get out of this racket.* He had not liked that Geralyn's family had watched the crime scene video. It had hurt him to see her like that, so he could only imagine what it must have been like for them. He had seen the photographs from most of the victims. Tony shivered in the darkness as the images churned through his mind. He rolled over, put his arm around Paula, and pulled her close into his body.

* * *

252 *Susan D. Mustafa, Tony Clayton, Sue Israel*

Tony strode into the courtroom, smiling, on August 9, no trace of his restless night on his face. He greeted his friend Sheriff Mike Cazes. Cazes observed that the courtroom was still split—blacks on one side and whites on the other—as he shook Tony's hand. "I noticed," Tony said, "and they don't think he did it. They don't believe that many white women would let a black man into their homes. Even my own mama says it—'He might have killed one, but he didn't kill all of them.' It's the DNA. They don't get it."

Tony took his seat as the court was called to order.

He noticed that Thompson was still sitting at the defense table. He and Todd had resolved their differences.

Tony's focus today would be the investigation into Geralyn's death and technical DNA evidence. Dannie Mixon, Todd Morris, and Ray Day testified about the swabbing. Detective John Colter told the jury how he had searched Consandra's home and found Todd's Wolverine boots, the same brand that had left a bloody footprint at Geralyn's house.

Tony called Consandra Green to the stand. She identified the boots as the ones that had been taken from her home in a search. Tony had to drag the answers he wanted out of Consandra. It was obvious she did not want to be there, testifying against the man she had loved.

Forensic scientist Kim Colomb was called next. Colomb went over what she had found at the crime scene. She told jurors how portions of the floor in the trailer had been removed—the portions with bloody boot prints.

"So the one we're about to talk about now, the Wolverine boot, it was only exiting the trailer?" Tony asked.

"Correct."

"Now, in your experience as a scientist and investigating crime scenes, what would that tell you?"

"It tells me that when the person wearing the shoes

entered the scene, there was no blood for him to step on prior to entrance, so he wasn't leaving any prints going to the bedroom area. So the blood had to have happened in the bedroom/hall area, and then as he exited, he left the shoe prints."

Colomb explained that the prints were matched to Todd's boots in tread design, class characteristic, and size, but that Todd's boots had experienced wear over time. She said that Todd's boot was the boot that had exited that home.

Chustz called Natasha Poe to the stand. Chustz asked her to explain DNA to the jury. "Everybody's DNA is exactly the same, about ninety-eight percent. There's only a small percentage of the DNA that makes us all different, which is what makes us look different. This small percent of the DNA is what we're actually looking at, and it's going on in these particular chromosomes."

Poe told the jury that STR means "short tandem repeats." She tried to keep it simple. She described how DNA had been extracted from under Geralyn's fingernails. Because of the amount of blood on her nails, the first profile had been only Geralyn's.

"At the time of this case, there was a new technology known as Y-STR, which our lab currently is not performing. Basically, what happens with Y-STR is it's looking for the male component of that sample. The type of testing we do amplifies anybody's DNA that's there, whether it's male or female. And with Y-STR, it does just the male.

"And so if there had been a sample underneath Mrs. DeSoto's fingernails, I couldn't see it because she was there in such a large quantity. That was when I called the district attorney's office and suggested that they maybe try this technique." Poe went on to describe how she had swabbed the boots to get a profile. She stated that the results were a mixture of Todd and someone unidentifiable.

* * *

Tony called Derrick Todd Lee Jr. to the stand. Everyone watched as the young man, who would suffer for the rest of his life the stigma of his dad being a serial killer, walked to the front. He was such a nice-looking boy. Even the families of the victims felt sorry for him.

Derrick told Tony that his nickname was D.L. He had taken on the nickname after his father's capture. He didn't want anyone to know his name was Derrick Todd Lee.

"D.L., look at those boots in front of you right there. Look familiar?"

"Yes, sir."

"Who they belong to?"

"My daddy," he said, glancing at Todd. Todd smiled at his son.

"Tell the jury what this is," Tony said.

"Pocketknife."

"And who does it belong to?"

"My daddy."

"Have you seen this knife with your daddy before?"

"Yes, sir. He always kept it in the house."

"He always kept it in the house? How would he keep it up?"

"In the jewelry box," Derrick said.

"The shape that it would be in—was it real sharp?"

"No, sir."

"Never was sharp. He never kept it sharp?"

"No, sir."

"You ever see him sharp it on a rod?"

"No, sir."

Tony knew the kid was lying, but he also knew that he would have offended everyone in the courtroom if he went on the attack. He tried a different strategy.

"All right," Tony said. "You remember talking to the police, the two detectives coming to talk to you?"

"Yes, sir."

"Do you remember them talking to you about that knife?"

"Yes, sir."

"What grade you in, D.L.?"

"Ninth."

"Ninth grade. You read and write, don't you?"

"Yes, sir."

"You read pretty good, huh? I could tell."

"Yes, sir."

"You play any sports?"

"I plan on playing football this year."

"All right. Let's see here, D.L. You were out of the state, I guess, but on August 4, 2003, remember the guys coming to talk to you?"

"Yes, sir."

"Read the highlighted portion. I want you to read it real loud, where they can hear all the way back there."

Derrick began reading his statement from the previous summer.

"Derrick Todd Lee Jr. acknowledge neither Derrick Todd Lee Sr. nor Jacqueline Lee own any type of . . ."

"Firearms," Tony helped him.

"Firearms. Derrick Todd Lee Sr., that on a . . ."

"Regularly," Tony prompted.

"Regularly carried a folding blade pocketknife. Derrick Lee Jr. described the knife as having a brown handgrip with a shiny blade, approximately three inches in length. Derrick Lee Sr. always kept a knife extremely sharp."

"Stop right there. You told them that your daddy always kept a knife extremely sharp?"

"No, sir."

"Okay. But go ahead. Continue."

"Seen Derrick Lee Sr. sharpen the knife on many occasions using sharpening rods."

"Stop right there. You saw your daddy sharpen a knife on many occasions using sharpening rods?"

"No, sir."

"That's what they say you said, though, right?"

Derrick nodded.

"Derrick Lee Jr. demonstrated for Thompson the sharpening motion when using sharpening rods as well as describing checking the blade edge by raking the thumb . . ."

"'By raking the thumb,'" Tony repeated.

"Across the blade edge."

"Like this?" Tony licked his thumb, then emulated the motion. "Your dad did that?"

"Yes, sir."

"A lot?"

"No, sir."

"But it was sharp, wasn't it? Real sharp knife, huh?"

"No, sir."

Derrick was mumbling his answers. Tony asked him to speak up.

"When's the last time you talked to your daddy?"

"Sir?"

"When's the last time he talked to you? He called you lately?"

"Yes, sir."

"He did? He knew you were going to take the stand? He knew you were going to testify at his trial?"

Todd was staring at his son intently, signaling with his hands for Derrick not to say anything.

"I don't know."

"You don't know?"

"No, sir."

"Did he talk to you about if you were going to take the stand?"

"No, sir."

"What did y'all talk about?"

Derrick looked at his dad. Thompson objected. Free overruled the objection.

"D.L., when is that last time y'all talked, man? On the phone. Tell me."

Tony moved so that Derrick could not see his father

and drew himself up to full height, intimidating the young man. He knew this was a golden opportunity—a way to get some sort of a confession from Todd in through the back door.

"I think last month," Derrick mumbled.

"Last month. Do you want to tell me what y'all talked about?"

Derrick looked down and shook his head.

"You don't want to tell me?"

"No, sir."

"I don't want to pick on you, but if I tell you you've got to answer my question, will you get mad at me if I say that?"

Derrick didn't respond.

"You understand that?"

"I don't care," Derrick said.

"You don't want to answer questions, do you?"

Again, no response. Tony felt sorry for the kid.

"You know what. I'm not going to ask you. Keep it to yourself. Thank you, man."

Tony knew by saying nothing, Derrick had said it all. It was obvious that Todd had tried to influence his son's testimony.

Derrick stepped down. Collette Walker Dwyer replaced him in the witness chair. She described how Todd had stalked her in 1999. She told jurors how Todd had walked into her apartment one night, sat down on her couch, told her he liked white women, and asked her out. "He just sat down, told me he's been watching me, and he thought we'd make a good couple, that he wanted to take care of me." She explained how Todd had asked her if she was afraid of him. She'd told him no. "'Well, if I wanted to rape you, I could,' he said, 'because your kids aren't here this weekend, and your neighbors aren't home.'" Collette said that she told Todd the conversation was over and opened her door for him to leave. Collette left instead.

Collette relayed how she had seen Todd in the parking lot of her apartment complex the night before he came into her apartment, and that he returned a few days later. She said she had reported him to police.

"Do you see that man in this courtroom who was inside your house?" Tony asked.

"Yes, I do."

"Can you point him out?"

"He's sitting between there," Collette said, pointing. "The gray pants and dark gray shirt."

Thompson tried to discredit her testimony, but there wasn't much he could do. Todd had been convicted of stalking her.

Carolyn Booker, of the Acadiana Crime Lab, was called to the stand. She explained how she had pulled DNA from Diane Alexander's dress. She told the court that Todd's DNA could not be excluded as a donor.

"And I believe your findings were that 99.9 percent of the African-American population could be excluded from this mixture. Is that correct?"

"That's correct."

She explained that rare markers, which Todd's DNA possessed, had been found on the dress—twenty-two, thirty-four, and nine (alleles not commonly found together).

"Is that unusual?" Tony asked.

"It's not unusual to find DNA markers in a stain, but those three rare alleles I had never seen together. And I've looked at several profiles and had never seen one person that possessed all three of those rare alleles."

"So not one person in any database that you've ever looked at possesses the three markers together as a set?"

"That's correct."

Booker then told jurors she had tested Dené Colomb's

vaginal swab. She said that the odds of the DNA being anyone other than Todd's was one in 30 trillion.

Gina Pineda was the next qualified expert to speak about DNA. She worked for ReliaGene, which, she said, was the leading authority in the country on DNA. Tony asked her to explain Y-STR.

"We have a total of forty-six chromosomes in each cell, and half of those come from mom and half from dad. There is also a sex identification chromosome. One person can have two X chromosomes, XX, which basically dictates the instructions to make that person a female. And the other choice is one person can have an X chromosome and a Y chromosome. Having that combination of chromosomes, an X and a Y, makes that person a male individual.

"The autosomal STRs that you've been hearing about are not on the sex chromosomes. They're on the autosomals, which you get half from mom, half from dad. And the Y-STR testing that I'm here to talk to you about today, and is actually the type of test that we performed in this particular case, is DNA that is only on the male Y chromosome."

Pineda explained that when there is too much blood, as in Geralyn's case, her DNA would overwhelm any other DNA that was present—that DNA would not show up in ordinary testing. She said that Y-STR testing targets the male chromosome.

"And Y-STRs get inherited straight from the father, so that one individual will have the same Y-STR profile as his father, as his brother, as his uncle."

Pineda told the jury that she had performed Y-STR tests on the DNA from under Geralyn's fingernails and DNA from Dené's vaginal swab. She verified that the Y-STR tests had shown that DNA taken from under Geralyn's fingernails was consistent with the DNA from Dené

Colomb. Pineda informed the jury that 99.8 percent of the world's African-American population could be excluded as donors.

"Mr. Lee is included as a potential contributor," she said.

Pineda detailed how the calculations were determined. She demonstrated the results of her calculations with a chart that showed Geralyn's DNA, along with Todd's, Darren's, and John Barr's. Todd's DNA matched the DNA under Geralyn's fingernails with markers thirteen, twenty-nine, twenty-two, ten, fourteen, twelve, eight, and eleven.

Tony knew that most of his evidence was circumstantial and that Y-STR testing was a new technology. He needed to tie it all together.

"In that article you read, you said you ought to go a step further when you're dealing with Y-STR, you ought to use other evidence, right?" he said.

"Correct."

"So what if I tell you that out of all of these people, his brothers and his cousins RayRay and Pookie, I would circle one of them, and I say that that person's Y-STR was in that crime scene. Are you with me?"

"Yes."

"And then I go a step further and say that that person had boots that were consistent with a print."

Thompson objected, stating that Pineda wasn't an expert in that area. "If she can answer the question, answer it. Go ahead," Free said.

"And then if I tell you there was a knife that his son identified that a doctor said was consistent with three-and-a-half-inch wounds to the body of the victim, and we tied to Derrick Todd Lee. Would you say that's a little bit of other evidence toward the Lee whose DNA, Y-STR—are you with me?"

Thompson objected again, but Tony was satisfied. He had made his connection for the jury. The prosecution rested. The court recessed.

* * *

Tony spent the evening mulling over his closing arguments. Again, he had a restless night as he thought about the cold-bloodedness of the man he was prosecuting. And again, he pulled Paula into a protective embrace while she slept.

Tommy Thompson knew that things were not going well for the defense. He also knew that his only hope was Darren. He hoped that Darren's abuse of Geralyn would be enough to persuade the jury that Todd was not her killer. Thompson's only chance for a not guilty verdict rested with Geralyn's friends. He began Todd's defense first thing the next morning.

Jonathan Soileau, who had worked with Geralyn at LSU, told jurors that everyone in their office knew that Darren abused Geralyn. He said that Darren was controlling and would rip up Geralyn's clothes if he didn't like them. The picture he painted of Darren was that of a man obsessed with overseeing every aspect of his wife's life—where she could go, what she could do, if she could smoke, what time she went to bed.

Sandy Gautreaux, Geralyn's neighbor, said that she had witnessed Darren abusing Geralyn.

"Well, our trailers were so close apart you can hear anything that was going on. And one night, I could hear them screaming and hollering. And he had her by the hair like this, and he drug her outside to her car, and he was beating her head onto the car because of a cigarette ash." Sandy started crying as she spoke about the incident.

"The next morning I spoke with her, and I said, 'Well, are you going to call the cops?' and she said no."

Thompson asked if Geralyn had ever told her about Darren's abuse.

"One time, she came over with a black eye, and I asked her what happened, and she didn't cook fresh rice from the night before. She had leftover rice from the night before, and he refused to eat leftover rice from the night before, so he punched her because he wanted fresh rice with his supper."

"What about the clothes she wore?"

"One night, they got in a fight because she had on a fitted shirt, and he ripped the shirt off of her and said, 'You're not going to dress like Sandy,' because he hated my guts."

Before the defense rested, Sandy testified about other incidents that indicated Geralyn was afraid of her husband. Thompson had done what he could, with what he had. Closing arguments would begin after lunch.

Tony began by thanking the jury for their service. Step by step, he connected the evidence he had presented: the DNA, the boot print, the knife, Diane Alexander, Dené Colomb, Collette Walker.

"And you heard the evidence. This is not me talking about it. The knife. We found the knife. They repossessed his Explorer. The repo man found the knife, called the Feds, we got the knife. We brought the knife in. His son identified it, and he told you, 'That's my daddy's knife.'

"The paycheck. He signed and cashed that check on January 15, 2002. Do you know what else was happening that day on January 15, 2002?" Tony said, pointing to Geralyn's family. "They were planting their child in a casket. He probably spent his money on the sixteenth. They were burying her on the sixteenth. While they were burying their child, he was spending his check."

Tony reminded the jury about the call to Todd's old place of employment and that the phone he had used to injure Geralyn had turned up missing. He asked why Darren would have stolen his own phone if he had killed Geralyn. He told the jury that the defense had put up "smoke screens, mirrors, hocus-pocus. You will never be as close to a cold-blooded vicious murderer. DNA ought to stand for 'Derrick's Now Accountable.' And you ought to say, 'Derrick, this is your DNA—Derrick's Now Accountable.'

"Ms. DeSoto has been with you for the last seven days. From the time we started jury selection to right now, and I'm telling you, she's screaming out to you. If there was a way we could have opened her eyes and got the picture of the man who stabbed her seven times and cut her throat open—but the good Lord has provided us with some new technology. Because when you're fighting a person, you're going to get a scratch on them. And look at her fist. It's clenched right there.

"You know, I don't like that *CSI,* but there's a little old lady who walks up to the body on *CSI.* She crawls up to the body, and she talks to the dead body. She says, 'Talk to me, baby. Tell me who did this to you, baby.' Geralyn has her fist right there. 'I know who did it. Just open my hand. Just open my hand, and you'll know who did it to me.'"

A hush fell over the packed courtroom as Tony continued, sounding every bit like an old Southern Baptist preacher. He told the jury that Todd had a signature, and he had left it on Diane Alexander. He had left it on Geralyn. He had stomped both of them. He had left it on Dené. Todd had watched all of them before attacking, Tony said, his voice rising and falling in a hypnotic rhythm.

"And I want you to imagine one second—bear with me, close your eyes. Imagine that girl in that trailer, and a stranger is in there with a knife. And you're just—you're just fighting for your life, and he's ripping her throat open. Imagine that.

"You can open your eyes. Imagine not being able to say, 'I'm going to call up my mama,' and 'Can I tell Mama bye? Can I tell Darren bye? Can I just hold my daddy's hand one more time? Can I see my little niece and nephew?'

"He took all that away from her. 'Can I call my grandmother? Can I call my aunts? Can I call my sister? Can I just tell them bye? Because when I woke up this morning,

I thought I was going to have a new career at LSU. I thought that if I worked hard, like my daddy told me and my mama told me, if I go to college, I can get a job as an occupational therapist. I thought I could do that. But what I didn't think is that if I was just kind enough to let a man use the phone, that he would suck the life out of me.'

"Folks, that's the evidence in this case, and I respectfully ask you to come back with a second-degree murder conviction."

Thompson asked Judge Free to declare a mistrial. He didn't like the fact that Tony had insinuated that Todd had stalked Geralyn without having submitted evidence to that effect. He didn't like much of what Tony had said.

"Motion for mistrial denied," Free said.

Thompson addressed the jury. He told them that the other victims that had been brought into this case were not relevant. "Now, if you're going to try this case on emotion and media hype, hell, let's drag him out right now and go stick him under a tree, hang him up, and let him die there, and we're done. We don't have to have a system."

Tony thought that sounded like an excellent idea, and it took everything he had not to jump up from his seat and say, "I would like to accept that as suitable punishment for this crime."

"Let's not fool each other," Thompson continued. "I know what would be a popular verdict in this case. I think everybody does. I'm asking you to be brave and courageous Americans and protect the rights, not only of Derrick Todd Lee, but of every citizen in this country and uphold the Constitution of the United States of America and the state of Louisiana and all of the laws of the state of Louisiana. Because if you let them fall, they fall for everybody."

Thompson attacked the state's evidence—the boots, the knife, the DNA—and noted that no blood had been found on the boots or the knife, no DNA. He questioned the date Todd had picked up his check from Dow Chemical, the phone call to Exxon. He noted that the numbers from Dené's autosomal DNA test had been one in 30 trillion, whereas the Y-STR test from Geralyn had only excluded 99.8 percent of the population—that the autosomal test didn't work on her. Thompson talked about Todd's extended family tree.

"You can follow it back up the ladder to every ascendant, father, grandfather, great-grandfather, on and on and on. And every time you go up one of those steps to the father, all of his brothers and theirs. The grandfather, all of his brothers. All of their children. All of theirs and all of theirs. All the way back up thousands of years to the first person that had that particular DNA. That person passed it on. We don't know how many people he passed it on to. I might have it. There's no way to tell how many people on Earth today have that same DNA prototype, that parental lineage. So don't be misled."

Thompson told the jury that Tony had not proved what he said he would, in his opening statements. Thompson did his job. He defended his client to the best of his ability.

"What I want you to do is this—whatever you do, do it from your heart and your soul and your mind. And do what you would have done if you or your son was sitting where Derrick is sitting. Thank you, and I do appreciate your time."

Tony didn't even wait for Thompson to sit down before he jumped up and addressed the jury.

"You know, I don't know if we were in the same courtroom. I don't know if we listened to the same evidence. But see, you ought not to put yourself in the case," he admonished Thompson. "But he said he could have been one to leave the DNA when the scientist told you

99.8 percent of black males can be excluded. That DNA is the DNA of a black male. Now, I've been black a little longer than Mr. Thompson, and it ain't Mr. Thompson. It's Derrick Todd Lee.

"And all that stuff he's talking about DNA—tie it back to one thing he said. He said to a medical certainty or scientific certainty Dené Colomb. Well, maybe we forgot that we extrapolated Mr. Lee's DNA from Colomb, and it was him, folks.

"And I wrote down copious notes—as my daddy used to say, 'copious notes'—about what he said. I mean, maybe Eve done it or Adam done it. I mean, he went way back looking for somebody who could have done this murder. King Tut, maybe. I don't know. Derrick Todd Lee killed Geralyn DeSoto."

Tony counteracted the rest of Thompson's argument, then urged the jury to come back with a swift verdict.

"And all of that about if you or your son was over there. You or your son are not going to be there ever. The person who is over there—judge him. He's trying to bring you over there. Let him take his own seat. And the DNA, I don't know what this last thing he was talking about when he said he could have left it. That just threw me off. Anything to get him out of here.

"Believe you me, the DNA—it's him. It's him. It's him. It's him. It's him. It's him. Look at him."

Judge Free gave the jury their instructions.

It was three-thirty in the afternoon on August 10, 2004, when the jurors filed into the jury room to decide if Derrick Todd Lee was Geralyn DeSoto's killer. It had been two years and seven months since the pretty young girl, who had suffered from the hand of one man, died from the hand of another.

Life for a Life

Kelli Hebert was nervous. This was only the second major trial, and the first murder trial, for which she had taken the minutes. Now it was her responsibility as deputy clerk to read the verdict. Like all of the other women in the Baton Rouge area, she had feared the serial killer. She looked at the families of the victims and could see the tension in their faces. The jury filed back into the room at 5:15 P.M., only one hour and forty-five minutes after they had left to deliberate.

Kelli's knees shook as she informed the families, the court, the world, that the jury had found Derrick Todd Lee guilty of second-degree murder. The vote had been eleven to one. The state only needed ten.

Todd sat quietly, his face showing no expression, as the courtroom broke out in applause. The Barrs cried and hugged the other families. Tony let out a huge sigh of relief.

Todd's family just sat there, stunned.

Judge Free set the sentencing date for August 16.

The following Monday, Todd entered the courtroom, looking more like a serial killer in his orange prison uniform and shackles.

Free explained that victims of a crime have the right to make a victim impact statement before sentencing.

John Barr approached the podium. He had waited impatiently for this day. He wanted to confront the man who had taken his daughter, his Sissy, away.

"I raised three girls," he began. "I tried to raise them in a Christian family. I tried to teach them about forgiveness. I love my children more than anything in the world. I've got a card from my daughter, Sissy. It's like a card bookmarker. I was searching for a sign, maybe to see, you know, what was going on after she got murdered. I didn't know what else to do, so I found my wife's Bible, and I picked it up. It was a card she gave me for Father's Day. I'm going to read what it said on the card.

"It said, *Dad, thanks for taking the time, for teaching me this love of God, for sharing God's heart and mind, for all these things and more. Dad, thanks for taking some time.*

"Because she knew how much I loved her. And this is one of the hardest things to do, to get up here and read this.

"I took some verses out of the Bible this morning. I got the Bible this morning. I've got it right here. I picked up Matthew 13:47. And it says, *Again the kingdom of heaven is like unto a net that was cast into the sea and gathered of every kind, which when it was full, they drew to shore and sat down and gathered the goods into the vessel, but cast the bad away. So shall it be at the end of the world. And you shall come forth and sever the wicked from among the just and shall cast them into the furnace of fire. There shall be wailing and gnashing of teeth.*"

John looked directly at Todd, who sat staring straight ahead.

"But that's how it was, huh? That's how you got into my daughter's house? Went there with a smile on your face and saying, 'Praise God,' huh? That's how you got into all these ladies' houses? You started talking about religion, and they just opened the doors. You had to use a weapon on some women. Big man. Big, big man.

"It's a good thing you used one on my daughter. She would have probably tore you up all over that house. You know, I have to forgive, but I don't see anywhere it says—today I have to forgive. If you would have any remorse at all, you wouldn't put these other families through what they're fixing to go through. Because you know you did it. I just wish I could have been at her house in time because I know you wouldn't have whipped my butt. And I know you still can't do it. Maybe God will have mercy on your soul, but I ain't."

John told Todd how he wanted revenge, pounding his fist on the podium for emphasis. He urged Todd not to put the other families through the torture of another trial. He attacked his manhood over and over.

"I never spoke my mind in court because I respected the court. A few times, I could have jumped on you, and nobody could have stopped me. Nobody. It wasn't because of you I did that. It was because of respect for my court and my family right there. And I'm like my daughter. If we start fighting, you're going to have to kill me, because I ain't letting up. But you wouldn't fight me, not unless you could get a sucker punch in on me, like you did those women. Big, bad man."

Todd looked at John. "That's the first time you looked me in the eyes. I wanted you to look at me all through court. But you couldn't look at me, because you know what you did. But you had to put me and my family through that torture to look at those pictures of my daughter—what you did to her."

John continued tearing into the man who had brought so much pain into his life. "Do you know every day, every day, five minutes doesn't go by that I don't think about my daughter. Not some days. Every day. Even while I'm up here looking at you old sorry thing, I think about her.

"You put my son-in-law through a lot of pain. You put my daughter through a lot of pain. You put our whole family—you know how they describe me when I go down the road now? 'That's John Barr, that's the one who had his daughter murdered.' They don't say, 'That's John Barr, my friend.' That's how they remember us. They come up to us with this sad face, instead of if all my kids would be living."

John was having his moment, and he didn't want it to end. He wanted to stand up there for hours, staring at Todd, telling him how much he had hurt not only his family, but everyone. He ranted. He raved. He hated. He hurt. John Barr put his pain on the table for everyone in that courtroom to see. He urged Todd to confess, to spare the other families the torture of seeing those pictures. Todd just stared angrily at him.

"And go ahead and look at me like you want to, buddy, because you don't scare me at all. You might scare those women, but you don't scare me. But if you want to get it right, it's up to you. It's up to you. You don't know how bad I want to be a little closer to you. And I wouldn't care if you didn't have those handcuffs on. That don't bother me. Nothing, nothing you do bothers me now.

"Thank God my daughter gave her soul to Christ before you took it. Thank God for that. But we know where your soul is going. I have nothing further to say at this time."

Everyone in the courtroom clapped and then quieted as Melanie Barr took her husband's place at the podium.

"Why? Why Geralyn?" Melanie began to cry as she looked at Todd. "Why does God allow such evil to exist in the world? He could probably never give me an answer that I could understand. I can't understand how a person like you could function with no heart.

"On January 14, 2002, you began to inflict your sadistic reign of terror upon my family. It began when you decided to take the life of my child—a child with so much left to give to this world. She had only just begun. A child who was still a baby to me and her father.

"You proclaim to be concerned about your family's safety. Where were your thoughts on their safety whenever you were killing innocent women? Were your thoughts on your parents, your wife, and your children? Were your thoughts on the pain that you're causing them? No, I doubt it. You were thinking of satisfying your own evil desires with no concerns for anyone, not even your own family.

"Your two-and-a-half-year reign of terror upon Geralyn and her family ends today. And hers upon you begins. When you close your eyes each night while you lay in your cell, I pray her face, as well as the faces of all of your other victims, burns into your memory until you're forced to think about the pain and agony you have inflicted upon countless people. Maybe your thoughts will even wander to your own family. What would it be like for you to bury your child? If there's still a heart in that body of yours, I pray that God touches it in some way and that you will begin your repentance by confessing to the authorities to the murders of all the other women you have taken from this earth."

Melanie finished by reading the Scripture on Geralyn's headstone. *"For the eyes of the Lord are over the righteous and his ears are open unto their prayers. But the face of the Lord is against them that do evil."*

Again, the audience clapped. Geralyn's mother stepped away from the podium, still crying.

Becky Chustz stepped up to read a letter from one of Geralyn's sisters. It was short and to the point. She revealed how much contempt she had for Todd, how incomprehensible it was to her for a husband and father to be capable of doing the horrible things he had done to women, who were other men's wives and children.

She commended the jury for putting a stop to his terrible crimes, and warned Todd that he could expect worse torment than he had ever inflicted when he was in hell.

Todd furrowed his brow.

Then Darren walked to the podium.

"I know the media is here today. I would like my statement to be quoted and not edited for the media to read it, like they want me to read.

"Nothing I can say, or anyone can say, can make Derrick Todd Lee remorseful or sorrowful for what he has done to everyone. Myself, my family, Geralyn especially, her family, and the numerous other victims that you have taken. God knows how many more victims there are than what was found so far. You will not be sorry for anything that you have ever done. You will just be sorry for being convicted, for spending the rest of your life in Angola. And I definitely couldn't say anything any better than what Geralyn's father has already said. They've expressed my feelings completely.

"Derrick Todd Lee, the police department, the judicial system in general, and, probably, especially the media has ruined my life. I'm sorry, not especially the media—it all starts with you, Derrick. As John Barr said, I'd love to have twenty or thirty minutes with you in a cell, hand to hand.

"The only people who stood by me were my family and a very good friend of mine that I didn't realize how special he was until all of this came about. His name is Bill Cody. John Barr, Melanie, Brandi, Heather, and any of the other victims, we're all Christians. And I don't know how many more of them could actually say that they will forgive you. I never will. Ever. I firmly believe in 'an eye for an eye and a tooth for a tooth.'

"Derrick Todd Lee, if there's any way possible, myself, and I'm sure if nobody else, John Barr, will be there when you are put to death. May Satan take you home."

* * *

It was time for Judge Free to pass down the sentence.

"I kept wondering, you know, what I would say to you," Free said as he looked down at Todd. "I think I understand you. I think we understand each other. I believe that. So I'm not going to waste a whole bunch of time. I'm not going to do that. You know what's right. You know what you need to do. It's up to you whether or not you do it. I can't do it for you, okay? I can't do it for you.

"But I still sit and I look, and I look at the pain, the pain that people brought with them today, and they will take back home with them today. Not just on Geralyn's family, but I'm looking at your family over there. And I look at the pain they deal with now. They've got to live under your shadow now. Think about that. Think about that.

"Your mother, the person who loves you the most, now has to live with 'My son got convicted of murder.' She has to live with that. But she will still love you. And that's the same thing these people are going through right now. They loved their child. It's unconditional. They don't—think about your own. It's unconditional. You don't ask for anything in return. You just give it because they're part of you.

"But Geralyn was somebody's sister. She was somebody's daughter. She was someone's wife. Somebody's cousin. Somebody's friend. And she was just another human being.

"There's nothing I can say any more than these people have said, and nothing more I can say than you've already felt. So with that, I'm going to go ahead and give you your sentence.

"It's the sentence of this court pursuant to Louisiana Revised Statute 14:30.1 that you be remanded to the custody of the Louisiana Department of Corrections for the term of your natural life. Said sentence to be served without benefit of parole, probation, or suspension of sentence. You have two years within which to seek application for postconviction relief."

* * *

For the Barr family, it was over. But Todd still held the other families in his grip. They would have to do this again—only this time, it would be their daughters up on the screen. In two months, Todd would face the death penalty for the murder of Charlotte Murray Pace. For now, though, they celebrated justice for Geralyn.

Lynne Marino waited on the courtroom steps as Todd was hurried from the building to a waiting van. "Hey, Mr. Lee. Who's laughing now, you big fat coward?" She watched as Todd got into the van. After the door was closed, she watched him deliberately bang his head against the interior wall of the van.

"Yep. He's got a date with Big Bubba," Tony told reporters as he watched the van pull away.

The Trial for Death

Television vans and camera crews lined St. Louis Street in downtown Baton Rouge on October 4, 2004. The Nineteenth Judicial District Courthouse was a hubbub of activity as the trial of Derrick Todd Lee for the murder of Charlotte Murray Pace was about to commence. Just two months after Todd was convicted of killing Geralyn, family members of all of the victims once again climbed marbled stairs to relive their nightmare while photographers frantically snapped photos of their nervous faces. Because a Prieur motion had been granted by Judge Richard Anderson, evidence from the murders of Gina, Pam, Dené, and Carrie would be introduced into the trial. Diane Alexander's attack and attempted rape were also being allowed. This trial was to be a bigger sensation than the first, as the district attorney's office had decided to go for the death penalty.

First Assistant District Attorney John Sinquefield, otherwise known as "Dr. Death," due to his reputation for winning capital trials, along with District Attorney Doug Moreau and Assistant District Attorney Dana Cummings, would represent the state in the *State of Louisiana* versus *Derrick Todd Lee.*

Todd would be represented by the public defender's office, including attorneys Mike Mitchell, who had never had a client sentenced to death, Nelvil Hollingsworth, and Bruce Unangst. Each side had formidable teams, veteran attorneys who knew their way around a courtroom. And each side was determined to win.

All eyes turned to Todd as he entered the courtroom surrounded by guards. Some of the victims' families glanced at him as if compelled to do so and then quickly looked away, unable to stand the sight again. Others, like Lynne Marino, glared at him, the hatred palpable. Onlookers simply stared at him, fascinated. Florence, Jackie, Tarshia, and Coleman smiled at him in encouragement, though the tension in their faces belied the gesture. Members of the press busily scribbled notes, carefully watching the reactions of everyone in the packed courthouse.

Todd seemed slightly more somber this time, not as robust and jovial as he had been at his first trial, but he betrayed no signs of nervousness. As he would throughout the trial, he repeatedly turned around and looked at his family sitting three rows behind the defense table, his eyes trying to reassure them that everything would be okay.

Sitting in the center row of the courtroom were the families of the victims. Each parent, brother, sister, husband, and child dreaded what they knew was coming—the gory details they did not want to know. They talked quietly with each other, sometimes letting a stray hand rest on the back of the person sitting next to them. They hugged. They fidgeted. Each felt the loss of the other. They had become bonded through death, and on this day, they were seeking death themselves—the death of the man responsible for their pain.

The bailiff called the court to order as Judge Anderson entered the room, followed by the members of the jury. Case number 6-03-655 had begun. Dana Cummings began opening arguments for the prosecution. Her strategy was to immediately garner sympathy from the jury by describing Murray's personality.

"Your Honor, counsel, ladies and gentlemen of the jury, Charlotte Murray Pace was a twenty-two-year-old beautiful young woman. She was the youngest recipient of an MBA degree from LSU. She graduated the week before she was killed. Murray, as her friends and family have always called her, was very outgoing, and she had a huge group of friends. Her friends and her family were critical to her. She had just landed the first, her first full-time job. She was set to go to Atlanta at the end of the summer and begin her life."

Cummings described how Murray had gone to work on May 31, 2002, and then hurried home to prepare to go to a friend's wedding. She described how Rebekah Yeager had come home, calling out to her friend: "Murray, I'm home. Murray, I'm ready."

She outlined the scene in graphic detail. Rebekah "walked through the kitchen, not noticing bloody footprints on the floor. Walked through the living room, not noticing Murray's half-empty food balanced on the edge of the sofa. She walked into her own bedroom, Rebekah's bedroom, not noticing the blood on the walls, not noticing the blood in the hall. What she noticed and noticed in waves of terror was her friend lying naked on the floor."

Cummings then told the jury that the prosecution's case would be based on DNA evidence collected from each of the victims. The men and women sitting in the jury box were enthralled.

Mike Mitchell immediately retaliated by attacking descriptions that the task force had disseminated about the serial killer. "After he [Todd] became known to law enforcement, and to a part of the multiagency task force, as a suspect, suddenly those descriptions morphed into the face of Derrick Todd Lee. How did it do that? A year later, a year after a description is given. Sometimes you may learn that there [were] three or four descriptions given. After those descriptions are given, they suddenly change and become Derrick Lee, but they don't change and become Derrick Lee until after his arrest."

He told the jury that Todd did not belong in the serial killer puzzle and that the state did not have any business bringing the other murders into the trial.

"Why is the state going to present evidence to you of the murders of Pamela Kinamore, Gina Green, Carrie Yoder, and Dené Colomb?" he asked. "We submit that that evidence that's presented proves nothing. Derrick has not been indicted for any one of those murders, not one of them. Derrick is under indictment for the murder of Charlotte Murray Pace. The evidence presented in this case of those murders is going to prove nothing as far as whether or not he is the person that killed Charlotte Murray Pace.

"So why is that evidence being presented to you? Well, we'll see. But what you will learn from the evidence that's presented is that the Charlotte Murray Pace case cannot, *cannot*, stand alone. If that was the only evidence that they were going to present, not evidence of other murders, but only evidence collected, analyzed, and presented to you in the Charlotte Murray Pace case, it couldn't stand alone. So they will come forward, and they will tell you that, well, he committed all of these other murders too. We ask and we thank you for your commitment to keep an open mind in this case, and believe if you do, the verdict at the end of the case will be not guilty."

The court recessed. Todd smiled at his family before he was led from the room. The victims' families thought Dana Cummings had done a good job of winning over the jury early on. Todd's family thought Mitchell had made good points. The Barrows didn't look at the families that had been hurt by their son as they walked out of the room, escorted by the guard designated to protect them. No one bothered them. Almost everyone felt sorry for Florence. They could relate to how horrible it must be for a mother to know her son was a serial killer. But Florence would never believe that. Todd was her baby boy. He was not a killer. The police needed a scapegoat, and Todd was it. But her step was weary on this day. Florence was afraid for her son's life.

An hour later, witness after witness began testifying, and the horrible recounting of rapes and stabbings and beatings began. It would last for eight days. Several witnesses testified about Murray's comings and goings on the morning of her death; then Rebekah Yeager took the stand.

In the ice-cold courtroom, made colder by the thought of a young woman being viciously killed, a nervous Rebekah told her story. Ann Pace's face turned pale as the young woman spoke.

"I did not see anyone when I went into the house. I could hear that the TV was on in the living room, and I called out to her, just 'I'm home. I'm late. How are you? How was your morning?' As I was walking very quickly through the kitchen and living room, I went into my bedroom, which was off of the living room at the back of the house, and when I walked in the door, I saw that Murray was lying on the floor between the door and the bed. I screamed and jumped back, and I'll tell you sort of how I noticed things, which was kind of in stages."

Rebekah's hands shook as she relived the scene. Taking a deep breath, she continued.

"I saw first that she was there on the floor, and then I noticed that she wasn't wearing any clothes, and again, this was all probably in one second, but I sort of saw it in pieces. I saw that she didn't have any clothes on, that she was nude, and then I saw that there was blood all over the room, on the walls, on the walls in places where I didn't understand how it could have gotten, on the furniture, all over the floor. The bed was made, but it was soaking, the bedspread on the bed. And then I looked at Murray, and I noticed that she had so many small holes in her chest and stomach, and I panicked."

The courtroom was silent, every eye and ear trained on Rebekah.

"I realized that I needed to call 911. So I looked for the handset of the portable phone, which we kept in the living room, and I couldn't find it. So I went back out through the kitchen, through the yard, into the garage, got my cell phone out of my car, dialed 911. While the phone was ringing, I screamed for help, but no one heard me.

"It was just a second before the 911 operator picked up. He had to calm me down. I was a little bit hysterical. I told him that someone had hurt my roommate, and I kept just saying that someone had hurt her. He needed the number of the house, and at that point, I didn't—we had just moved in. I didn't remember the exact address. So I went back in through the kitchen, through the living room, out the front door, looked at the number, gave it to the officer—or to the 911 operator.

"I went with the phone while I was talking to him back into the bedroom, and he asked me to let him know if—to touch her and to tell him if she was warm or if she was cold. I knelt down next to her, and I touched her arm, and she wasn't cold. I told him that, and at this point, it just—it was not in any way conceivable to me that she could be dead. That was not a thought that entered my mind, even though the evidence was completely contrary to that fact."

"Did you see her throat?" John Sinquefield asked.

"Yes."

"What was it?"

"It was cut open wide. He asked me if I wanted to do CPR, and I said yes, I would try that, so I leaned over her, and that's when I saw that her throat was not just slit, but cut open, and her hair was soaked with blood and sort of

pushed back from her face. So I continued to talk to the
911 operator. I ran outside. There was a police car in the
front of the house, just sort of—I don't know if it was from
the 911 call or if he was just passing by. He didn't have
his lights on or his siren, but I flagged him down. He came
into the house with me, and I pointed to the bedroom,
and he went into the bedroom. He drew his gun and told
me to get out of the house, but I went back in anyway, and
he told me again to get out. I just sort of sat on the porch
for a minute, and I dropped my phone there, and then I
heard the sirens and the ambulance, and the other police
cars were arriving."

Ann Pace's face turned whiter as she listened.

"And so I went down, and someone put me in one of
the police cars, and more and more cars were arriving. I
saw them putting crime-scene tape around the house,
and I was still in the back of the car. Then someone let
me out, and I asked them if she was dead, and they said
yes. I never went back to the house again after that day."

As she identified crime-scene photographs for the prosecution, Rebekah glanced as briefly as possible at each
one, obviously shaken by the ordeal of seeing those sights
again, but she maintained her composure. As she left the
stand and passed by the center row, she reached out to
touch Ann Pace's hand before leaving the courtroom.

Ann's ordeal was only getting worse as Dr. Alfredo
Suarez took the stand.

John Sinquefield, who looked every bit like Burl Ives,
offered thirty-nine pictures of eighty-three stab wounds
into evidence and asked Suarez to identify each one individually for the jury.

"Tell me about the wounds to the body of Charlotte
Murray Pace," he said in his slow Southern drawl.

"Well, this young lady sustained multiple injuries to the
body. Most of them were stab wounds. Dr. [Michael]

Cramer, [a contract worker with the Coroner's Office] enumerated them and added them up together to eighty-three different wounds. She also sustained blunt injuries to predominantly the head, with a fractured skull and bruises to the ocular globes—that means the eyeballs—and also multiple bruises to the upper and lower extremities. These latter bruises were not fatal. I think the most fatal wounds were located in the neck area.

"There's also perforation of the heart three times, the liver three times, and the lungs three times. These injuries by themselves that I mentioned, these nine wounds, penetrating wounds to important vital organs of the body, like I said—the lungs, the heart, and the liver—were, by themselves, fatal wounds. However, this is what I call an overkill, because there were too many wounds. I think some of them were probably inflicted postmortem."

Suarez went on to say that stab wounds to Murray's left frontal lobe near her eye caused bleeding in her brain, which would have also killed her. He described thirty wounds on her thorax and abdomen, then the slit to the young woman's jugular vein. He also mentioned defensive wounds on her arms, hands, and wrists that Murray had sustained while fighting for her life.

Ann Pace was visibly shaken, but sat quietly as she had been told to do. All of the families had been warned against emotional outbursts. But for Ann, the hardest part was over. For the jury, it was just beginning as the photographs were passed from one to the other, and they were exposed to violence the likes of which they had never seen. For thirty minutes, they looked at those pictures—some unable to give more than just glance at them, others studying them like professionals. One juror seemed to become slightly ill as he viewed the brutality.

Sinquefield realized that the jurors had been exposed to enough violence for one day and switched tracks. It was time to teach them how DNA works. He called forensic analyst Julia Naylor to the stand.

Dana Cummings stood up to question the witness. "I'd like to show you what I've marked as State's Exhibit Number 25. Actually, let's go with 24. Can you identify that for the members of the jury?" Cummings said, showing Naylor the report.

"This is a chart of the profile I obtained from the sperm fraction of the left buttocks swab, exhibit 24-A, and a profile from the reference blood sample of Derrick Todd Lee," Naylor responded.

"Do these numbers accurately reflect the numbers that you came to in the analysis of this case?"

"Yes, they do."

"And you said on the far left, what is that column, the very far left?"

"The very far left is the STR marker column. That's just the addresses of the thirteen markers, including the sex determinant that we look for."

"What is the next column?" Cummings asked.

"That is the profile I obtained in July of 2002 from the left buttock of the swab of the victim's body."

"And what is in the right column?"

"That is the DNA profile I obtained from the reference blood sample of Derrick Todd Lee in May of 2003. I'm sorry, June of 2003."

"What is your finding as a DNA forensic analyst?"

"That the numbers in the 24-A column and the numbers in the 76-A column match exactly, all the way down, at all thirteen markers."

"No questions? Nothing missing? Nothing different?" Cummings probed.

"No, ma'am."

"And does that tell you that the seminal fluid that was found on the buttocks of Murray Pace came from that man, Derrick Todd Lee?"

"Yes, ma'am."

"Doubt in your mind?" Cummings posited.

"No, ma'am."

Naylor continued to discuss alleles and peaks and baselines for each of the thirteen markers. The jury struggled to keep up, to understand the scientific explanation of how DNA works, as Naylor testified for three hours. But they did understand one thing: Todd and Murray could not be excluded as contributors of that DNA.

"If I were to remove the victim's types, which would be all of the blue numbers, that profile would be consistent with the profile from the reference sample of Derrick Todd Lee," Naylor explained.

Cummings homed in on that. "So if you take the victim out—*boom*—you've got him. That's who it is?"

"Yes, ma'am."

Again, Cummings asked, "Any doubt in your mind that Derrick Todd Lee is the person that left his seminal fluid in Murray Pace?"

"No, ma'am."

Cummings tendered the witness to the defense. Mitchell questioned all of the DNA analysts vigorously about their experience, hoping to convince the jury that they were not experienced enough to competently evaluate DNA. He tried to show that DNA can never produce a positive match—that it can only determine who can and cannot be excluded. That approach would later backfire on him as witness after witness testified that Todd's DNA could not be excluded from all of the victims presented to the court. The odds that it was not Todd who had contributed his DNA to each of them would be staggering.

The prosecution decided it was time to introduce the other victims.

Eight Days in Hell

As the trial wore on, the crowd that had been in attendance on the first day thinned, until only victims' family members, Todd's family, and the media, along with a few die-hard spectators, remained to witness the proceedings. The material being presented was too graphic, too gruesome, for those who had simply been interested in the case to return to the courtroom. The jury, too, had difficulty dealing with the evidence, and as witnesses testified about the lives of the young women who had been killed, jurors tried to stem their tears.

Family members and friends of the victims who were called to testify had a difficult time speaking about their loved ones, but they tried valiantly not to break down.

"Gina was very, very intelligent, well-rounded," Amy Sanders, Gina Wilson Green's sister, told the jury. "When she walked in a room she had a presence about her, and people immediately noticed her and gravitated toward her. She was very funny, had an incredible sense of humor. And she could describe the day's events and just have you falling out laughing, with just the simplest things."

"Was she a smart girl?" Sinquefield asked.

"Extremely."

"A pretty girl?"

"Beautiful."

"Well-paid?"

"Very well-paid, and she worked very hard for everything she got."

Amy described the Saturday night before Gina's death that she had spent with her sister.

"Where did y'all go, and what did y'all do?" the prosecutor asked.

Amy told him that she and her daughter had gone out to dinner with Gina and then watched a movie.

"What time did she leave?"

"She left my house at eleven-thirty that night."

"And that was the last time you saw her alive?"

"Yes, it is. I walked her out the door to her car and watched her drive off."

"You recall what she was wearing?"

"Yes, I do. It was a—it looked like a T-shirt. I believe it was a crew neck, and I think a three-quarter sleeve. And it kind of looked like—maybe an Easter egg is the best way to describe it, with the colors kind of bleeding into each other. And she had on some denim blue jean shorts and a pair of Liz Claiborne blue shoes."

Sinquefield asked Amy to identify the shirt, which contained Todd's DNA. He tendered the witness. After being cross-examined by the defense, Amy was excused and left the room in tears, only to return a few minutes later after she composed herself.

Gregg LeBlanc, Gina Wilson Green's friend and coworker, was next. He was asked to describe what he had found when he went to Gina's house to look for her.

"At first, when I finally saw her face, it looked like she was sleeping. She was laying in the bed. The covers were covering her from the position I was at, at that point, and it looked like she was sleeping. And when I approached the left side of the bed, I saw her right side of her body exposed, and I could tell that she was dead."

"What indication did you have, or what did you see, that caused you to learn or believe that she was dead?"

Sinquefield asked, hoping his witness would paint a clear picture for the jury.

"Her right arm was draped over the side of the bed, hanging downward. And you can tell when a person has been lying there for a while. The blood in the body will settle down, in which her entire hand was bruised. The lower part of her body that I saw was all bruised down."

"When you say bruised, is that the blood?"

"The blood seeping out of the vessels," Gregg explained. "I immediately took off, ran out of the house, thought I was going to be sick. And then I got on my cell phone and called 911."

Prosecutors later showed the jury photographs of Gina's autopsy and a video of her home during the police investigation. Gina's sisters, unable to take it anymore, hurried out of the courtroom during the latter part of the video. The defense took exception to that. Nelvil Hollingsworth addressed the judge.

"I want to note for the record that during the latter part of the playing of the videotape, two family members of Gina Green stood up and walked out of the courtroom," he said. "They caught the attention of at least part of the jury right there, and I do not want this to be a pattern in future pictures or videos. If they—they have been instructed, they know that these are going to be explicit and painful. And if they feel a need to leave the courtroom, then I prefer that they do that prior. This caused needless attention to their suffering and grief, which is not part of this case."

Sinquefield argued that the jury was watching the tape and didn't even notice. The court did not see this as a disruption that had unduly influenced the jury.

* * *

This scenario played out, over and over, as family members struggled to keep their emotions in check, their pain from overflowing. Lynne Marino sobbed silently, her thin shoulder, shaking and tears flowing down her face from under the dark glasses she wore to hide her grief, as Byron Kinamore testified about Pam's life and their marriage.

Byron wheeled himself toward the witness stand. "We would have been married twenty years in October," he said, speaking slowly and softly.

"Did y'all have a child?" Sinquefield asked.

"Yes, sir."

"What's the child's name and age?"

"His name is Jacob, and he is fourteen years old right now."

"Tell me just a little bit about Pam."

"She was born and raised in New Orleans. She came to Baton Rouge to attend LSU and graduated with a degree in fine arts and started out in real estate and eventually went into the mortgage business and did that for several years. Ultimately she was able to do what she always wanted to, and that was to open up an antiques and interiors shop in Denham Springs. For about the last four or five years of her life, that's what she was doing."

"Was she a pretty lady?"

"She was beautiful."

"Good wife?"

"A wonderful wife," he said, with a sad smile.

Byron went on to describe what had happened the night he discovered Pam was missing.

"When I got home, her van was home. I parked in the carport next to her van, got out, came to the back door. Her keys were stuck in the back door. The back door was just barely open. It was shut to the point of the door being against the doorjamb with the keys in the door, which really didn't alarm me too bad. She had done that on several occasions. Being in the business she was in, she often carried things in the house with her, and often had her hands full of whatever—boxes, lamps, et cetera. So she did occasionally bring things in and maybe kick the door with her foot behind her and brought her materials in, set them down or whatever, and just didn't immediately go back and lock the door and forgot to grab her keys or whatever."

"So that's not the first time you had found keys in the door?"

"No, sir."

"Had anyone cautioned her about that or got onto her about it?"

"Several times, yes. I would always fuss at her and tell her, 'You left the keys in the door again,' you know. So, anyway, I took the keys out of the door, closed the door, locked the door, came into the house. That's at the kitchen, and just made my way back to the bedroom. The lights were on in the bedroom, and I just went to the bathroom area and started calling her name and didn't see her at first and went into the bathroom. The tub water was run, and she wasn't in the bathroom."

Byron told the jury that he had noticed that some things in the bedroom were not in their usual places, and he had become concerned when he could not find Pam.

"I could see that she had been in the bathroom, but she wasn't there. So her not being in the bathroom, coming back into the bedroom, seeing those things ajar, I immediately started to become very alarmed. My first inclination was to call her best friend, who lived down the street, because she did go visit her quite often, you know, whether I was home or not. So I picked up the phone, called our neighbor, asked her if she had seen Pam, and she said no. I asked her if she talked to her in the last hour or two, and she said no. So my next thing to do was to call 911 and tell them what I had seen and found, and that's what I did."

Byron testified that he had identified his wife's body from the wedding ring she wore, with the date of their marriage inscribed on the inside.

The Kinamore family then got a lucky break. The judge decided that showing video of Pam's body, which was in advanced stages of decomposition when she was found, would be too disturbing and inflammatory for the jury to view, although the jury was shown pictures. Judge Anderson made the same ruling for a video of Carrie Yoder, who had been found so close to Pam's body.

Lee Stanton, Carrie's boyfriend, would tell the jury about the young girl he had loved.

"Carrie was very outgoing. She was motivated. She was extremely smart and articulate. She was the kind of person that didn't just talk about doing things. She did them. And she always made whoever she was with feel good about themselves and empowered them to do things on their own as well.

"Her outside hobbies included dancing," Lee went on, sometimes speaking so low that Sinquefield had to ask him on several occasions to repeat what he said and to speak louder. "She was gifted at ballroom dancing and did exhibitions through the Baton Rouge area with a dance partner there. She loved to cook. She enjoyed taking trips and traveling. She always had her nose in a travel book and had a map in her house with all these pins in it that—the places that she visited and all the places she wanted to visit. So she was a girl very interested in the world around her."

"She was an attractive woman?"

"She was beautiful."

Lee told the court that he and Carrie had gone to Mardi Gras the weekend before she died. When they got back, she spent the night with him before leaving the next morning. "The last time that I saw Carrie was right around nine, nine-thirty that morning."

Lee explained how he had called and called, but had gotten no response from Carrie. He described how he had gone over to her house twice and had become convinced that something was wrong.

"And then later on, on or about March 13 of 2003, did you learn that her body had been found—in fact, she was dead?" Sinquefield questioned.

"I did," Lee said.

The defense had no questions.

As pathologists testified about Carrie's autopsy results—how she had been strangled, beaten, murdered, and then dropped from the Whiskey Bay Bridge—Ann Pace reached out and placed her arm around the shaking shoulders of Linda Yoder. The testimony was difficult for all of the families, and they strived hard to comfort one another.

Todd just watched with his chin always resting on his hand, seemingly unaffected by the horrific details that had everyone else in the courtroom in tears. For the most part, he sat perfectly still, unless someone walked into the room. Then he would turn around to see who it was. He would listen to the testimony about Dené Colomb as dispassionately as he had the others.

Chester Cedars, district attorney for St. Martin Parish, would be allowed to question witnesses in the Colomb case. Jillian Sura, a lifetime friend of Dené's, would paint a picture of Dené's personality for the jury.

"We met when I was four years old," Jillian said. "Everyone called her Dené. She was so intelligent, taught herself to speak foreign languages. She joined the army, then tried out for the Marine Corps. Dené was a bookworm. She attended Nichols State University and quit to join the army.

"She was so beautiful," Jillian said, tears gathering in her eyes.

Again, everyone was subjected to the brutality of another murder—crime-scene photos from the woods located off Renaud Drive in Scott, Louisiana, the graphic details of how Dené was raped and killed against a tree, the autopsy report explaining every wound.

Investigators reported that a white male in a white pickup truck had been spotted near where Dené's car was parked in the cemetery where her mother was buried. Jurors listened as witnesses explained that Dené had been traumatized by her mother's death and had visited that cemetery often, how a killer had taken her from the cemetery as she visited with the woman she loved so much.

Sterling Colomb and his son sat stoically on their seats throughout. Sterling Jr. stared daggers into the back of Todd's head as Todd sat there doing what he did best—watching.

No one would come away from these eight days unaffected. Many would have nightmares for months. And the most effective witness was yet to come, the witness who could point her finger at Todd and say with certainty that he was the man who had attacked her.

No Defense

Mitchell, Hollingsworth, and Unangst struggled to tear holes into the evidence. They brought up Sean Gillis, the white serial killer who had been operating in the Baton Rouge area during the same years as Todd, to present an alternate theory to the jury. They tried desperately to create reasonable doubt. They told the court how Gillis had killed Ann Bryan, who lived in St. James Place on Lee Drive, close to LSU's campus, in the same vicinity that some of the victims in this case were killed.

They questioned investigators relentlessly about all of the witnesses who had reported seeing a white man in a white pickup truck around four of the murder scenes. They questioned Todd Morris from the attorney general's office about the subpoena used to swab Todd. They asked why the normal method of using a body search warrant was not utilized, perhaps already preparing for the appeal. They asked Morris about the various concrete slabs that had been dug up, the creeks that had been drained. They asked him if anything of significance had been found. Nothing had.

It didn't matter, though. The DNA evidence was too damning. And as forensic analyst Angela Ross testified, the defense watched the faces of the jurors, trying to gauge if they were able to comprehend such technical subject matter. As Ross discussed the odds of the DNA being anyone other than Todd's, the defense knew they were sunk.

"The murder had occurred of Charlotte Murray Pace, and my coworker [Julia Naylor], who I actually share an office with, she was doing her analysis on her own, and over the weekend or the next week after she had begun working the case, she developed a male DNA profile. A coworker of ours had actually asked us if we had compared the two [Gina and Murray], because I had already established—I had already had the profile from my case, and we actually said—we told them no. We hadn't done a comparison on our own. And initially in our minds, the crime scenes seemed very different, so we didn't really see a similarity, but we said, well, we need to compare them anyway. We did. She held up her profile. I held up mine. And we noticed that they were exactly the same at every location."

Ross explained how she had examined DNA evidence from Gina's shirt and the gourmet kitchen towel from Gina's home that had contained Todd's blood. She told the jury that no DNA had been found on Gina's cell phone, nor had any been obtained from the rape kit. Cummings asked Ross to describe the meaning of "random match probability."

"What they look at is all of these different numbers you saw on the chart. We look at how frequently that particular number is found in the population, and we designate—you find that frequency and then as a product—it's called the product rule. You multiply those frequencies together to have an overall number that represents the entire profile. I do want to briefly explain what the product rule is.

"What you would take into consideration is, let's say every one in ten individuals has naturally blond hair, and then you say every one in ten has blue eyes. Then that would mean that every one in one hundred has that combination of blond hair and blue eyes. That is just basically what the product rule means. And then we turn around and apply that to the frequencies that each of those numbers has been found in the population. We multiply those together to get our number that would represent for an entire profile."

"Okay," Cummings said. "And what that means is that's the probability of finding anyone randomly that has the same profile as Derrick Todd Lee?"

"That's correct," Ross responded.

"And what is the random match probability from the evidence that you worked in this case, specifically the shirt and the towel?"

"That random match probability was 3.6 quadrillion."

"And put that in terms of the earth's population."

"Currently the earth's population is approximately seven billion in population right now, and that's living. You would actually have to take over five hundred thousand earth populations to have the chance of finding an individual that has the same exact combinations of numbers at those locations."

The jury was impressed. They had heard about the random match probabilities to Todd and the other victims as well. But the prosecution had saved the best for last. Chester Cedars called Diane Alexander to the stand.

Todd perked up, more interested now than he had been throughout the trial. He chewed his gum vigorously and fidgeted with the leg of his pants.

Cedars showed the jury photographs of Diane's mobile home in Breaux Bridge, where the attack had occurred. They saw the front steps, where Todd had stood while looking at her phone book. They saw the living room, where Todd had tried to strangle Diane while attempting to rape her. Cedars asked Diane about her history, where she worked, where her husband worked, where her son, Herman, was at the time of the attack. Diane described what she had done that morning, then what had happened next.

"He was clean-shaven and neat. He wore blue jean shorts, a white shirt, ankle socks, and sneakers. I didn't see him as a problem. He seemed lost," Diane said. "When I went back to the door to get the phone and phone book, he heard the gospel music I was playing. He said he sang with a gospel choir and asked if I had heard of him. I was getting aggravated. He asked if my husband knew the Montgomerys. I said, 'Look, my husband's not home.' He rushed me into the house."

Diane went on to explain how Todd had caught her by the throat and told her he had a knife. "He laid me on the floor and told me to take my panties off. I said, 'Your hand is on my throat.' He said, 'Shut up. Shut up.' Then he said, 'I've been watching you.'"

Diane recited details of the attack matter-of-factly. "He couldn't get an erection. He laid the knife on the side of him. I grabbed for it and realized the knife wouldn't do him harm. He took it away from me. He called me out of my name."

"What does that mean?" Cedars queried.

"He called me bitch."

Diane talked about how she had tried to reason with Todd, to appeal to him, to compliment him. She explained that he had cut the phone cord to the computer and how she had put her finger in front of the cord so that it would not touch her neck. She told the jury that he had changed shirts, then straddled her shoulders and began hitting her in the head. She said that he was still trying to rape her when he heard something.

"I saw him. It looked like he heard something. Then he stomped me in the lower part of my abdomen with all his might and ran out."

"Is the man who did this to you in this courtroom?"

Diane looked directly at Todd and pointed her finger at him.

"Are you sure?"

"Positive. Without a shadow of a doubt. I'll never forget that face."

Todd looked back at his family before smiling in a flirtatious manner at the blond reporter sitting in front of them.

Again, Diane was an excellent witness, confident, poised, and sympathetic. The jury felt her pain, and some winced as they viewed photographs of the swollen black circles around her eyes and her head soaked in blood. They studied the bloodied dress Diane was wearing that day. She went on to tell them how she had described her attacker to Detective Arthur Boyd and how she had identified him in a lineup sent to her by e-mail on May 26, 2003, the day after the DNA connection was made.

The defense was about to make a mistake. Bruce Unangst, trying to discredit Diane's story, went on the attack. No one in the courtroom enjoyed watching this nice lady being treated like that, including the jurors. Diane stood her ground.

Unangst began by questioning Diane about her relationship with Arthur Boyd and Chester Cedars.

"In all your conversations with Detective Boyd, did you ever talk to him about getting parole granted for your other son?"

The prosecution objected. Unangst moved on.

"On July ninth, did you tell Linda Fontenot that you barely remembered your attacker?"

"I don't recall. I was in and out of it."

Unangst tried to discredit Diane's description, to show that the information she had provided police had changed over time. "I described him as a black male, light-skinned, approximately five feet nine inches. I asked Lieutenant Boyd to stand up so I could have some gauge to understand how tall he was," Diane said.

Unangst asked her to identify the composite. Diane was getting testy. She felt like she was being disrespected, that the defense was saying she was a liar. They were trying to say that her description had changed after Todd had been arrested.

"Do you remember giving a taped statement after Derrick Todd Lee was arrested?"

"I don't recall. You're trying to confuse me." Diane appeared increasingly uncomfortable.

Unangst told Diane that she had not made statements about Todd sweating profusely in earlier reports, that there was no previous mention that Todd said he was going to stick Diane in the eye.

"You did not say before that you told him he was good-looking. Is it safe to say your memory has grown since the event of July 9, 2002?" Unangst accused.

"Objection."

"My memory is the same," Diane said.

"She's getting caught in her lies," Florence whispered to Tarshia.

"Uh-huh," Tarshia responded. "She a liar."

"The first time in any report you discussed a poke in the eye is January 2004," Unangst continued, unrelenting.

"I remember it happening."

"In a hearing on June fifteenth, you didn't mention that he sang in a gospel choir."

"I started to remember." Diane was getting rattled.

"What stimuli caused you to remember? Was it conversations with Boyd, with Cedars?"

"No."

"Do you deny that you told the jury on August fifth that you said it was knee socks? I don't believe your testimony has been consistent."

Diane was becoming angry.

"I want to question you about the observation that your attacker was clean-shaven. On August fifth, you said you could not look at him and tell that. Why did you say he was clean-shaven?"

"He laid his head next to my ear. That's how I knew."

"You said that you could feel roughness when he put his face next to yours."

"He had a mustache that was neatly shaved, eyebrows that were not too heavy."

"Do you admit that your testimony has grown?"

"What do you mean that it has grown?" Diane shot back.

Unangst questioned Diane for a few more minutes before he tendered his witness, but the damage had been done. The jury hated him.

Cedars redirected. "Is there any doubt in your mind that the man who you see in the blue shirt is your attacker?"

"No doubt in my mind." Diane stepped down and hurried out of the courtroom, back to Kentucky, where she had made a more peaceful and safe life for herself.

Detective Sammy Inzerella was called to testify next. He told the jury how he had noticed a missing section of a phone cord as he was collecting evidence from Diane's home, and how he had tied a control knot on the end he had cut to use as a reference sample.

Lieutenant Arthur Boyd would be the final witness in the trial, although no one in the courtroom knew that. The attractive black man with a receding hairline told the jury how the phone cord found at Whiskey Bay had been matched to the one at Diane's house.

"We were able to obtain the phone cord, State Exhibit [Number] 122, from the Louisiana State Police Crime Lab. We took it to the Acadiana Crime Lab in New Iberia for comparison purposes, to see if it was part of the same cord. It matched."

The defense didn't harp on that. They were still more

interested in Diane's original description of Todd. Boyd
was shown the composite drawing. The description read:
*White T-shirt, blue shorts, five-foot-nine-inch man, heavy, black,
complexion smooth, yellowish skin color, eyes light brown.*

"The defense stipulates that Derrick Todd Lee's height
is six foot one-and-a-half inches."

The prosecution rested.

"In that case, the defense rests as well," Mitchell announced. A collective gasp went through the courtroom.

Outside of the presence of the jury, Anderson informed Todd that he had the right to testify in his own defense.

"I don't want to testify if I ain't going to get to say what
I want, really want to say," Todd said. "I been getting
threatening, threatening letters. I want to let you know,
aware how I been treated in that jail."

Anderson had given Todd the opportunity to defend
himself. Todd simply wanted to complain.

The court recessed as Sinquefield and Mitchell prepared to present their closing arguments.

It was almost over.

In Closing

The only sound in the packed courtroom on a sunny Tuesday morning was that of John Sinquefield's drawl as the silver-haired prosecutor addressed the jury. The families of the victims held hands as he explained the meaning of first-degree murder and how a murder must be accompanied by an underlying felony, such as rape, burglary, arson, or kidnapping, to be considered a capital offense. Jurors listened intently as he informed them that it was to be first-degree murder, or nothing. Some leaned forward as Sinquefield launched into the reason why all of the other victims had been introduced into the trial, and the motive for the crimes.

"We produced a lot of evidence in this case—five first-degree murders, one attempted first-degree murder, with underlying felonies of rape, robbery, aggravated burglary, and, in some cases, second-degree kidnapping. Why, you say? Mr. Mitchell told you in opening statement that the reason is that the Charlotte Murray Pace case couldn't stand alone on the evidence in that case. I say that it can. I say that it did. I say that on that evidence you have more than sufficient evidence to find Derrick Todd Lee guilty as charged.

"So why the additional evidence? Because Louisiana law permits it. It allows us to bring you the additional

evidence within the limited purpose of Article 404 (B),
and we wanted you to have all of the information, all of
the evidence that we could give you to make this very important decision hopefully easier.

"Think about it a minute. Think about my victims in this
case. Think about something that they had in common—
all of them. They were beautiful women. They were physically attractive women. They were smart women. They
were accomplished women. They were educated women.
They were women that had an attractiveness to them, not
only from the outside, not their physical beauty, but they
were nice women, the kind of women that people are attracted to—all of them. And I may not be politically correct, and forgive me if I offend anybody, but I believe that
beautiful women, highly intelligent women, accomplished
women, they are a gift to this earth. They bring a softness,
an attractiveness, a beauty, to what sometimes can be an
ugly world. And people are attracted to them.

"But in this beauty, in this attractiveness, in this allure
that they may have through their intelligence and their
physical beauty, there can be a danger. It can attract the
wrong type of person. It can attract sexual predators. It
can attract people that want them for sordid purposes.

"What was the motive in all of these cases if you compare them? Why were they slaughtered? Each and every
one of these women, the evidence shows you, was raped.
Some of them anally, some of them vaginally, some of
them both. They were all raped, with the exception of
Ms. Alexander, and Derrick Todd Lee was in the process
of raping and killing her when her son interrupted him.
She would have been like the rest of them.

"'I've been watching you.' That's what he told Ms.
Alexander. 'I've been watching you.' He didn't pick
them out of the sky. He watched them. He waited. He
waited for the right opportunity. He checked. He made
sure they were alone, and then he strikes."

Sinquefield's words had the desired effect. The thought

that Todd had not only viciously murdered his victims but had watched them, waiting for the right moment, struck at the heart of every woman in the courtroom's worst fear—that this was possible, that, but by the grace of God, it could have happened to her. The air thickened as all eyes focused on the distinguished attorney whose voice chanted its tale of depravity.

The intent, he told the jurors, was certainly to kill—eighty-three stab wounds, a cut throat, a beating, defensive wounds—the intent to kill Murray Pace was there. Sinquefield spoke of Todd's preparation, the planning that went into the murders. He talked about Todd's strength, how he could kill a person easily with his bare hands, as he had done in some of the cases. He reiterated the DNA evidence that had been presented, explaining how the DNA from Gina and Murray had been linked, then brought his argument back to the circumstantial evidence in each case.

"So one thing is certain, on that night after four P.M., March 3, 2003, Carrie Yoder was abducted, raped, murdered, and dumped off the Whiskey Bay Bridge. Well, let's see, Derrick Todd Lee had a prepaid cell phone, and it just so happens at nine fifty-one and nine fifty-two that night, he was making calls. They will say maybe he lent that cell phone to somebody. Those two calls hit two towers moving west to east away from Whiskey Bay Bridge very close to where you come off I-10. So with the DNA from Carrie Yoder's body, you add the phone calls, and what happened? He dumped her body, and he is on his way back, and he is making phone calls. That corroborates the DNA, the Ramah Tower, seven miles from Whiskey Bay, less than thirty-five miles from Baton Rouge."

Sinquefield moved to Diane Alexander's identification of Todd as her attacker. "Who would find a lady like that and go in her house and make her take off her clothes and try to strangle and rape her? What kind of man would do that to a lady like that? What kind of man, through his own failure, his own inability to achieve an erection to rape her, would take it out on her? That's when he became violent, through his own failures. What kind of man? A man like Derrick Todd Lee, and that was a mean, cruel, senseless thing to do to a nice lady like that.

"Did you watch her when she identified him?" Sinquefield asked. "Did you watch her face? I hope you did, because she looked at him, and she said, 'That's him,' and she stared at him. She didn't take her eyes off him. She didn't have a bit of hesitation. She didn't have any doubt."

Todd's leg shook as he listened, but he showed no other emotion.

Sinquefield knew he had the jury. He had vested all of his years of experience into these closing arguments, and he knew he had them. He could feel it. Everyone in the room could feel it. He went for the kill.

He explained how three days after Diane Alexander's attack, Pam Kinamore died. "She is raped. She is murdered. Her body is put over there at Whiskey Bay, but a hundred and fifty yards from her body is the phone cord from Diane Alexander's house, and the pieces exactly match. So let's see if we can figure this out. After he finished with Ms. Alexander and wasn't successful, he had that cord in his car. Then he kills Pam Kinamore, and he dumps her body, and he decides to get rid of the cord while he is over there. I think we just figured it out. And I say that marries the DNA, which is one in 3.6 quadrillion. That marries that DNA to Diane Alexander's identification.

"So, ladies and gentlemen, there is no question in the evidence in the case. Derrick Todd Lee is the person that committed all of these crimes. And what are these crimes that we've proved that he committed?"

Sinquefield picked up a pile of photographs. He held up Gina Wilson Green's smiling face for the jury to see as he spoke. "Gina Green—what a beautiful woman. A registered nurse, practices her trade, a specialty. Nice automobile, highly paid, everything to live for. Beautiful home, very neat except for the part disturbed when Derrick Todd Lee entered. And what did he do to her? He attacked her. He strangled her. He raped her anally and vaginally. He killed her. That beautiful woman that hadn't done anything to him. He killed her. Why? Just for that few minutes of sexual gratification with that beautiful woman. He was willing to take her life and take her away from us. I say he should pay for that."

Sinquefield held up a picture of another victim. "Pam Kinamore—what a beautiful woman. Do you realize the loss to her husband and her family? One little thing about Pam Kinamore—just think about it. What was the name of her antiques shop? Comforts and Joys. I say this woman was a comfort. I say she was the joy, and he took her from us. He killed her. He killed her. He cut her throat for that few minutes of sexual gratification with this beautiful woman that he craved, and he dumped her body in a ravine, where it was found. He destroyed her, and I say he should pay for that."

In the hand that Sinquefield held up, Pam Kinamore's face was replaced with a new woman's. "Carrie Yoder—what an interesting, beautiful, physically attractive young woman. But how smart—she is working on coastal erosion. She is adventurous. She is spirited. She likes to skydive. She likes to dress up. She likes to do ballroom dancing. She likes to cook. A young, adventurous, spirited woman with everything to live for. What might she have done? What might she have produced? And Derrick Todd Lee took her away from us for just that few minutes of sexual gratification that he craved. He killed her, and I say he should pay."

Carrie Yoder's face morphed into Trineisha Dené Colomb's. Some of the jurors were in tears. It was too much, too terrible to listen to impassively. "Look at Dené Colomb—young lady so smart she taught herself foreign languages. A young lady bothered, devastated, by her mother's death from cancer, such that on the day she was abducted, raped, and killed, she was visiting her mother's grave. An athletic young woman who was trying to get back in the Marine Corps because she wanted to serve her country. What a beautiful young woman, and he took her away from us just for that few minutes of sexual gratification that he craved. And to eliminate her as a witness, he destroyed this young life."

Murray Pace's beautiful smile was last. Sinquefield held it high for all to see. "And last, but certainly not least, look at Charlotte Murray Pace. She was smart. She was the youngest person to get an MBA in internal auditing in the history of LSU. She just got a wonderful new job in Atlanta, going to finally make some money, treat herself to a BMW. Her and Rebekah Yeager talked about what they were going to do with their lives. Spirited, never went out without her makeup, hair—everything perfect. Good worker. And Derrick Todd Lee took her away from us.

"And how did he do it? That's the case in chief. What happened that day? She shares something with us, something we'll all have. You don't know when it's coming. You don't know under what circumstance. You don't know when, but all of us have a last day on this earth. We just don't know when. And death can come suddenly, and it can come unexpectedly. And sometimes it's understandable if it's caused from cancer or if it's from a wreck or it's from natural causes. But under some circumstances, it's not understandable, and it's not justifiable."

Sinquefield described the last day of Murray Pace's life, how she had come home from LSU and sat down to relax while she ate her lunch. He spoke of the safety that everyone feels in their home. He admonished the Southern culture for not locking their doors, for being too polite. He noted how this society feels it is rude not to answer a door when someone knocks, but that it was much better to be rude than to be dead.

"All of these women were dead when they unlocked the door, and when he found out nobody was home.

They were dead, but it would be smarter, I guess, to submit—you might buy time. But they are women. They are not to do that. And Charlotte Murray Pace was one of these women. She is young. She is strong. She is athletic, and when he grabbed her and made his intent known, she fought. She fought back with him.

"She clawed. She hit. She fought.

"The battle went from one part of that apartment to the other, blood on the walls. And what goes through a person's mind when that's happening? This polite stranger—all of a sudden, the terror of him grabbing you, and you know he's going to try to rape you, and when he starts injuring you, you know that he's going to try to kill you. You fight back, and that's what she did.

"And as her young, strong heart pumped her life's blood out of those holes he cut out of her, you can believe that she realized that she wasn't going to survive this. She was alone. No help was coming. She wasn't going to survive, but she fought and she continued to fight. He picked the wrong victim that day. It wasn't easy.

"And in the fight, he took her life. He took her body. But he couldn't take her honor. She wouldn't give it to him, and he couldn't take it. She preserved her honor forever by the way she lived, and by the way she died. And that fight—he didn't win it. It's not over. It's here. It's alive in this courtroom. She brought it to you when she trapped his DNA in her body and on her body, and when she reached out and clawed his skin. She brought the fight to you. I say if he doesn't get away with it, he doesn't win it.

"I respectfully request that you return a verdict of guilty as charged of first-degree murder. Thank you."

Those in the courtroom sat in a stunned silence, tears openly streaming down the faces of the jurors, the families of the victims, the reporters, the onlookers.

Mitchell's task had just become that much more daunting.

Judge Anderson called a recess. Everyone needed it.

* * *

Mike Mitchell steeled himself. He knew how much damage had been done to his client through the course of the trial. Sinquefield's closing arguments had put the nail in Todd's coffin. But Mitchell gave it his all as he tried to undo what had been done.

"This is one thing I want to point out," he began. "I understand that this is a tragic case. The case of Charlotte Murray Pace is tragic. The cases that he, Derrick Todd Lee, is not indicted for, but have been presented in this case, are tragic cases, but the judge will instruct you that you cannot decide, you cannot make your decision based on bias, prejudice, or sympathy. And I realize that may be hard to do in a case like this.

"Now, what you have seen for the last eight days or so is what can happen when the state decides that an individual citizen is guilty of a crime, and it brings its awesome, awesome power against that individual." Mitchell reminded the jury of their promise to deliberate sincerely and honestly, of their promise to give Todd his presumption of innocence.

Then he set about attacking the competency of the DNA analysts who had matched Todd's DNA to the victims. He again questioned why the other cases were brought in if Murray's case could have stood on its own. His point was that it couldn't.

Next he attacked the Zachary Police Department, questioning how they could have had Todd under surveillance all those years, and not have known he was the murderer—if, in fact, he was. "How does he commit all of these crimes while he is under surveillance by law enforcement? How does he do that? Derrick Lee—special education dropout. How does he do that? Well, I don't know, but I know, and you know from testimony, that Derrick has had problems with the Zachary Police Department, that he doesn't want anything to do with them, that they have harassed him. They have followed him. They surveilled him for years, so that when Dannie Mixon comes to him to take a swab from him, he says to Dannie Mixon, 'I don't want Ray Day taking it.'

"And why doesn't he want Ray Day taking it? Because he doesn't trust Ray Day. He doesn't know what Ray Day is going to do with it. He says, 'Mr. Mixon, you can take it. I don't have any problems with you. I don't know you. You say you're with the attorney general's office. You can take the swab. Come on in the house and take the swab.'"

Mitchell asked the jury to think about why Sergeant Ray Day, who thought Todd was the serial killer, would wait until the next day to take the swab to the lab. "Now, you know what happens with the swab between the time he takes it and eventually gets to the crime lab? I don't know. We don't know. But we do know that it's a few weeks or later before it's even run. And at the time it's run, it's run by Natasha Poe, who knows and is acquainted with, professionally, Mr. Day, or Officer Day. And she goes in on her day off before the day of a holiday, and—lo and behold— she finds that that swab matches Derrick Lee, and then we extrapolate everything from that point out, and everything else matches, supposedly, Derrick Lee. Well, I'm going to submit to you that there's an error in there somewhere."

No one in the courtroom, aside from Todd's family, was buying it. Mitchell moved on to the blood in Murray's apartment.

"The question I have for the state, the thing that raises a reasonable doubt in this case about Derrick Lee being the perpetrator, is this—if there is blood in that house everywhere, and it's slinging all over the place, why is there no one, not anyone anywhere, who sees Derrick Lee either that day, that afternoon, that evening, with bloody clothes? Why is it that when they search anybody who's ever been connected to him, they find nothing, nothing that ties him to Charlotte Pace, except the DNA? Nothing else. How is that?

"We go to Gina Green. We essentially have the same problem. Are there fingerprints at Charlotte Pace's place? There's fingerprints at Gina Green's home. In fact, in Gina Green's home, there are fingerprints that are on the headboard, the bedpost, and they manage to get the fingerprints off of there. The problem is, they are not able to match them to anyone, but guess who they are especially not able to·match them to? Derrick Lee. Why is that? Why is it that—and how could it be that in that home there is nothing, nothing at all, that ties Derrick Lee to that crime, other than, of course, the DNA?

"I want to move down to Pamela Kinamore. Ms. Kinamore—in her home. Again, there is nothing at all, not a hair, not a piece of skin, not a piece of clothing, not a footprint, nothing that fits Derrick Lee. Except, of course, the DNA.

"In the Carrie Yoder case, we have exactly the same problem. There is not any evidence at all that ties Derrick Lee to that case other than the DNA.

"The last unfortunate death that we had that you heard about was Dené Colomb from Lafayette. And in that case, in that case, we have evidence collected at the scene where her body was found. You have a cast of a tire print. The tire print doesn't match anything that Derrick Lee ever owned. Was there any other evidence at that scene that tied Derrick Lee, other than the DNA, that tied Derrick Lee to this case?"

Mitchell was just warming up, the direction of his argument resting on the hope that the jury had not been able to understand all of the DNA evidence.

"When Derrick Lee is arrested, and you heard Officer Colter, Dannie Mixon from the AG's office, other witnesses from the attorney general's office, all testified that when he was arrested, they got search warrants for his family's home. They got search warrants for his friends' homes. They got search warrants for every automobile that he ever touched. They got search warrants for cars

that he had either lost at foreclosure or traded in, and
were now owned by somebody else. They searched cars
in Dallas, Texas, and they found not a trace of evidence
in any of those automobiles that ties Derrick Lee to any
of these cases, not a trace."

Mitchell realized that it was time to do some damage
control, as he had recognized the jury's anger at the an-
tagonistic questioning of Diane Alexander.

"Now, I want to at this point, I want to apologize to
you, apologize to Diane Alexander. We understand that
she's a victim in the case, and we don't come into this
courtroom to beat up on anybody. But the fact of the
matter is when a witness takes the witness stand and
holds their hand up to tell the truth, the whole truth,
and nothing but the truth, when the whole truth doesn't
come out, you've got to bring it out," he said, defending
Bruce Unangst's tactics.

Mitchell went on to say that eyewitness identifications
are notoriously flawed, that Diane was under stress when
she identified Todd. "Now, she didn't come into this courtroom to deliberately lie, I don't think, but she's wrong.
She's in error. She has been convinced that she's right. She
has met with the DA in Breaux Bridge. She has met with
the investigators over and over and over and over again,
and gone over this story over and over and over again, but
the first descriptions that she gave of her attacker did not
match Derrick Lee—and if any description is going to be
reliable, it's going to be that first one. By the time she
picked out Derrick Lee, Derrick Lee's picture was on *America's Most Wanted*."

Mitchell talked about the unreliability of DNA, how
it wasn't conclusive because DNA analysts could only
give random match probabilities of who could not be excluded as a donor. He tried to make the numbers—in the
quadrillions—appear to be numbers the forensic scientists
pulled out of thin air. Then he moved on to the task force.

"The task force put out a bulletin that there was a white

312 Susan D. Mustafa, Tony Clayton, Sue Israel

guy in a white truck, white pickup truck, that was their main person of interest. Today, the prosecution tells you that was wrong. Well, it just happens to be coincidental that in the Pam Kinamore case, we have three people who see a white guy in a white truck leaving that neighborhood somewhere around the time that she would have been home. Is that just coincidence? Is it just coincidence that we have the same thing in the Charlotte Murray Pace case? Is it just coincidence that in the Gina Green case we have a vehicle leaving her driveway, or someone's close to it the same day that she is murdered, at a high rate of speed? Is it just coincidence that in the Dené Colomb case, her car is parked near—on Robbie Road, near her mother's grave site—and there's a witness who sees a white truck with a white male parked right behind her car?"

Mitchell told the jury they had only two pieces of direct evidence: the testimony of Diane Alexander and the not guilty plea of Derrick Todd Lee. "The other piece of direct evidence that you have is the record in this case that was read to you at the beginning, where the indictment was read to Derrick Lee, and Derrick Lee entered his own plea of not guilty. He was not guilty then. I believe after your deliberations, the verdict will be the same.

"Now, I don't know about the scientists, but I make mistakes. When I make a mistake in this courtroom, Judge Anderson corrects me. The prosecutor makes a mistake in this courtroom, Judge Anderson corrects them. I'm asking that you, in your deliberations, deliberate carefully and not make the mistake of finding Derrick Lee guilty in this case."

Mitchell had given it his best—a valiant effort, considering the DNA evidence against Todd. But few in the courtroom felt that it would be a mistake to convict Todd. And no one, aside from Todd's family, felt an ounce of sympathy for the man after what they had witnessed in that court.

* * *

In his rebuttal, John Sinquefield complimented Mike Mitchell on his excellent representation of Derrick Todd Lee. He pointed out that some of Mitchell's argument was not factual—especially the point he had made about Todd being under constant surveillance. Sinquefield explained that every home has many fingerprints that cannot be identified—basically anyone who has been in the house at any time could leave a print. He told the jury that the reason no one had seen any blood on Todd was that the victims had been unable to injure him—that he was too strong and had disabled them. He defended the accuracy of DNA, the competency of the scientists. He defended Diane Alexander.

"Eyewitness identification. Notoriously flawed. They don't like DNA. They don't like eyewitness identification. I assume they figure if they can get rid of DNA, get rid of eyewitnesses, people like Derrick Todd Lee, they can just rape and murder at will."

Sinquefield submitted that the evidence was overwhelming. The case went to the jury.

The Jury Deliberates

Things had not been going well for Barbara Helms Bass in 2004. She lived in a one-room apartment in a complex on Sharp Road in Baton Rouge. She was in the middle of a divorce and was heavily in debt. But there was a bounce in the sixty-one-year-old woman's step as she went to check her mail one day early that fall. The slight breeze in the air had revived her spirit.

The metal mailboxes were attached to the wall in row upon row, small boxes that required keys for entry. As Barbara inserted her key, she happened to look up and noticed an envelope resting on top of the boxes. Curious, she reached up and grabbed it, surprised to see that her name was on the envelope, along with a note that read: *Not at this address.* She tore open the envelope. It was a summons for jury duty.

"Finding that letter like that made me feel like I was supposed to do that, be on a jury, but at that time, I did not know it would be Derrick Todd Lee."

Barbara arrived at the Centroplex early on the day she was to report. Soon the auditorium filled with hundreds of people. The word passed around quickly that this was to be the trial of the South Louisiana Serial Killer. It would take twelve days for attorneys to choose an acceptable jury, which would consist of six men, six women, including ten white members and two black, and three alternate jurors. Mitchell had raised serious doubts as to whether a fair jury could be found in East Baton Rouge Parish and had requested a change of venue. Judge Anderson had refused that request, but he had ordered that the jury be sequestered.

Barbara was among those chosen. She was brought with the other women in a van to the Marriott Hotel, off Corporate Boulevard. The women stayed on one floor of the hotel, the men on the floor below them. They were under constant guard by sheriff's deputies, who also attended to their needs.

The group was a diverse one, fifteen people with differing political beliefs, religious beliefs, and socioeconomic backgrounds. But they all had one thing in common: if warranted, they could sentence someone to die. That had been a key factor for John Sinquefield when questioning prospective jurors because the death penalty requires a unanimous decision. None of the jurors, who had taken an oath to be impartial, had any idea how this trial would affect their lives. By the time the case went to the jury, the men and women were worn out, tired of being away from their families and sickened by what they had witnessed.

"I did not realize that we would have to go through all the deaths," Barbara said. "I thought it would just be Charlotte Pace. Nobody on this jury can say those pictures didn't affect them. Some of the pictures seemed worse than the ones of the Holocaust. You couldn't make out Charlotte's face—or Pam's. I couldn't believe a human being could do that to another human being."

And after spending so much time together, some of the jurors were sick of each other. Barbara was the feisty one—an opinionated, talkative mother figure who did not get along with several men on the jury, including the foreman, Ronald Venable.

"Two of the jurors, in particular, thought of me as a domineering female," Barbara said, shrugging. "You have to understand that we had fifteen people living together, eating together, for almost two weeks, with a lot of different personalities involved. It was difficult at times. As the trial wore on, it got worse. All of the other women had nightmares, and some of the men too. My faith kept me from getting them. I knew I was where God wanted me to be, and I brought a rosary with me every day to trial. I always faced the cross toward Derrick Todd Lee."

And so on October 11, 2004, late in the afternoon, these jurors, who had spent more than a week observing Todd, listening to the evidence, watching video, viewing horrific pictures, and learning about the victims, gathered together in a room to decide his fate. Many had openly cried during the trial. All had seen the worst of human depravity. None would return to their lives unaffected.

The families of the victims didn't know whether to leave or stay. So much evidence had been presented, but they knew that the jury in Geralyn DeSoto's trial had not taken much time, and they hoped this jury would follow suit. So they waited, chatting with each other uneasily, impatiently, hoping for the outcome they wanted. Praying that justice would be done.

Judge Anderson had given the jurors their instructions. After a few minutes of discussion, they decided they wanted to see a part of the court record of the trial. Anderson called the jury back in to refuse that request, citing that the record was not yet transcribed. They returned to the jury room.

The group decided to take a tentative vote. All twelve jurors agreed that Todd was guilty of first-degree murder.

"We decided in five minutes that this man was guilty. Diane Alexander and her son were the most convincing witnesses. And the district attorneys and the scientists that taught us about DNA were superb in their presentations. Once they got to the phone cord that connected

Pam and Diane, you could see the serial killings," Barbara explained. "We asked if anyone had a doubt, and no one did. We knew we couldn't go back in there in just ten minutes, so we took a smoke break and a bathroom break. Some of the guys played cards. We wasted time until we decided the parents had waited long enough."

After one hour and twenty minutes, the jury returned to the courtroom. Todd sat stoically in his chair, not a flicker of an eyelash, as the verdict was read. Anderson polled the jury. The verdict was unanimous. Todd's luck had run out. He had just been convicted of a capital offense.

Jackie and Florence sat silently as they listened to a jury find their beloved Todd guilty of murder, once again. Still, they did not believe he was capable of doing the things two courts had agreed he had done. He just couldn't have.

The families of the victims celebrated quietly, hugging each other fiercely, with tears of joy streaming down their faces. "Thank you, God. Thank you, God" reverberated throughout the courtroom.

Through the conviction of Todd for Murray's death, the families of Gina, Dené, Carrie, and Pam had also received vindication. Diane Alexander had received vindication for her attack. None of the other cases of murder for which Todd could be tried would ever go to trial. No one wanted to go through this again. And as Connie Warner's family celebrated with the others, they knew that they would never have that same vindication, nor would Randi Mebruer's family or Eugenie Boisfontaine's or Christine Moore's.

The penalty phase was set to begin the next morning.

Eye for an Eye

The jury convened at nine o'clock Wednesday morning. It was Todd's turn to fight for his life. And this time, his only weapon was mental retardation. According to Louisiana law, a mentally retarded person could not be put to death. The defense would try to convince the jury that Todd should be given a life sentence because his mental incapacities prevented him from acting in a rational manner. But first, the jury would hear from Murray's family. Her father, Casey Pace, was called to the stand.

Casey took a deep breath, then described for the jury what his daughter Murray had been like, how she collected friends so easily, how he was in awe of her. Then he described how her death had affected his life.

"Like most men, I spent a lifetime trying to hide emotions from the world, trying to hide from myself. But when you lose a child, they're too strong. You can't do it anymore. I learned how to cry. I don't remember crying any time in my adult life until Murray died. Now it's something you read, a phrase you hear, a song. You don't know what's going to trigger things. But it's too strong to hold back. I learned what heartache really means.

"One of the hardest moments for me was at Murray's

memorial service when her mother spoke about her, her preacher spoke about her. And I can remember a little piece of my mind being shocked that your heart can still beat when it hurts that bad. I can't say it's a bad thing to learn about emotions. It probably makes me a better person. It's probably a gift from Murray, my daughter. Unfortunately, there's some bad ones that come with it—anger, rage, hate. These are things that you—I pray that I learn how to deal with it in a constructive way."

Casey read a letter to the jury that Murray had sent to her mom that told of Murray's love for her mother and her regret that she had not appreciated Ann as much as she should have. The letter expressed Murray's dreams and hopes for her future: *I want to see for myself and become the endlessly able sparkling beauty that my mother envisions me to be,* Murray wrote.

"That's the kind of relationship that was taken from us, and that's the kind of person that my daughter, Murray Pace, was, and that the world lost," Casey said.

Murray's sister, Sam, was next. "How did you learn of her death?" Sinquefield asked.

"It was a Friday. I live in Texas, so I was far away from home. And it was Friday after work, and I had come home. A friend was moving, and so I had gotten home from work late, stopping to help her pack up her moving van. My husband was already there. I hit play on the answering machine, and there was my mother's voice telling me to call her, but it was that voice that you don't know what happened, but that you know whatever it was, that it's horrible.

"And so, Scott, my husband, and I, of course, immediately called. And my mother was who I was able to get in touch with first. And I remember her saying, 'Murray's dead.' And that—that just couldn't be. I mean, this person, she was so larger than life. She couldn't die. She couldn't be dead.

"And I said, 'What happened?' because you don't expect to hear that. But what you expect is there was a car crash or something. And all she said was 'A man broke in, and she's dead.' And that's how I found out. I don't even remember much after that. My husband packed our suitcases, and we drove all night to get here. And it's been a cascading nightmare ever since."

Sinquefield called Ann Pace to the stand. Todd sat impassively looking on. Everyone else in the courtroom dabbed at their eyes.

Sinquefield showed Ann pictures and asked her to identify them. "That's Murray's preschool picture from Beth Israel School. And when she was that small, she had curls and big—big blue eyes. And in this picture, she in her pink tutu with her legs straddled out and her hands on her hips. That's Murray's picture with her brother. And they were both going to the prom with other people. And it's—she has on a very glamorous, beautiful dress. That's a picture from her graduation from LSU, where she was the youngest person ever to receive an MBA. That's Murray with her dad. Her dad coached her through seasons and seasons of soccer, and they were soccer pals. In this picture, her dad has on his soccer things, but Murray, of course, has on a strapless black gown. That was a picture of us at Millsaps. I think it was a mother-daughter day."

"Tell me how her murder has affected your life," Sinquefield requested.

"It's affected everything. It's—there's—there's no peace in sleep. There's no joy in holidays. There's—you—it has changed who I even thought myself to be. It's changed—it's changed the world. It's a hotter, darker, more frightening place than I ever imagined it could be. It feels like maybe soldiers feel when they come back from a war, and they're missing parts of their body. It feels like that. You know you're not dead, and you keep

going, but it—you're missing things. It—you're just—that
won't ever come back."

Ann went back to her seat. She reached for the hands
of her family and held them close.

Some of Todd's teachers and a principal from the
schools he had attended in St. Francisville were called by
the defense to testify. They reported that he had some difficulty in school. "He wasn't the best student, nor was he
the worst," recalled Michael Thornhill, principal of West
Feliciana High School. "It seemed like if he got angry or
something, he got over it quickly. He seemed to enjoy PE."

"The most I remember about Derrick is more about
behavior than academics," said Dorothy Temple, principal of Bains Elementary. "Very sociable, very talkative,
hard to keep focused. The type of child that you want by
your desk to keep him focused."

Mike Mitchell called Tarshia to the stand. "Before I
get into the specifics of your relationship with Derrick,
was there something you wanted to say?"

"That on behalf of my family, my mother, my dad, my
entire family, for the Pace family and all of—all of y'all,
we are so sorry for y'all loss. And I promise you there's
not a day that goes by—before this happened, I could remember one New Year's Eve, the pastor calling me to
pray. And I prayed for the families and the victims of the
serial killer. And even when Derrick was accused of this,
I never stopped praying for y'all. Never. We are sorry.
I'm sorry. My family is sorry for your loss."

Tarshia was crying. Mitchell asked her if she was okay.
She nodded as she went into a description of what is was
like to grow up with Todd, how they had always been
close, how she and Todd had the same smile. She talked

about how they had always squabbled, but they had always made up.

"Anything else about your relationship that you would like this jury to know about Derrick or the family?" Mitchell asked.

Tarshia stuttered through it, nervously aware that she was fighting for her brother's life.

In his first display of emotion throughout the entire trial, Todd cried openly as he listened to his sister.

"That Derrick, Derrick is, he's—he's still my brother, and I—and I love him. I love him. And he's just, he's been there for me. No matter how many arguments you have as siblings or fuss and fights you have, you're always there for each other. And I do, I miss him, not, you know, just not being right. It's been hard. It's been hard. And it's, I just miss having, you know, I just, even having the kids at my house and having to face those, an eleven-year-old child and a fifteen-year-old child, and having to give them answers and having to help them cope with everyday life. It's been hard because I know they love their dad. And we love him too."

There was not a person in that courtroom who did not feel sympathy for what Todd's family must have been going through.

Prosecutor Sinquefield showed Tarshia a police report that had been filed in which Todd had tried to get into her house, cursing and threatening her. He had made his point.

Each side had enlisted two experts to interview Todd and determine his mental abilities. One by one, they were called to the stand.

Dr. William Drew Gouvier, a professor at LSU, where some of the victims had attended school, and Dr. Sarah DeLand, a board-certified forensic psychiatrist, would testify for the defense. Dr. Donald Hoppe, a board-certified psychologist who had interned at Johns Hopkins in Baltimore, and Dr. Robert Blanche, a geriatric psychiatric pratitioner, would testify for the prosecution.

Dr. Gouvier reported that he had discovered significant deficiencies in intellectual functioning in two of five important domains of adaptive functioning in Todd. He reported that Todd had a long history of having speech and communication disorders. Todd's capacity for self-direction was also limited, he said, which is the ability to make planned, wise choices about what Todd did with his time, with his life.

To the victims' families, that analysis was laughable. Todd planned very well—every detail of every murder and rape was planned as he stalked each of his victims.

Gouvier also found Todd's IQ to be sixty-five, five points below the standard measure of retardation. He told the jury that Todd's habits of drinking a lot, hanging out in bars, and trying to make people think highly of him were coping mechanisms. He explained that he had administered a grip test on Todd, and that he was mild to impaired in the right hand and had average grip strength in his left hand.

"Did you let him try your throat?" prosecutor Sinquefield asked. "You think he could have done better?"

"I wouldn't want to invite anybody that demonstrates a mildly impaired 41.5 kilogram, approximately ninety pounds of grip strength, to wrap his fingers around any of my private parts," Gouvier retorted.

Dr. Sarah DeLand agreed with Gouvier's findings that Todd was retarded. She told the jury that Todd had been knocked out as a child, that he had hit his nose and had stitches, which could have affected him. She said that he had been classified in school as a slow learner, that he couldn't handle a checkbook, that he needed help with logs when he drove trucks. She said that she had performed three interviews with Todd and had tried to trip him up. She noted that he had trouble with chronology, that he couldn't remember what happened three years, five years, ten years ago. "Everything is five years to him."

She said that Todd was narcissistic, self-centered, and selfish.

Dr. Hoppe went over Dr. Gouvier's reports and disagreed. He said that there is room for error in IQ tests, that Todd had equally developed verbal and nonverbal skills. He told the jury that IQ constantly changes over time.

The law requires that the onset of mental retardation must occur before the age of eighteen. Dr. Blanche explained that Todd's IQ had slipped below seventy occasionally throughout his early school years, but on average, that it had stayed around seventy-five and had even gotten as high as ninety-one at one point.

Doctors Hoppe and Blanche both agreed that Todd was not mentally retarded. He had learned to cope in a work environment, had driven big trucks, and had maintained relationships—not one, but two, for many years.

In closing arguments, Sinquefield explained the law about mental retardation to the jury. He stressed that mental retardation had nothing to do with a person's IQ. "Mental retardation means a disability characterized by significant limitations in both intellectual functioning, and the second part that's a requirement—it requires two—adaptive behavior as expressed in conceptual, social, and practical adaptive skills."

He reminded the jury that they must consider all of the evidence from the first part of the trial in addition to what had been presented during the penalty phase.

"So you ask yourself here, do you have a mentally retarded person that should be exempt from capital punishment, or do you have a murderer sitting over there, a serial killer that's trying to hide behind a claim of mental retardation to escape the punishment that he so richly deserves? And I just didn't say it. The evidence said it. My psychologist, 'He's not mentally retarded.' My psychiatrist, 'He's not mentally retarded.' The people from JE Merit—'He is not mentally retarded. He worked his way up. He is like everybody else out there.'

"Look at his background. He functions. He gets commercial driver's licenses. He has cell phones. He has families. He has wives. He functions in society. He is not mentally retarded under that definition. Ask yourself one more question. How could a person that played so dumb with his mental experts—how could he get in there, kill, rape, abduct those women, and avoid detection for the length of time that he did, with hundreds of law enforcement officers looking for him all over the area, with the TV looking for him, everybody looking for him? I say he is smart. He is clever. It takes a smart, clever individual to do that and get away with it. And I say if you are that smart and you're that clever in murdering people, if you're intelligent enough to carry that out and not get caught, then you're smart enough to be executed for it.

"How much pain, how much misery, how much destruction, how much damage, can one person do before somebody puts a stop to it?"

It was the defense's turn, and Bruce Unangst defended his experts, explaining the results they had determined to the jury. "Dr. Gouvier has everything to lose by being associated on this side," he said. "He had the courage to speak. He had the courage to do the right thing.

"I told you in opening, I looked at Derrick. I didn't see mental retardation. I had to learn what it was. I didn't realize you could function. I didn't realize you could have a driver's license. I didn't realize one in fifty people suffer from mild mental retardation, and eighty percent of those fall into mild category, the functioning category. I didn't know that.

"Now, I told you in opening that I had seen those pictures, and I had seen a monster in my mind that's presented by those pictures, but I'll tell you, in the eighteen months that I've represented Derrick Lee, that's not the side of Derrick Lee that I've seen. He is childlike. He is simple. And he is human. And I don't know what kind of evil must have descended upon that man to produce what I saw in those pictures. I don't understand that kind of evil. I don't fathom that kind of evil, but I do know one thing. That evil is not defeated by sticking a needle in an arm. That evil is not deterred by a death penalty."

Unangst went on and on, doing his best to convince the jury to spare Todd's life. "I feel like the death penalty, putting him to sleep, is too easy. I think life in prison for the rest of your life in a jail cell half the size of this—no windows, the stench of mildewed cement and iron, twenty-three hours out of the day, living with this—is worse.

"You can choose life. You may say, 'No. The death penalty is worse, but I'm going to say mercy.' You can choose life. You say, 'Mercy? He didn't have mercy on Murray Pace,' and I say you don't have to make the same choice Derrick Lee made. You say, 'He doesn't deserve mercy,' and I say that's not what mercy is. If you earn it or you deserve it, it's not mercy. The only way mercy is extended is if necessarily it's not earned or deserved."

Unangst returned to his seat, hoping that at least one person on the jury would have mercy.

One hour and thirty-three minutes later, as the verdict was read, family members of the victims held hands and held their breath. No one on the jury had had mercy. They voted unanimously that monsters have no place on this earth. Derrick Todd Lee must die.

As Todd was taken from the courtroom, Florence,

with a mother's pain etched into her face, screamed to her son, "I love you, son. Always." Tarshia cried aloud, "I love you, Todd."

Todd raised his hand, making the peace sign to his family. "They won't say about the DNA they took eight times," he yelled, still proclaiming his innocence to the very end.

On the steps of the courthouse, family members were mobbed by the media. "I feel like they are finally, finally, finally given some measure of peace and justice," a relieved Ann Pace told reporters.

An ecstatic John Sinquefield celebrated. "Let me say tonight that South Louisiana Serial Killer Derrick Todd Lee got South Louisiana justice."

Lynne Marino also celebrated with reporters, but she still wasn't letting up. Her convictions were too strong to forgive so easily. "I knew he wasn't retarded," she said. "If that man's retarded, what does that say about our task force?"

Death Row

White wooden crosses line up over graves in cemeteries that house the remains of those who have lived and died at the Louisiana State Penitentiary at Angola. There are no names on the markers through which to remember the dead, only numbers—numbers prisoners were assigned as they entered the system. There is nothing to represent that these men had a mother or a father who loved them, who gave them a name. There are no loving epitaphs to depict accomplishments. The number on the cross is simply an indication that once there was a life, and now that life is gone. The sight is an eerie one, a premonition of what awaits lifers and those assigned to Angola's death row. And a numbered white cross is the fate that awaits Derrick Todd Lee.

Under heavy guard, Todd made the long trip from Baton Rouge to Angola. The road he traveled was a familiar one, a road he had traveled all of his life. Sometimes it had led him home to the house he had bought with Jackie's inheritance, the home where he had raised young Doris and Derrick Jr. Sometimes it had led to his favorite fishing haunts and to the homes of his family. Other times to Liz's Lounge and Bailey's Lounge to drink with his friends and play his games with the women there. On this day in October of 2004, that road led to death row.

Todd was familiar with prison life, had spent many

years in and out of the system. But he had never been to Angola, and this prison is not the average, everyday prison. Many consider it to be the Alcatraz of the South, and at one time, it was the bloodiest prison in Louisiana.

In 1869, Samuel James, owner of a steamship line, acquired the lease to the land upon which the penitentiary sits. By 1880, James had moved prisoners to Angola Plantation and was becoming wealthy on the backs of those he forced into hard labor. The plantation was a way to continue slavery legally after the Civil War simply by arresting people, bringing them to the prison, and forcing them into slave labor. The average life span of the prisoners was ten years at that time—ten years spent breaking their backs to increase the coffers of their warden. James died in 1894, and the state of Louisiana bought the leases to the prison in 1901.

Surrounded by a naturally rugged terrain, including Tunica Hills, swamps, the Mississippi River, and the oxbow-shaped Lake Killarney, the setting is perfect to discourage those who might wish to escape the hell that is life within the walls of the compound. The prison's history throughout the twentieth century is peppered with stories of murders and rapes and attempted escapes—not very successful attempts—and corruption and bloodshed, lots and lots of bloodshed. It began in 1916 when the state's efforts to save money resulted in the firing of all of the prison's guards. Trustees were elevated to the position of guards, which led to abuses of prisoners and general chaos.

Conditions at the facility continued to deteriorate over the years, and by the early 1950s, prisoners were cutting their own Achilles tendons to protest the brutality they suffered and the hard labor to which they were subjected. Finally the situation became so intolerable and such an embarrassment to the state that the then-governor Edwin Edwards appointed a reforming director of corrections when the U.S. courts ordered the prison be reformed in 1972. Thus, the Angola that would welcome Todd to Tier A was a different Angola from years past. Within the last twenty years, this prison that boasted one of the worst reputations in the country had turned around under the wardenship of Burl Cain, and had become a model among U.S. penal establishments in many ways.

With an agricultural background, Burl Cain utilized his expertise to take advantage of the eighteen thousand acres on which the prison rests by raising cattle and growing corn, cotton, soybeans, and wheat. Selling millions of pounds of these items on the commodities market each year has turned Angola into a moneymaking machine and reduced the cost to feed its 5,108 "regular" inmates to $1.42 per day.

While Cain worked to increase Angola's efficiency, he also determined to restore moral order to the prison. This warden believes in moral rehabilitation and brought religion to his inmates in an effort to give them hope. His efforts paid off through improved relations between prisoners, and over a period of a few years, Angola began functioning less as a hellhole and more like a well-oiled machine, with prisoners being rewarded for good behavior, given hope that God will be merciful, and understanding that idleness is unacceptable. Aside from minor incidents here and there, most prisoners came to understand that it was in their best interests to make their time as easy as possible. Cain gave to the prisoners their own community and much-needed pride.

But for those inmates who don't buy into Cain's philosophies, Camp J lies waiting and ready for the most hardened offenders. And for those who dream of escape, the howling of the wolves at night serves as a reminder that attempting that might not be the best of ideas.

Cain loves his wolves. Although the prison is surrounded with chain-link fences, decorated with razor wire, there is really no need for that. All of the inmates know about the wolves, and are duly respectful of what they represent. Because it is illegal to breed a pure wolf, Cain

brings to Angola beautiful animals of black and white and
beige that are 95 percent wolf, then breeds them with
German shepherds and Belgian Malinois. The mixed
wolf-dogs are then trained to become ferocious attack
dogs. Living among bloodhounds, like Missy and Heidi
and Calypso and Old Red, the latter making it to fame in
Blake Shelton's country song by the same name, these animals with the piercing eyes and sleek coats provide all the
security that the prison needs. When asked why he would
even contemplate breeding these wolves, Cain simply responded, "Wasn't it the wolf that ate Grandma?"

So it is this prison, surrounded by beautiful rolling hills
and imbued with a serenity that belies the blood and
sweat that are soaked into its fields, that Todd will forever
call home. And there's really no place like Todd's new
home. Death row is built at the highest point in Angola,
with $30 million having been invested in the last few years
to shore up the levees that surround the compound to
avoid ever having to evacuate the most lethal of prisoners in the state—an irony in that these prisoners are saved
from the floods known to devastate Louisiana only to be
put to death. Solid concrete walls, one foot thick and re-
inforced with steel, surround the compound. Twelve-foot-
high razor-wired fence secures the perimeter. Guards in
towers—Cain likes to use females, as they are better able
to stay awake—overlook death row, ever watchful of anything out of the ordinary.

Six tiers—Upper A and B, Lower A and B, and Upper
C and D—currently house eighty-eight inmates convicted
of capital offenses. Hopeless eyes peer out from behind
thick white bars at passersby visiting the prison or guards
watching their every move. Some of those eyes are men-
acing, reflecting the beasts that live within. Some are
despairing as the realization of hopelessness has long
since settled in. And there are the lustful eyes, and the
ones that reveal no soul, and the ones that seem simply re-
signed to their fate. Each copes with being caged in his
own way, but no inmate could have dreamed what would

become of his existence as he raped and kidnapped and murdered his way through life.

The cells, six feet by nine feet, each contain a bed along one wall, with a shelf for personal items above, a table connected to the opposite wall, and a toilet, which sits only inches from the head of the bed, where they sleep. Each prisoner is confined to his cell for twenty-three hours per day. Three times each week, they are brought individually and restrained into the exercise yard—six pens about twenty feet long and three feet wide, encased in high fences topped with the jagged points of tumbled razor wire, which can easily tear flesh from bone. Only one prisoner at a time is allowed in each pen, but they can converse and throw Nerf balls to the prisoners in the other pens, if they behave.

Death row inmates are allowed one hour of sunlight each day in fifteen-minute increments and are unrestrained during showers. They are allowed visitors from the ten people on their approved list, twice each month, but these visits are conducted from behind a screen. Twice each year, usually in July and August or December and January, they are allowed contact visits. But as the years go by, it is usually the case that fewer and fewer visitors come. For many death row prisoners and lifers, when the mother in the family dies, usually other family members stop coming, too disheartened by watching their loved one rotting away in prison to continue with the self-torture. By the time some prisoners become a number on a white cross, the only people they've had contact with in years are the guards, other prisoners, and those on the four televisions that line the halls of the tiers.

Todd is the most notorious killer on death row. As you walk into the compound, his photograph is pinned at the top of the row of photographs identifying all of the death row inmates. For Todd, life now is a monotonous routine of eating, exercising, watching television, and looking forward to occasional visits. There are no more beautiful women to stalk and kill, no more bragging to friends about his conquests, nothing more to life than looking forward to death.

For the most part, he is quiet, although guards report that he did get into one altercation with another inmate, a dispute over the television. Todd spit on him. But other than that, he paces his cell, listening to the conversation around him. Picking up his toilet paper from the back of his toilet and putting it under his bed, then retrieving it and putting it back. Again and again. His every movement watched on a closed-circuit television.

Todd is the only inmate on death row who is monitored twenty-four hours per day, seven days per week. This monitoring resulted from a promise that Cain made to the families of Todd's victims, that he would watch him at all times to make sure he never had the opportunity to escape. Cain kept that promise. Every move that Todd makes is watched: when he sleeps, when he eats, when he uses the toilet, when he plays with his toilet paper. It is a fitting punishment. There is never a moment of privacy for this man who spent so much of his life watching, then raping and murdering, innocent, beautiful women. It is poetic justice that he must endure being watched for the rest of his life.

And after all of his appeals are exhausted, Derrick Todd Lee will be watched once again, by the families whose lives were torn apart by his deeds; they will watch as his life is taken from him in a much more humane manner than the lives he took. On that day, he will be brought to a holding cell twelve hours before his execution, where he will be visited by his attorneys and spiritual advisers. He will pray for a stay of execution while those outside will pray that the call from the governor does not come. He will eat his last meal while a minister prays for his soul.

As the hours and minutes tick away, the IV Team will prepare the lethal injection that will take Todd's life. Inside the Lethal Injection Chamber, the team will run the IV tubes into a hole in the wall that conceals the executioner.

No one knows who the executioner is, except Warden Cain. Between six-thirty and eight-thirty that evening, Todd will be escorted into the room, about fifteen minutes before he will die. The Strap-Down Team will lay him down and place his arms and legs into restraints on the gurney. Five belts will make an eerie sound as they are clicked into place over him.

Perhaps Todd will look toward the wall to his left, to the two red phones that are his only lifeline. Perhaps he will say a final prayer for mercy before Warden Cain opens the blue curtain that covers the glass windows of the two viewing rooms. In one room, the eyes that will watch him are the eyes of those families he destroyed. In the other, two media representatives, the coroner of West Feliciana Parish, and other selected dignitaries, whose eyes simply reflect distaste, will watch him take his final breath.

If he wishes, Todd can say a few last words. Will he say he's sorry? It doesn't seem likely, as he still admits to nothing. But then, "sorry" would ring hollow to the ears of those who have to live the nightmare he created.

And then the executioner in the next room will dispense the drugs. It will be over for Derrick Todd Lee, and he will soon be marked with a numbered white cross.

But it will never be over for the families of Randi Mebruer, Geralyn DeSoto, Gina Wilson Green, Charlotte Murray Pace, Pam Kinamore, Trineisha Dené Colomb, and Carrie Lynn Yoder. And for the families of Connie Warner, Eugenie Boisfontaine, Christine Moore, and Mari Ann Fowler, who may never know for sure if Todd was the killer of their loved ones, the nightmare that was Derrick Todd Lee will continue long past the time that justice was administered through a simple IV.

Revelations

In the end, seven victims were linked through DNA to Derrick Todd Lee:

Randi Mebruer
Geralyn Barr DeSoto
Gina Wilson Green
Charlotte Murray Pace
Pamela Piglia Kinamore
Trineisha Dené Colomb
Carrie Lynn Yoder

And there are others who have not been linked through DNA, but are believed by many to be Todd's victims through strong circumstantial evidence. These women were included in preceding chapters:

Connie Lynn Warner
Eugenie Boisfontaine
Christine Moore
Mari Ann Fowler

But there are still others whom we feel it necessary to mention, women who were killed over a span of almost two decades—women who may possibly be victims of the South Louisiana Serial Killer.

Melissa Montz was twenty-seven years old when she disappeared on October 4, 1985. She was an LSU student, earning her doctorate in geology and was out for her morning run on Brightside Lane, near LSU, the last time anyone saw her alive. Her route took her from Brightside to River Road, then Gourrier Avenue to Nicholson. Her body was discovered on November 24 by a golfer who had gone to retrieve his golf ball in a wooded area along the LSU golf course. Melissa had been strangled. Her murderer has never been apprehended.

Todd would have been seventeen at this time, and it is possible for several reasons that Melissa may have been his first victim. Gourrier Avenue turns into Dodson Avenue, where Carrie Lynn Yoder lived. Murray Pace lived just off Brightside Lane. It is evident that Todd liked to return to the same areas, both to find murder victims and to dispose of their bodies. Christine Moore's body was also found in that area a few more miles down River Road.

Todd's propensity for violence had emerged by that time as he had been arrested just a few months earlier that year for cutting Roy Raiford in a knife fight. Melissa also fit the general description of the other victims—pretty and dark-haired, with high cheekbones. If Melissa is indeed a victim of Todd's, his killing spree would have lasted eighteen years.

Joyce Taylor was an older black woman, age fifty-nine, who many would not consider to be one of Todd's victims, due to her age, but the disappearance of Mari Ann Fowler, who was sixty-five, tells us that age was not a prerequisite on Todd's victim preference list. Joyce lived a good distance away from Todd's other victims, in North

Baton Rouge. She was found stabbed to death in her home. No signs of forced entry were evident, and although she had money and jewelry there, nothing was taken. She was killed on May 30, 1992, almost three months before the death of Connie Warner.

Joyce taught physical education at West Feliciana High School and was a close friend of Liz Lee, even lived with her for several years before she moved to the home where she was murdered. "Joyce would never have let anyone into her home that she didn't know," Liz said. "She had one of those voice boxes and would always ask who was there before she opened her door."

Todd had attended West Feliciana High while Joyce was teaching there, playing basketball and exercising in the gym while Joyce's class was gathered nearby. Joyce knew him, and she was known to be tough on all the students. "It would break my heart to think that Derrick Todd Lee killed Joyce. I couldn't bear that," Liz said, tears still welling in her eyes more than thirteen years later.

Patricia Carter was twenty-five years old when her body was found severely beaten in the parking lot of a church on Winnebago Street in Baton Rouge. Witnesses reported seeing a black pickup truck dumping her into the lot on April 17, 1996. Todd had been hired by JE Merit as a pipe fitter in a conditional capacity that morning, but was notified later that day that he was to report to the West Feliciana Parish Courthouse on April 25. Todd was still on parole at this time. Patricia would spend several days fighting for her life before she died, becoming just another of Baton Rouge's many unsolved murders.

Aside from the fact that Patricia was beaten, there are several other indicators that she may have been one of Todd's victims. Christine Moore would be discovered near the grounds of a church seven years later. And Patricia's body was found just a few blocks from the home of Todd's cousin and friend, Kenny Ray Lee.

Elizabeth Darensbourg's body was discovered on Zeb Chaney Road on June 6, 1999, near Doyle's Bayou Park. She was thirty years old. Police have not released an actual cause of death, but Elizabeth was found partially undressed. We include her on our list because Todd was working for Ascension Ready Mix at the time, and in the days prior to Elizabeth's death, he picked up and delivered several truckloads of concrete in that area. He called in to report he would not be at work on June 5, and he did not work on the day she was discovered as well.

Robin Gremillion's body was found on January 18, 2000, in City Park Lake, which is right next to the LSU lakes. She was naked and had been drowned, apparently only hours before her body was found. Although Todd is not known to have drowned any of his other victims, we know that he was fond of stalking and finding women in the LSU area. Again, things were not going well for Todd, and he did not work on this date. He had been found guilty of stalking Collette Walker the month before, but he had received a suspended sentence and probation. Four days after Robin's body was discovered, Todd would be arrested for aggravated battery, aggravated flight, simple criminal damage to property, and attempted first-degree murder of a police officer. This was the night he beat Consandra in the parking lot of Liz's Lounge.

Francis Baldwin was forty-seven when she was beaten to death in the town of Scotlandville on August 30, 2002. She lived on Progress Road, and this was not her first experience with being attacked. Her throat had been slit in a robbery attempt four years earlier, but she had survived. This time, the only thing taken was her life. This murder occurred at the height of Todd's frenzy. Christine Moore had been killed on May 23 and Murray Pace on May 31. Diane Alexander had been attacked on July 9, and Pam Kinamore was killed on July 12. Todd was employed by JE Merit at this time, but he did not work from August 29 to September 3, which follows his pattern of not being at work on the days murders were committed. He lost $180 at Casino Rouge at some point during this day.

These murders bring our count of victims and possible victims to seventeen. It is important to note that Sean Gillis is also a suspect in some of these cases, but he has confessed to eight murders, none of which appear on this list. Unless Todd eventually confesses, we may never know how many women he killed, not only in Louisiana, but in other states in which he worked as well.

But the dead are not Todd's only victims. Every woman who locked her doors and windows obsessively, who was afraid to go outside of her home at night, to answer a knock at her door—every woman in the Baton Rouge area was a victim. And these murders tore a whole region of Louisiana apart, from the law enforcement agencies that were pitted against one another to break the case to the public officials who faced ridicule in the media for their inability to catch the serial killer to the numerous white men who were pulled over on the side of the road to be swabbed for DNA. So many lives were changed by the acts of one man, who held a whole region of the South in his terrible grip.

After more than thirty years in law enforcement, Chief of Police Pat Englade was forced to retire, reportedly so that Mayor-President Bobby Simpson would have a chance to be reelected in 2004. Voters had not forgotten what it was like to live in fear under his administration, and Simpson lost his bid for reelection to Kip Holden, Baton Rouge's first black mayor. We offered Englade the opportunity to tell us his side of the story. His response: "This has left such a bitter taste in my mouth that I can't even talk about it."

"But we've got so much information that is negative about the task force and your investigation. We'd like your perspective about what happened," we persuaded.

"I'm not getting into a pissing contest with Lynne Marino," he said, and that was that.

Other members of the task force were also approached in our efforts to give an accurate account of the events as they took place. All refused, citing the fact that the case is on appeal, and they did not want to do anything to influence the outcome. That is certainly an understandable reason, but their silence has become almost deafening to those who are still waiting for answers as to why so many women had to die before Todd was caught.

But Dannie Mixon did not hesitate to admit the mistakes he made. Within a few weeks of Todd's conviction for the murder of Murray Pace, Dannie suffered a stroke, brought on by the stress of the aftermath of his apprehension of Louisiana's most notorious murderer. Dannie suddenly found himself an outcast among many detectives and police officers he had worked with in his fifty years of law enforcement. As he walked into the grand jury room after Todd's capture, many of his fellow officers turned their backs to him. Many on the task force felt that Dannie had hijacked them, even after they had refused to listen to him and called him crazy. Their disdain stung and preyed on Dannie's mind. But that wasn't all that bothered the investigator.

"I'm not the same person I was, not the hotshot

go-getter anymore, and I'm finding it real hard to adjust to retirement. But most of all, the thing that bothers me is that I wish I would have been able to put this together two or three years sooner. I would have been able to save lives, beginning with Geralyn and Gina and continuing through Carrie. Sometimes I get so down on myself because I feel like I failed them," Dannie said as tears gathered in his eyes and spilled onto his ruddy cheeks. "I tried so hard. I had my maps and zones and flags and pins. I tried to stay on top of it, but I failed them. I simply failed them."

The women of Baton Rouge would disagree. To them, Dannie Mixon was a hero, the man who saved their lives, who gave them a very special gift—peace of mind. And for the families of the victims, Dannie gave them a face to hate, an evil to put behind bars, a feeling that there was some semblance of justice for what was done to those they loved.

Sadly, Dannie passed away from acute leukemia on September 30, 2008, only days after being diagnosed. His wife Kathryn says he died of a broken heart. Despite Dannie's efforts, things will never really be made right for these families who are tortured by the knowledge of the horror and pain that embodied their loved ones' last moments. They live that knowledge every day and every night. They try to go on, to forget that which cannot be forgotten. They go through the motions of their lives, but the memories live on, lingering persistently in the background on some days, rising up to taunt them on others. Birthdays, anniversaries, holidays, now bitter reminders of their losses. They try to laugh. They try not to cry, but tears come unbidden. They toss and turn at night, sleep elusive as they recall a special moment—a hug, an accomplishment, a smile. They cling to those memories before sorrow once again takes hold. And then they hate the man who took from them the ability to make new memories—like they've never hated before.

And they each question God: Why Connie? Why Randi? Why Geralyn? Why Eugenie? Why Gina? Why Christine? Why Murray? Why Pam? Why Dené? Why Mari Ann? Why Carrie?

While in a dark cell, amidst the souls of the damned, the monster closes its eyes and lets memories of its conquests lull it into a peaceful sleep. A small smile curves its lips. . . .

Authors' Note

Soon after Derrick Todd Lee's conviction in West Baton Rouge Parish, Sue Israel and I [Susan Mustafs] went to Tony Clayton's law firm to conduct an interview with him about the serial killer. We had featured Tony a few years earlier on the cover of *City Social* magazine. Sue and I were happy in our positions as editorial director and managing editor, respectively, of the magazine and had no particular aspirations to do anything else at the time.

As the interview progressed, Tony mentioned that several well-known writers had approached him about writing a book about Derrick Todd Lee. He was concerned because he didn't know if he wanted to write a book, and he didn't know whom he could trust to tell the story the way he wanted it told—with a heavy emphasis on the victims and the significance of their loss. In the middle of his sentence, and without forethought, I found myself raising my hand.

Tony looked at me incredulously. "You would be willing to write this book, Susan? Do you know what it would involve?"

"Yes," I said. "Sue and I could do it."

Sue nodded her agreement.

Tony was familiar with our work, and we contracted to become a partnership on the spot.

None of us had any idea of what we were getting into. Sue and I went from writing about artists and musicians and beautiful homes to riding around looking for the locations of where the bodies of victims had been found. The experience changed our lives.

We had lived the fear that all the women in South Louisiana felt when Derrick Todd Lee was on his rampage, but as we gained intimate knowledge of the murders and the victims, we began to feel their loss very deeply. We began to empathize with the families on a more profound level. We had come to admire the victims, to know them, and we hurt for them. We hurt for their families. And we began to question why we were doing this.

I expressed our feelings and concerns about how the families might react to Lynne Marino on the phone one night. Lynne had been very helpful to us and believed in our project. Her response: "This is a story that needs to be told. I want everyone to know what a beautiful person my daughter was and how horrible this monster was."

So we had our answer. This was a story that needed to be told. And the telling was not easy. As we sifted through crime-scene photographs of the women we had come to care so much about, we sometimes had difficulty sleeping at night. As we tried to get information from the task force, we were met with brick walls. As we mulled over police reports and began to put the facts together, the enormity of our task became daunting.

This project that we originally thought would take only a few months took more than a year to complete. We could not have done it without those who were brave enough to talk with us, as well as our families, who loved and supported us throughout the course of this project. We would like to take this opportunity to thank them:

To Lynne Marino—you are one brave lady. We are proud of your outspokenness, your single-minded determination to see that your daughter's murderer was caught.

We thank you for believing in us and for sharing your experiences, painful though that was for you. You are always in our prayers.

To Dannie Mixon—you were a hero. We will always appreciate your honesty and your willingness to tell us your story. South Louisiana owes you a debt of gratitude that could never be repaid.

To Sid Newman—Baton Rouge Crime Stoppers is lucky to have you. We thank you for your insight and wish you every success in your continued endeavor to get criminals off the streets.

And to the families of the victims—we pray that you find your way back to happiness and peace.

To Angel and Brandon—thank you for all of the love and laughter you bring to my life. You have been my greatest blessings. To my sister, Brenda—I will always miss you. To B-Bunny, Bridget, Cathy, Mark, Bruce, Danny, Sue, Belinda, Laura, and Rebecca, I don't even have to say it. You already know. And to my two Mikes in Nashville—Mike Kinnamon and Michael McCall—thank you for believing in me and for all of your advice, support, and encouragement.

—Susan

To Paula—thank you for loving me and for bringing so much happiness to my life. To my mom—thank you for being the guiding light that inspired me to be the best that I can be. To my dad—thank you for being the strong influence that kept me on the straight and narrow. To Ricky Ward—I couldn't ask for a better boss. You are a great partner to try cases with, and an even better friend. To Becky Chustz—you did an excellent job of putting this trial together. I couldn't have done it without you. And to my children—Brillant´, Jené, Austin, Brandon, and T.J.— I love you.

—Tony

To my sweet Bob, who has supported me every inch of the way, and to my mom, who has always been my greatest cheerleader and best friend—I can't thank you enough. To my brother, sister, extended family, and dear friends— thank you for your love, friendship, and faith. To Patt, Steve, Gina, and Susan—thanks for helping me learn how to believe in myself. I love you all.

—Sue